THE FOOTBALL CODE

THE FOOTBALL CODE

THE SCIENCE OF PREDICTING
THE BEAUTIFUL GAME

―――――

James Tippett

First published in 2017

Published in the United Kingdom

©James Tippett

The right of James Tippett to be identified as the author of this work has been asserted in accordance with the Copyright, Designs and Patents Act 1988.

ISBN 9781527211940
ISBN: 1527211940

Printed in Great Britain

Website: www.thefootballcode.com

Twitter: @TheFootballCodeUK

Facebook: The Football Code

Email: TheFootballCodeUK@gmail.com

To Adam Manley and Anne Griffiths

Contents

1. A GOAL IS MORE THAN A GOAL · *1*

Why the best teams often lose and the worst teams often win; why it is difficult to accurately assess the ability of young players; how we are regularly fooled by the randomness which occurs within football; a methodology that can help us win (or not lose) the lottery; the science of penalties; how Opta revolutionised football.

2. SENTIMENTS ARE DETRIMENTS ·*34*

Why head coaches are irrelevant; what makes clubs overpay for strikers; correlation and causation within football; the fallacy that prompts managers to become wildly overconfident; why humans overvalue the role of skill and undervalue the role of luck; in order to win big you must risk losing big.

3. THE FLAWED WORLD OF PUNDITRY ·*78*

The similarities between Man City and Salford City; why pundits are the worst footballing predictors; how sports media is intrinsically flawed; why owners are considered tyrannical; what happens when fans take charge of their clubs; what Ancient Athens can teach football teams; how success turns luck into genius.

How Leicester won the Premier League; Britain's greatest gambling triumph; why the house always wins; how to turn the tables on the bookies; why it is better to be uncertain than overconfident; why you should never cash out or place accumulators; the secret rivalry between two pioneering gambling syndicates.

The flawed nature of football's conventional stats; a new metric (xG) that will modernise the sport; how xG reveals who the best teams really are; why it is better to have fewer shots; how to rank every football team in Europe in one huge table; the secret training it takes to work at a leading betting consultancy.

How to succeed in the transfer market; why it is naïve to believe that loyalty exists in football; why the poorest teams are often the most innovative; how statistics are conventionally used by clubs; a revolutionary analytical player recruitment system; the radical, ground-breaking structure that every club will eventually adopt.

PRE-FACE

———

ON MY FIRST DAY OF work at Smartodds, a betting consultancy that turns over hundreds of millions of pounds each year, I instinctively wore my finest suit. I was shocked when I entered the offices for the first time. What stretched out to my right-hand side was a large floor space filled with around one hundred employees, some collecting data, some analysing the gambling markets and some betting millions on football matches. The overwhelming majority were men aged between twenty-five and forty. Each desk housed four or five monitors, every screen showing either a football match or a copious amount of data. More screens lined the walls of the office, showing sports news, game highlights, interviews with managers and any other feed which could be of interest to the bettors who inhabited the workspace. There was an atmosphere I could only compare to the trading floors of investment banks I had seen in movies. However, there was one glaring difference; most of the employees in the office at Smartodds were wearing khaki shorts, football shirts and other casual attire. I later found out that most of the men had just returned from a kick about at a nearby pitch owned by one of the clients. Needless to say, many of them stared bemusedly at the eighteen-year-old suit-wearing newbie that was being led to his desk.

The company lives and breathes football. If this hadn't been given away by the countless number of screens showing football related activity, or the series of framed signed football shirts that lined the walls of the offices, then it certainly was by conversing with other analysts. Almost every discussion was about a recent development in the world of football. Everyone had an opinion on managerial decisions, refereeing mistakes, set-piece routines and the like. Often I would find myself overhearing debates over such obscure things as who the best player in the Azerbaijan Premier League was.

The only rule of the office was that you were not allowed to celebrate a goal under any circumstances. Some fixtures would have millions of pounds riding on their outcome. Clients and bettors who had just lost big as a result of a team scoring did not want to hear other employees revelling in that very same goal. On the other hand, swearing, cursing and execrating were practically encouraged. When a punter did lose big, you would often hear a barrage of expletives resonate around the office.

The "Watchers" team, the subdivision of the company that I had joined, are responsible for collecting match data. These analysts watch between three and six hours of football each day. They are paid £20 for each match they collect data on, a salary that adds up to over thirteen pounds per hour. The data that these employees collect is scrutinised by another subdivision of analysts, before being sold to professional gamblers. These clients occupy a different area of the trading floor, and pay Smartodds to supply them with statistics which can inform their betting. The company also places bets of its own accord, using their state-of-the-art models to consistently beat the bookmakers. The Watchers team that I was a part of are trained by Smartodds to collect and analyse the innovative, ground-breaking stats upon which the company founds its success.

The owner of Smartodds, Matthew Benham, has also utilised the company's data to run the football club he owns. Brentford FC, a West London side currently residing in the second tier of English football, have found incredible success under Benham's analytically driven approach. Despite having the fourth lowest playing budget in the twenty-four team league, the Bees have managed three consecutive top ten finishes. Their £172k per week wage bill is less than half the average for the division (£375k), and three times less than the average of the rest of the 2016/17 top ten sides (£511k). Benham's team have managed to thrive in the second tier, despite having a budget lower than many *third* tier sides. Brentford's success has been founded on their use of Smartodds' statistics to exploit inefficiencies in the transfer market.

Having been through the company's training programme, I will never watch a match of football in the same way again. Their philosophy has given me a completely different outlook on the beautiful game, one that incites me to approach it in a much more intelligent manner. Much of what I believed about the sport was proven false, and incredible insights into how it *should* be played were revealed. In *The Football Code*, I wish to share these insights so that the sport may become shrewder, smarter and more rational.

At several points in the ensuing pages I will single out individuals for criticism. José Mourinho, Gary Neville and Alan Hansen are examples of those who come under particular scrutiny. In each of these cases, I simply wish to emphasise a particular point. Readers should bear in mind that many others have fallen victim to the same mistakes as those that I single out in the following pages. This book intends to instruct and inform the reader on how to approach football and, more broadly, life in a more rational manner. I hope to lay out some basic principles that may assist in this task, using stories and examples to help explain the philosophy. Those who are singled out for failing in their predictive endeavours are part of a large sample of incompetent forecasters. Hopefully we can learn from the mistakes of these unsuccessful speculators, whilst simultaneously studying the top secret analytical methods of companies such as Smartodds, with the ultimate aim of making more accurate footballing judgements and predictions.

INTRODUCTION

———

FORECASTING THE OUTCOME OF FOOTBALL matches is incredibly difficult. The correct formula has eluded fans, managers and analysts for over a century. Many have concluded that it can't be done; football is simply too fluid and dynamic to correctly prophesise. However, through the furthering of our predictive abilities, through adopting a shrewder approach to the sport, and through embracing new methods of analysis, the game loved by millions has the potential to be changed forever. This book aims to promote a new, smarter football philosophy.

The beauty of the sport lies in its objectiveness. No clear answer often prevails, with every fan possessing a different set of beliefs. Supporters might ponder over who is the best player in the world. Managers might wonder which formation best suits their playing staff. Analysts might speculate how the total number of passes a player makes in the final third relates to his attacking output. Everyone has a different outlook on how the beautiful game should be played. With so many different opinions looking to prevail, deciphering which of these opinions are actually correct becomes a great challenge.

Never before has there been such a fervent interest in the ability to calculate the future results of football matches. This is a rapidly growing area of interest, as indicated by the booming gambling market in recent years. Since the sport was formed, many have tried their hand at forecasting the outcome of matches. Pundits and fans have struggled with their endeavours, whilst bookmakers earn fortunes off of those bold enough to take them on. When it comes to gambling, the bookies nearly always come out on top. For everyday punters, betting is essentially a tax on those who don't understand the laws of probability. This book will attempt to decipher the methods that can be used to crack the code.

The science of prediction is essential in all walks of life. Every day, the human brain makes thousands of calculations in an attempt to predict the outcome of our actions, thus allowing us to choose a path which leads to the greatest happiness. Because of the definitive rules by which they are governed, sports make for a fantastic playground in which forecasters of every nature can test their own judgement and ability. The principles which will be laid out in this book carry far greater implications than simply being able to accurately determine the outcome of sporting fixtures. This book aims to improve the inherent forecasting ability of any individual, whether that be in sport, politics, economics or everyday life.

Hopefully this book will give rise to a new footballing philosophy; a fresh way of viewing a sport which has been approached in the same manner for over a century. The following chapters should each contribute their share to an innovative outlook of the beautiful game. An understanding of the rules of probability, a more rational demeanour, and a foxier approach are all essential if we wish to excel in the world of forecasting. By studying the science of predicting football, we may begin to make more clear and concise judgements about the world that we live in.

FOOTBALLING PREDICTIONS

Prediction is an intrinsic aspect of football, just as it is an intrinsic part of human nature. Evolution has wired humans to recognise patterns and trends, and to use that information to anticipate the future. Every action that we make involves a forecast, be it conscious or unconscious, as to whether that action will have positive or negative implications. Whether deciding which route to take home, where to go on holiday, or whether to buy the latest Apple product, we habitually weigh up the outcome of the event and decide what will give us the greatest fulfilment.

Forecasting takes a leading role in the realms of sport. Fans, managers, television pundits, bettors and even the players themselves all rely on their ability to successfully determine the outcome of various events. The supporter will subconsciously make thousands of pre-match predictions. Whenever a fan goes to a match, they will hold a series of expectations. How likely is it that their team will win? Will the game be open and attacking, or tense and closed up? Which players are most likely to score? Whether they realise it or not, fans will make a great deal of calculations based on various information that they have gathered from previous matches. This book will study how biases, both natural and unnatural, can undermine the predictions of fans.

The football manager faces a plethora of choices every day; from signing players to naming a starting eleven, from making substitutions to negotiating players' wages. Good predictive skills are essential for any management position, not least in the world of modern-day football. The head coach of a club must be able to distinguish the truth from all the noise distracting his attention.

Television punditry is one of the more interesting areas of footballing prediction. In Chapter 3 we will delve more deeply into why "expert" analysts are often hindrances to us when it comes to predicting football. Sports media filter a vast amount of inaccurate information through to the fans. In fact, the higher the profile of the source, the less likely they are to be correct. We will learn why television pundits, in particular, are the worst predictors of them all.

Professional gambling is perceived as a dream job. People generally place bets (whether that be in a casino, in a bookmakers or simply amongst comrades) because they want to make quick money without doing too much hard work. However, betting in order to generate enough money to make a living off commands incredible predictive skills. Successful professional gamblers live their lives around the principles of this book. These men base their whole wellbeing around *the ability to be consistently correct*. The people who run football clubs could learn a lot by studying the methods of those who professionally bet on the sport, as this book will do.

Football holds a sort of middle ground between predictability and unpredictability. Whilst it is impossible to correctly forecast the outcome of every single match[1], we are able to distinguish between favourites and underdogs fairly easily. In a match between Arsenal and Wycombe, although we cannot say who will emerge victorious with absolute certainty, we can conclude that the Premier League team have a much better chance of doing so than their opposition. This relationship between assurance and uncertainty is what makes football so fascinating. Any team, on any given day, has a *chance* of winning. The combination of skill and luck lies at the heart of our interest the game. A team can play well and lose, whilst another could play poorly but emerge triumphant. This makes it challenging to make accurate predictions.

A New Method of Lawn-Mowing

I once read about an old man who was too infirm to mow his garden. He lived alone and was not strong enough to push his lawnmower across the grass. His solution was to erect a pole in the middle of his garden, tie one end of a rope to the middle of the pole and the other end of the rope to the lawnmower. He set off the mower, designed to run of its own accord, from the edge of the grass. The rope tightened and the vehicle started doing laps around the lawn. The rope tightened further with each lap which occurred, drawing the mower ever closer to the pole. At last, the lawnmower found its way to the middle of the lawn, leaving the whole garden with a fresh trim.

The footballing philosophy which this book outlines was developed by a football team too financially weak to mow their metaphorical lawn. They had to develop a more intelligent system of operating in order to do what other, stronger teams could do. What the old man lacked in brawn, he more than made up for in brain. Bill Gates allegedly said that he would

---

1 BBC Sport football pundit Mark Lawrenson managed to correctly predict 52.8% of the outcomes of Premier League fixtures in the 2012/13 season. The fact that such a record was deemed "impressive" is a testament to the difficulty that faces us when trying to forecast the outcome of football matches.

always pick a lazy person to do a difficult job, because a lazy person would find an easy way to do it. Whilst hard work is often instrumental, innovation is often invaluable. Whether weak, poor or lazy, discovering a pioneering means of operating can lead to great accomplishment.

Michael Lewis's famous book *Moneyball* tracks one of the greatest successes in predictive history. One which helped a baseball team with a budget of roughly $44million compete against clubs with a $125million pay-roll.

"There is an epidemic failure within the game to understand what is really happening", says Peter Brend, assistant general manager at the Oakland Athletics baseball team, in Aaron Sorkin's film adaptation of Lewis' book. Oakland's financial disadvantage to other teams in the league means they must play by different rules in order to achieve the same success. If they do not innovate, adapt and gamble, their final position in the table will reflect their financial situation and they will be rooted to the bottom of the league.

The central hypothesis of *Moneyball* is that the traditional methods used by baseball insiders (in particular those of managers, coaches and scouts) over the past century were subjective and often flawed. Statistics such as stolen bases, runs batted in and batting average, typically used to gauge player ability, were relics of a 19th-century view of the game and the statistics available at that time. Beane believed that the future of baseball lay in a broader statistical approach based on numerical models, rather than the traditional scouting methods which had dominated the sport for over a century. The Oakland A's' realised that the methods used by every other team were outdated, and they used this to their advantage. They developed more analytical gauges of player performance to field a team that could better compete against their far richer opponents.

General manager Billy Beane, the man tasked with recruiting players for the A's, employed the services of Paul DePodesta, who had just graduated from Harvard with a degree in Economics. Together they developed a system of finding undervalued baseball players, whom they could purchase for little money but who could have a large positive impact on the team's performance. At first, Beane's revolutionary and previously unheard of methods were met with rigid opposition; not only from outsiders but also from the manager and scouts of the Oakland A's. There were several reasons for this.

Firstly, sport is steeped in tradition. This is especially true for sports such as baseball, and indeed football. It is very hard to amend the way sport is played because it is governed by such strict rules. Players, fans and managers take comfort in what is familiar to them. For example, the introduction of goal-line technology into football was met with a great deal of resistance, despite the fact that it has momentously increased the number of correct decisions made in-play. This resistance to change seems to be intrinsic to the sport. Indeed, goals did not have nets when football was first formed. Despite the obvious need for change, the introduction of football nets did not happen until 1891 and was first used in an FA Cup final in 1892. For the decades up until that point, referees often had to guess whether the ball had in fact gone in, or whether it had simply whistled past the post.

Baseball suffers from a similar rigidness. It is of little surprise that Bill James, the American baseball writer, historian and statistician whose work Beane based his philosophy around, was widely hated in baseball for proposing a new and revolutionary thesis. His approach, which he termed sabermetrics, analyses baseball scientifically. He was the analytical pioneer who first attempted to use statistical data to determine why teams win and lose.

The second reason why new ideas are often rejected by sport, particularly ideas based on statistical mechanisms, is because managers, coaches and scouts are afraid they may lose their jobs. They feel threatened by the fact that computational data is being used more and more, replacing the more traditional methods based on experience and "gut feeling". Following the success of Beane's *Moneyball* system, virtually every baseball team has now employed analytical departments to lead the recruiting of players. This has left many of the "old-school" scouts out of a job. Football scouts are wary of letting statistical analysis permeate into their sport, having seen what fate became their kind when baseball adopted such an approach. Slowly but surely, the traditional scouts are being replaced by statisticians and their computers.

The final reason why the use of analytics is often met with scepticism is because it doesn't yield results overnight. Every new system needs time to settle, and often requires fine-tuning. The Oakland A's started the 2002 season badly, to such an extent that Beane came under real pressure and nearly lost his job. The media attacked him, as the media are inclined to do, and dismissed his methods before they had had a chance to have an impact. Beane had tried something revolutionary, discounting over a century of tradition, and many people were eager to see him fail. These people concluded that sabermetrics were useless as soon as the Oakland A's started losing games. However, Beane's side of undervalued misfits, purchased on a shoe-string budget using statistical models, went on to become one of the most overachieving sides in sporting history. Beane has irreversibly changed the way that baseball is played and thought about.

A Brave New World

The question is often posed, "Why has *Moneyball* taken so long to come to football?" This query not only refers to the unnatural scepticism within football to embrace statistical analysis as a form of scouting, but the fact that, as of yet, there has been no footballing equivalent of the Oakland A's. There has been no Billy Beane to have revolutionised the sport of football. There has been no identification of a key undervalued metric which could change the way the sport is played[2]. That is, until now.

The strategy of using statistical analysis to gauge the true skill of baseball players has been proven to work. The first team to master the same approach in football will gain an enormous edge over the competition.

2 In baseball, this metric was On-Base Percentage. The regularity with which a player got on base was identified by Bill James as a highly undervalued statistic. Beane looked closely at the OBP of his players, and valued this as a key performance indicator. Such an undervalued metric has been incredibly hard to find in football.

Billy Beane's revolutionary style of looking at baseball came about well over a decade ago, so why has football been lagging so far behind? It's not as though people haven't been searching for it; a plethora of journalists and analysts have all dedicated themselves to finding "the secret formula".

The answer is that baseball and football are very different sports. Whilst baseball consists of only a few, easily definable actions (the pitch, the swing of the bat and the fielding of the ball being the key events), football is a lot more fluid. This makes it hard to know where to look when it comes to creating statistical models. When it came to separating the truth from the noise, Billy Beane was looking for a needle in a haystack. Football analysts are looking for a needle in a stack of broken needle parts.

Additionally, it is logical that the best football analysts are employed by the best clubs. These top teams have so much money that there isn't an urgent need to innovate. They don't need to find an edge over their opponents; they already have an advantage in the form of huge amounts of wealth. The top clubs don't need to focus their attention on finding undervalued players, they tend to concentrate on making big-name signings that keep their fans happy.

The teams who need to innovate are the ones who have a minimal pay-roll. They must adapt and evolve in order to survive. However, there is an innate fear inside football to be the first one to break the mould. The first one through the wall is always going to get bloody. Even Beane, the pioneer of baseball who revolutionised the way the game was played, was on the verge of losing his job before Oakland's results made a miraculous turn-around. Add this risk to the difficulty of applying a mathematical philosophy to the sport of football, and you would need a very brave individual to take on the pile of broken needle parts.

The truth is that one man has already provided football's answer to *Moneyball*. He has revolutionised the whole structure of his two football clubs in order to accommodate his statistically driven methods, with the ultimate aim of competing against much bigger clubs on a much smaller budget. This man's name is Matthew Benham, and he has developed the most effective system of analysing football that the beautiful game has ever seen.

Benham worked as a trader in the city for eight years before setting up his own betting consultancy called Smartodds. This company collects innovative data, which it then sells to professional gamblers. Benham's statistically-driven methods are also used by Smartodds to place bets of their own, allowing the company to make millions of pounds through accurately predicting the outcome of football matches. Smartodds made Benham enough money to buy the football club he has supported since childhood; Brentford FC. When Benham purchased the West London outfit, they were a League One side who had yo-yoed between the third and fourth divisions for the vast majority of their existence, their only real spell of success coming before the Second World War. Brentford were struggling financially when Benham decided to invest.

Attending his first Brentford game as an 11-year-old in 1979, Benham has shared an affinity with the Bees for nearly four decades. In 2012, Benham became owner of the West London club, bailing Brentford out of a £500,000 hole. Realising that lowly Brentford did not have the finances to compete with bigger clubs, Benham began slowly implementing an analytically-driven philosophy on the club. He used the same approach that had made him millions in the betting markets to run the club, and, in particular, in the recruitment of players.

In 2014, Benham bought Danish club FC Midtjylland, who were in a similar financial position as Brentford were two years earlier. Virtually broke and struggling in the top flight of Danish football, Midtjylland were desperate for a backer and Benham sensed an opportunity. He transformed the Danish club into a laboratory for his revolutionary ideas and philosophies. Midtjylland's players and coaches were sceptical of Benham's statistical methods, but did little to oppose his takeover. They needed the money that Benham pumped into the club, realising that beggars couldn't be choosers.

Benham has used the radical methods that brought him success as a trader and in the betting world in order to bring success to both Brentford and Midtjylland. Both of these clubs have hugely over-achieved since Benham took over. A year after Benham bought them, FC Midtjylland won the Danish Superliga for the first time in their history. In the process they qualified for the early stages of the Europa League. In order to progress to the group stage, they had to overcome Southampton, a club of much greater size and wealth, over two legs. They managed a 2-1 aggregate win which saw them qualify for the group stage of the competition for the first time in their history. They progressed through to the knock-out stage, before being drawn against Louis Van Gaal's Manchester United, a club that had won the treble the year before the Danish side were formed in 1999. Midtjylland pulled off one of the upsets of the decade to defeat United 2-1 in the first leg of the tie, but were comfortably beaten at Old Trafford in the second leg.

The resemblances between Billy Beane's influence at the Oakland A's and Matthew Benham's impact on FC Midtjylland and Brentford have been uncanny. Benham's two teams could be considered footballing equivalents of the Oakland. They are both comparatively small, financially timid clubs who were tasked with competing against much bigger sides. Something needed to change in order to take the clubs to the next level.

Whilst the success of Brentford and Midtjylland may seem insignificant when compared to the giants of the sport, they are two of the most overachieving sides in the whole of Europe. Fans and the media consider success in terms of how many trophies a team wins. Manchester United and Liverpool are often the given examples for English football's most successful ever sides. However, a more accurate gauge of success would be attained by looking at the performance of teams compared to their *expected performance based on finances*. Manchester United and Liverpool, and Chelsea and Manchester City in more modern times, are extremely wealthy sides. Success, as it is traditionally assessed, is guaranteed for such clubs. Players are drawn to money like moths to a flame, meaning the clubs who can pay the highest wages will undoubtedly be the most successful. Outside of the media attention, there are clubs much more deserving of praise, clubs who should be commended for *overachieving*.

Should one assign each team an expected league position based on finances and compare it to their *actual* position in the EFL, Brentford's three consecutive top ten finishes in the Championship would render them one of the most overachieving teams in footballing history. In their most recent campaign, the 2016/17 Championship season, Brentford had a wage budget of roughly £172k per week. This meant that they were ranked 21st out of the twenty-four teams financially. Only three sides spent less on player wages than the West London outfit. The average amount that Championship clubs spent per week on player salaries in 2016/17 was £375k. This meant that *the average team could have bankrolled Brentford's player wages twice over*. The Bees finished above teams like Aston Villa (who spent £951k per week), Cardiff City (£440k), Nottingham Forest (£339k), QPR (£402k) and Wolves (£444k). Brentford's finances should have seen them fighting a relegation battle. Benham's analytical system and innovative approach to football meant they were able to finish in the top ten of the Championship. To put this achievement into perspective, the average wage budget of the other nine teams in the top ten was £511k, three times larger than Brentford's. Bear in mind the Bees also finished 9th in 2015/16, and an incredible 5th in 2014/15. Benham's system has consistently enabled Brentford to defy the odds.

It may seem strange that the Oakland Athletics achieved such prominence within the sport of baseball so quickly, whilst Brentford have almost completely slipped under the radar of the footballing world. This can be explained by the fact that, whilst the Oakland A's are competing against fourteen other teams in Major League Baseball, Brentford are essentially competing against ninety-one other teams in the English Football League. It is easier to spot an overachieving team in a smaller league than in a large one.

The fact that Brentford are able to slip under the radar allows their pioneering methods to go unnoticed. The Bees share the limelight with almost one hundred other professional clubs, meaning that Benham and his club are able to hide in the shadows of football's giants. Billy Beane's methods were outed fairly quickly because his Oakland team had nowhere to hide. The English football media pay little attention to teams outside of the top divisions of European football, allowing Benham's revolutionary analytical approach to remain virtually undetected.

Both Beane and Benham faced criticism for their drastic neglecting of tradition. Beane came into particular conflict with the manager of the Oakland A's, Art Howe. Howe refused to play the players that Beane recommended to him because of a scepticism towards Beane's mathematical methods. Beane's calculations showed that playing Scott Hatteburg at first base would increase Oakland's chances of victory. However, Howe went with the seemingly obvious choice of Carlos Pena because it would be "easier to explain in job interviews" come the end of the season. The relationship between Beane and Howe is easily comparable to that between Benham and Mark Warburton, a Brentford manager who left the club under one of the most fascinating and misreported media stories English football has ever seen.

The following chapters will unveil the secret story of football's answer to baseball's *Moneyball*. Just as Beane overcame his critics and revolutionised the sport of baseball, so too does Benham appear to be following the same path within the sport of football. Brentford managed three consecutive top ten finishes in the Championship, despite having the budget of a team who should be fighting relegation. This incredible record is down to the revolutionary statistical methods that Benham has deployed. Benham has shown that, by exploiting the many inefficiencies that exist within football, any team has the potential to overachieve. This book outlines how two small fish, Brentford and Midtjylland, are surviving in an enormous pond. A pond filled with sharks.

THE FOOTBALL CODE
This book will be broken down into two coherent parts.

The first section will aim to deal with failed predictions, and study how to avoid making poor judgements when it comes to distinguishing between luck and skill. We cannot attempt to implement a new and revolutionary brand of football thinking without first understanding what we must *avoid* doing. In football, the best way to be smart is to not be stupid. This opening half will assess the intrinsic errors that we are all prone to making. Benham's success has been founded on the knowledge of what pitfalls he must avoid; knowledge that he has picked up through years of working as a trader, as a professional gambler, and as an owner of two football clubs.

The second section will attempt to unravel Benham's innovative methods, secret formula, and world-shattering philosophy that has enabled him to succeed in the betting markets and in the guiding of his two teams. We will see how his approach allows him to develop a clearer image of what is really happening on the pitch. These pages also study the broader applications that Benham's approach can supply us with, with the ultimate aim of advancing our own predictive skills.

Over the course of the next few years the science of football looks set to change irreversibly. In recent history, seismic shifts have been occurring under the surface of the footballing landscape. New means of operating have been developed, but have gone unbeknownst to the public given the vital importance of keeping them secret. This book aims to bring the analytical conversation within football into the mainstream. By revealing how Smartodds' work could revolutionise how we assess the sport, hopefully a lot more voices will join the discussion.

The success that Benham's *Moneyball* approach has already attained with both Midtjylland and Brentford, as well as the monetary success that his betting consultancy has achieved, serves as a testament to the fact that there is an inherent fault within football. The inability to see what is *actually* happening out on the field of play is a disease that has infested the beautiful game for over a century. A disease that we don't even realise we are infected with. Furthermore, it is a disease that has disguised itself as an intrinsic part of the game. However, it is a disease that there is a cure for.

A Goal is More Than a Goal

Marcello Trotta placed the ball on the penalty spot and took several, confident strides back. The referee held up his whistle, ensuring that the rest of the players were not encroaching on the eighteen-yard box. Trotta glanced up at the scoreboard. The match had entered its 95th minute. Twelve thousand fans held their breath inside the packed stadium. Many turned away, not daring to watch.

The date was the 27th April 2013, the final day of the Football League season. The League One promotion race had boiled down to one match. Third-placed Brentford were playing second-placed Doncaster Rovers, knowing that a win would see them automatically promoted to the second tier of English football for the first time since 1992.

Before the match, Bournemouth sat at the top of the table on 82 points, Doncaster in second on 81 points and Brentford in third on 79 points. The first and second placed team would win automatic promotion, whilst the third place team would enter the play-offs, in which they would have to compete with the three teams below them for promotion.

The equation was simple. Bournemouth had already been promoted, as it was mathematically impossible for *both* Brentford and Doncaster to overtake them. Doncaster simply needed to draw at Brentford to ensure promotion. However, if Brentford defeated Doncaster then they would automatically be promoted to the Championship, and handed the chance to compete with the likes of QPR, Nottingham Forest and Leeds in the second tier. As well as competing in the higher division, they would earn an extra £4m from the increased television rights, merchandise and ticket sales if they went up.

The match was too close to call. Doncaster had the best defence in the whole of the division that year, whilst Brentford had the best home record. Rovers had the advantage of only needing a draw to win promotion, whilst Brentford *had* to win. From the opening minutes, it was clear that Doncaster's intention was to sit deep and contain Brentford. They had no intention of going forward in search of a goal, choosing instead to try and see the game out for a draw. The match seemed to be heading for stalemate. By the time the ninety minutes were up and the referee had indicated five minutes of added time, the only chance of note had been when Bradley Wright-Phillips hit the post for the Home side.

As the scoreboard ticked over to the ninety-fifth minute, Brentford lumped a hopeful ball forward in a final attempt to snatch a winner. The ball made its way to Clayton Donaldson, Brentford's top scorer, in a wide position just outside the penalty area. Donaldson chipped a cross towards the melee of players who were waiting in the Doncaster penalty area. The ball was flicked on and looped dangerously into the air, where it met the flailing arm of a Rovers defender. The whistle blew and the referee pointed to the penalty spot.

The thousands of Brentford fans who were tightly packed into Griffin Park were euphoric. The whole season, all forty-five matches and 94 minutes, came down to this one kick of the ball. If Brentford were to score the penalty then they would be promoted to the second division for the first time since 1992, and for only the second time in over fifty years. This was arguably Brentford's most crucial single kick of a football in their 124-year history.

However, there was a problem. Harry Forrester, Brentford's designated penalty-taker, had been substituted in the seventieth minute. Club captain Kevin O'Connor, on the pitch in the right-back position, had a proven record of scoring penalties. O'Connor had made his debut for Brentford in 1999, and had played for the Bees for fourteen years. Manager Uwe Rösler signalled from the touchline that O'Connor should take the spot-kick. There was a wonderful sense of romance in the story; the man who had devoted his entire career to Brentford FC would be the one to complete the fairy-tale.

Italian forward Marcello Trotta, on loan from Brentford's West London rivals Fulham, had other ideas. Trotta picked up the ball, and engaged in a fiery quarrel with O'Connor. The captain tried to reason with Trotta, gesturing towards the manager who indicated that he wanted O'Connor to take the penalty. Eventually Trotta's stubbornness prevailed and O'Connor conceded defeat.

The referee blew his whistle and Trotta sent the ball high to Neil Sullivan's right. The goalkeeper watched as it smashed hard into the underside of the crossbar and bounce down back into the penalty area. There was a momentary scramble in the Rovers box, before they eventually cleared the ball to the half-way line where it found Billy Paynter. Brentford had committed men forward in an attempt to scramble in the rebound. As a result, Paynter found himself one-on-one with the Brentford goalkeeper. The Rovers player raced into the Brentford half unopposed and was joined by James Coppinger on his left. Bees goalkeeper Simon Moore was left helpless as Coppinger received the ball from Paynter and tapped into an empty Brentford net. The visiting support erupted in euphoria.

Doncaster had sealed the victory and Brentford were heading for the play-offs. It transpired that Bournemouth had only managed a draw at Tranmere, meaning that Doncaster's last second goal had won them the league. They had been one kick away from heading into the play-offs in third position, but twenty seconds later had secured the title.

THE NOISY GAME

The hardest thing to do when attempting to predict football is to define the truth. Once you correctly locate the direction in which the data is pointing, you can begin to draw accurate conclusions. The problem with football is that the truth is hidden in a whole batch of noise. The vast volume of noise that exists within football data can be attributed to the fact that goals are extremely rare. It is for this reason that in no other sport is a score celebrated with such passion.

On average, there is a score every nine minutes in American football, every thirteen minutes in rugby, and every twenty-two minutes in hockey. In these sports scoring opportunities present themselves regularly. However, in football a goal is scored on average every thirty-five minutes, whilst around 8% of matches finish goalless. A team scoring is celebrated in football with a degree of ecstasy that no other sport can parallel. Spectators are made to wait for the ultimate reward, the reward that wins matches and rockets players to untold fame. However, the fact that goals are scored so infrequently is problematic for those trying to accurately analyse and forecast football.

Commentators can often be heard saying that "at the end of the day there's only one stat that counts". That statistic is how many goals a team has scored. Thousands of actions take place each match: passes, tackles, shots, duels, sprints and so on. However, at the end of the match these events are all rendered inconsequential. The only thing that impacts the league table is the scoreline – how many goals a team scores and how many they concede.

One match of football contains an infinite amount of information, far too much for the human brain to comprehend. We cannot possibly keep track of *every* nugget of data that presents itself in a game. If one were to try and log everything which happens in a match (the position of every player during every second the ninety minutes, the speed at which the ball is travelling, the curvature with which each corner is struck out, etc.) it would take decades for just one fixture to be fully analysed. Even the most in-depth statistical analyses performed by companies such as Opta are relatively shallow. It is impossible to account for *everything* which takes place in each match.

Instead what happens is that the thousands of actions are summarised and broken down into more digestible stats. Possession, shots, shots on target and corners are all frequently used match facts that reflect to some extent the shape of a game. However, by condensing such a vast amount of information into just a few simple stats, a great deal of noise is introduced. Indeed, the more information they try to summarise, the more noise the stats induct. Trying to picture a game of football by looking at such basic statistics is like trying to read a book by glancing over the blurb. You may get a sense of what is going on, but you are missing out on a lot of vital information.

Data on the "shots on target" that teams take are a great example of this. When a player shoots and hits the bar it is deemed a shot off target. A team may hit the bar five times, thus amassing five shots off target, whereas their opposition may have five shots on target which are comfortably saved by the goalkeeper. The first team have clearly come a lot closer to scoring, but this is not reflected in the data. The scoreline is the ultimate summarisation, and therefore is the least precise statistic. The final score only takes into account the number of goals a team has amassed. It doesn't register how many times a team has hit the bar, the amount of possession that each side has had, or any other stat that might give a more precise representation of a team's ability.

Precision is something that football lacks, particularly in England. Managers, fans and the media all prefer to offer generalisations than specificities. This promotes a culture of vagueness. The traditional match stats give us a vague idea of which team is better, but lack a degree of exactness that is needed to make better predictions. Another example of this is how English football categorises certain positions. The only phrase we hold synonymous with "attacking midfielder" is "number ten". Other footballing cultures, particularly in other European countries, have several different names for an attacking midfielder. Each label specifies precisely what traits he has, what role he plays, how fluid his positioning is, and other in-depth characteristics of the particular position. We must attempt to define the beautiful game in more specific terms if we are to make more accurate assessments.

The low-scoring nature of the game means that football is inherently random. Most matches are defined by the smallest of margins. Teams are often separated by only one or two goals, and draws occur around 28% of the time. The cliché is true; goals do change games. Had Trotta taken his season-defining penalty one thousand times, it is probable that he would have scored much more often than not. However, on that particular occasion, the Italian happened to miss, resulting in Brentford missing out on promotion to the Championship.

Goals also incorporate a huge amount of luck, both in terms of how they are scored and when they are scored. Every goal in the history of the game has had a series of events align perfectly for the scoring team, whether that be defensive error, attacking brilliance or a combination of the two. Some goals carry more fortune than others. Own goals are considered particularly lucky, as no defender intends on putting the ball into his own net. Similarly, a shot which goes in off the post or bar carries a large degree of providence. The salient point is that *every* goal carries at least an element of chance.

Goals are the single most important events that take place in football. The dynamic between their incredible significance and their complete unpredictability is what makes the sport so entertaining. The Trotta penalty miss serves to outline the fine lines which exist between success and failure within football, and emphasises the randomness which gilds the beautiful game. When there is so little to choose from between victory and defeat, the role of luck becomes pivotal. It is crucial that we acknowledge and accept this randomness.

SAMPLE SIZE: THE PATH TO FAILED PREDICTIONS

When attempting to make accurate predictions, a forecaster must recognise the size of the sample of data that has been collected. When we have a large sample of data, we must make sure the information that we are analysing is relevant. More importantly, we must be cautious when deal-ing with small samples of data. Making overconfident predictions based on a small amount of information is one of the most common pitfalls that befalls us. For instance, too much is made of the opening sets of results at the beginning of each season. Fans will read heavily into a sample of data that is too small to draw accurate conclusions. The positioning of a team in the league table bears very little indication of their ability until at least the tenth game of the season. Before this point, there is simply not enough data to make accurate forecasts of where the teams will end up after the completion of the campaign.

The danger of making assumptions based on small sample sizes is far-reaching and inherent. Scouts will collect as much information as pos-sible on a player in an attempt to counter this problem. They normally work for a club, but some are employed by agencies, who will in turn ap-proach a club. Football scouts will watch players, file reports detailing the strengths and weaknesses of a player, and will earn a monetary reward if that player gets picked up by the club. However, analytical pioneers will tell you that the traditional methods of scouting players are inherently flawed. A scout can only realistically attend a handful of matches to watch a player. At most, a Premier League scout might watch a target play live about ten times before compiling his report. This leaves the scout with a small sample size, and his opinion of the player's ability may be based on anomalous performances. A scout may overvalue a player who hap-pens to be on form during the ten or so games that he is being watched, whilst a player who plays unusually poorly during these matches may be dismissed too easily.

Matthew Benham likes to tell the story of when he went to a match many years ago to watch a young player. The striker was drawing a lot of attention from some of the top clubs. This hot prospect apparently had the potential to become a great player. However, when Benham went to see the forward with his own eyes, he was awful. Every touch he made was too heavy, and every shot he took was either blazed over or sliced wide. "That player will never amount to anything", Benham thought.

That player was Zlatan Ibrahimovic.

The dangers of a small sample size can also be accentuated by how humans naturally process information. We are quick to judge, and are prone to form opinions with great haste. The eminent saying that we decide whether we like someone within the first seven seconds of meeting them serves testament to this. Studies done by researchers at Stanford, Tufts, and NYU have revealed that the brain makes eleven rapid-fire decisions within the first few seconds of meeting someone. The ultimate conclusion is that first impressions are remarkably hard to overcome. Neuroscientists generally agree that a substantial opinion is formed after three to seven seconds. Nearly everyone forms a first impression in less than half a minute. After that, opinions are slow and difficult to change. Growing familiarity can alter them, but a negative first impression creates a reluctance to engage for long enough (or often enough) for us to want to draw a second opinion. It's this lack of new information that makes a change of view hard to muster.

Football fans suffer from this quirk in the wiring of the human brain. If a player has a poor performance on his debut, he will be deemed a poor signing by the fans. Conversely, a player who puts in a good performance on his debut may be hailed as the team's new super-star.

When Anthony Martial signed for Manchester United in 2015 for £36m, he became the most expensive teenager in the history of the game. Expectation was high for Martial, and on his debut the youngster duly delivered. Not only did he score on his debut, but he scored a glorious goal, taking on several Liverpool defenders before slotting into the bottom corner. Football fans everywhere overreacted. Martial was hailed as "the next Thierry Henry", with Manchester United legend Alex Ferguson claiming that "he can do anything".

Martial was clearly a good player, but after a blistering start to his Manchester United career, he put in a string of average performances. However, due to the buzz created from his debut – and more specifically his debut goal, his mediocre displays were overlooked. First impressions matter. What would have happened if Martial had put in an average performance in his first match? Would there have been as much hype? Would Van Gaal have been criticised for splashing out so much money on a player who was so young? In the seasons following Martial's breakthrough, he has gradually fallen out of favour at United. As his data sample has increased with each performance, his career has seemed increasingly ordinary.

As a footballer gets older, the sample size of his performance data grows larger. When a player has played for several years, it is easy to measure his ability. There is a large amount of information that we can analyse in order to assess how good he really is. However, when we do the same with young players we can often be misled. They have played fewer matches, meaning that their sample size is shrouded in noise. We have already seen that if we judge a team too early on in a season then our predictions can turn out disastrously wrong. The same can be true for players' careers.

When Manchester United signed Martial they believed that they were signing a world-class superstar. They thought that his record at AS Monaco, where Martial scored eleven goals in forty-nine appearances despite being just eighteen years of age, was a true reflection of the striker's ability. It was a risky move. With such a small sample size to consider, Martial could have simply been lucky to have attained such a good record. It is obvious that players such as Beckham, Lampard and Gerrard were greats, as consistently performing well over an extended period removes the element of luck. The truth prevails over the noise. This is the result of ergodicity, which we will study in the next section.

If mediocre young players are mistaken for being highly talented, then the reverse is also true. Youthful footballers who have great ability may be dismissed if they go through a slump in form. Even Benham, the pioneering mastermind of this book, fell victim to this when he dismissed Ibrahimovic based on a miniscule sample size. Scouts are forced to make predictions about the future ability of a player based on similarly small sample sizes. Every day, multiple young players who have great potential are dismissed because scouts mistake a drop in form for a lack of ability. The saying goes that form is temporary, class is permanent. When faced with a small sample size, we can find it difficult to differentiate between the two.

In November 2008, *The Guardian* asked its football writers to select the twenty players under nineteen years of age that were playing in England at the time who they thought would be most successful in the future. Nearly a decade later, most of these footballers are now at the peak of their playing ability, and are performing at the highest level that they are likely to perform at. Assessing the success of the pundits' predictions reveals the difficult nature of forecasting the future ability of young players.

Figure 1-1 shows the eighteen players who finished the 2014-15 season in the English Football League system. The fourth column shows their age in 2008, when *The Guardian* published their predictions, whilst the fifth column shows what club they played for at that time. The seventh column shows their age at the end of the 2014-15 season, and the eighth shows the club that they played for at that point. The ninth and final column tells us the ranking of that club in the English Football League. For example, Arsenal finished third in the Premier League, and thus are ranked third overall, whereas Hartlepool finished twenty-second in League Two, earning them 90th position in the Football League[3].

It immediately becomes apparent how difficult it is to predict the future ability of young players. *The Guardian* correctly projected that players such as Jack Wilshere and Danny Welbeck, who both resided at Arsenal in 2015, would go on to become successful footballers. Players such as Victor Moses, Jonjo Shelvey and Jordan Henderson were also on their list, and also serve to illustrate that it is possible to forecast which young footballers will achieve success.

---

3 The Football League is taken to mean the Premier League, Championship, League One and League Two – the top four divisions of English football.

Figure 1-1: The Guardian's Best Young Players in England Development

Player	Position	Age (2008)	Club (2008)	Club (2015)	Rank of club
Mark Beevers	Defender	18	Sheffield Wednesday	Millwall	42nd
Nathan Delfouneso	Striker	17	Aston Villa	Blackburn	29th
Fabian Delph	Midfielder	18	Leeds United	Aston Villa	17th
Daniel Drinkwater	Midfielder	18	Manchester United	Leicester City	14th
Jordan Henderson	Midfielder	18	Sunderland	Liverpool	6th
Gavin Hoyte	Defender	18	Arsenal	Gillingham	56th
Henri Lansbury	Midfielder	18	Arsenal	Nottingham Forest	38th
Jacob Mellis	Midfielder	17	Chelsea	Bury	61st
Victor Moses	Striker	17	Crystal Palace	Stoke City	9th
Nile Ranger	Striker	17	Newcastle	Blackpool	44th
Jack Rodwell	Midfielder	17	Everton	Sunderland	16th
Freddie Sears	Striker	18	West Ham	Ipswich	30th
Jonjo Shelvey	Midfielder	16	Charlton	Swansea	8th
Danny Welbeck	Striker	17	Manchester United	Arsenal	3rd
Aiden White	Defender	17	Leeds United	Rotherham	41st
Jack Wilshere	Midfielder	16	Arsenal	Arsenal	3rd
Michael Woods	Midfielder	18	Chelsea	Hartlepool	90th
Jose Baxter	Striker	16	Everton	Sheffield United	49th

This is to be expected; to a certain extent, the pundits at *The Guardian* had had half their work done for them. Every young player who is contracted to a leading football club is expected to achieve great things. The club has put faith in them by offering them a contract. In theory, the best young footballers will be contracted to the best football clubs. To make a reasonable prediction of who are the future superstars, all one has to do is look at the Under 18 squad of a top Premier League football club.

The Guardian's forecasts were ultimately failures. Only eight of the eighteen players were playing in the Premier League at the end of the 2014-15 season, with 22.2% of the selected eighteen playing for a club who weren't even in the top two divisions of English football. Only two of the eighteen players who were allegedly the future of football in England were playing for clubs who finished in the top four positions of the Premier League table; Danny Welbeck and Jack Wilshere at Arsenal. Indeed, Michael Woods, the Chelsea midfielder who was eighteen at the time that the predictions were made, played for Hartlepool in 2015, a club who only narrowly avoided relegation from League Two. These results serve as a testament to the difficulty of making forecasts based on a small amount of data.

The Guardian's 2008 predictions also highlight that it is a lot harder to determine whether a defender is destined to achieve success than it is to do so with a striker or midfielder. The average ranking of a defender's team was forty-sixth position on the Football League pyramid, the equivalent of second position in League One. Comparatively, midfielders proved to be playing for the highest ranked teams. On average, a midfielder in The Guardian's eighteen top young players in 2008 was playing in twenty-sixth position in the Football League pyramid. That is the equivalent to sixth in the Championship. Strikers were similarly successful as midfielders, with an average ranking of twenty-seventh between them.

Why did defenders fare so badly? The answer lies in the fact that it is much harder to gauge the ability of a defensive player than an attacking player. Scoring a goal is a fairly individual activity; the scorer often gets most of the credit. However, whereas a goal is scored by a *player*, a goal is conceded by a *team*. Letting a goal in is considered a failure of the collective. Additionally, much of what a defender does goes unnoticed. It is said that the best defenders hardly ever touch the ball, because their excellent positioning means that they are not required to. Paolo Maldini, the legendary Italian defender, said, "If I have to make a tackle then I have already made a mistake".

The Guardian's predictions show us is that it is hazardous to make predictions based on small sample sizes. The best approach is to try and recognise when we may be making assumptions based on a small amount of information. If we become more vigilant when it comes to judging new players, new managers or early-season performances, then we will become infinitely better at separating truth from noise, and ability from luck.

RANKING SAMPLES, ERGODICITY AND VARIANCE

The less data we have at our disposal, the more extreme our findings will be. This seems obvious, but can make it difficult to create ranking systems for entities with different sample sizes. We tend to overlook this fact when making predictions. Media companies will often compare the records of two different managers, or, more dangerously, the record of two different players. They may compare the scoring records of two strikers, one who has played thirty games and one who has played just eight. Obviously, the striker who has played more games is likely to have scored more goals, so they account for this by offering a "Goals scored per ninety minutes" stat. This displays the average amount of goals the striker has scored for every ninety minutes he has completed.

It can be easy to fool oneself into believing that these stats offer any meaningful indication of which striker is likely to score more goals in a match. If the two players had played the exact same number of minutes, we might be more inclined to take notice of the graphic. However, the fact that the two strikers have such different sample sizes creates a huge problem with the data. The striker who has played less games is much more likely to have scored a more extreme number of goals per ninety minutes.

Allow me to use the example of goalkeepers to illustrate the problem with ranking players (or teams, or managers, or whatever) that have dispensed different quantities of data. I once came across a graphic on a blog displaying the average "Goals per game" that various goalkeepers had conceded. The blogger was attempting to define the best goalkeeper in the Premier League, and was claiming to have made a miraculous discovery. The shot-stoppers who had conceded the least amount of goals per game weren't the players you would have expected. The keepers who are commonly considered the best, the Cechs, the Harts, the De Geas, were all placed about halfway down the rankings, whilst some of the more obscure goalkeepers dominated the upper echelons of the table. In fact, the best goalkeeper, this blogger concluded, was Wayne Hennessey. Crystal Palace had conceded just 0.69 goals per game when Hennessey had been between the sticks.

In actuality, Hennessey was almost certainly not the best goalkeeper in the Premier League. The blogger had fallen victim to the pitfalls of ranking entities with different sample sizes against one another. What had happened was that Hennessey had played less games than most of the better goalkeepers in the sample, meaning his data was more prone to deviance. The Crystal Palace goalkeeper had only played thirteen games at that point in the season, whilst most of the top goalkeepers had played nineteen.

To further explain what went wrong with the blogger's analysis, we must introduce the statistical phenomenon of variance. In short, variance tells us how much a statistic deviates from the norm. For example, the average goalkeeper in the analysis conceded 1.3 goals per game. Hennessey's record of conceding 0.69 goals per game is quite a large deviance from the average figure. A goalkeeper who conceded 2 goals per game would have a similar deviation from the norm, simply in the opposite direction. Every data point in a sample has a degree of variance, which is known as *standard deviation*.

Another important factor to introduce is ergodicity. Ergodicity, essentially, is a way to describe how the effect of randomness diminishes over time. This links with the fact that the larger sample size you collect, the less noisy the data will be and the easier it will become to perform an accurate analysis. Here is an example of ergodicity: you decide to flip a coin multiple times to find out whether it is weighted fairly. A fair coin should land on "heads" just as regularly as it lands on "tails". Flipping it over and over again will leave you with a satisfactory conclusion.

You flip the coin once and it lands on "heads". This tells you basically nothing about the fairness of the coin. It could still be heavily weighted towards one side or the other. All you can really determine from this flip is that the outcome "heads" is possible. You flip it six times. Now, it had landed on "heads" five times and "tails" once. Do you conclude that the coin is heavily weighted towards "heads"? Whilst you should at this point be suspicious about the fairness of the coin, you should not yet draw any conclusions. The sample size is still too small to make an accurate assessment. You flip the coin another ninety-four times, and end up with a total score of fifty-three to "heads" and forty-seven to "tails". With this large sample size, you can now conclude that the coin is pretty fairly weighted. There is only a slight difference between number of times that the coin lands on each side, a small enough disparity to attribute this variation down to luck. What you have just witnessed is ergodicity. The more you flip the coin, the less the impact that chance has on your findings. If you were to flip the coin another ten thousand times, you would be able to draw even more conclusive results.

This ties in neatly with variance. Were you to flip the coin four times, and "heads" showed up on three occasions, you probably wouldn't be that surprised. There is a fairly large probability that the coin would land on either "heads" or "tails" on three of the four occasions. However, were you to flip the coin one thousand times, and the coin turned up "heads" 75% of the time (or on 750 occasions), you would probably be incredibly shocked, and begin to question the fairness of the coin. Due to ergodicity, the annoying effects of randomness should have been removed by the time you reach the one thousandth toss.

How does this tie in with our table ranking the Premier League goalkeepers? Essentially, Hennessey came out top of the list because he had played less matches, meaning that his results were more prone to variance. Whilst the top goalkeepers had played lots of matches, meaning that their "Goals conceded per game" score moved more towards the average, Hennessey's score had remained further away from the mean.

This phenomenon also works the other way. The goalkeepers at the bottom of the rankings had also played very few matches, but had just happened to concede lots of goals in those matches. Had these players played every game of the season, they would have moved more towards the middle of the table. The more tosses of the coin that you get, the less extreme your results will become.

Here is one more example that further explains the potential impacts of ergodicity and variance. Consider an insurance company that has two million customers each paying £100 to be insured for a year, meaning that they take in £200m each year. Each time someone makes a claim, they pay out £1m to the customer. This happens about one hundred times a year, meaning they pay out £100m each year in claims. Thus, the company is collecting £200m a year (£100 from each of their two million customers), and are generally paying out £100m a year (£1m to each of the one hundred customers who claim the insurance), meaning that they are able to pocket the remaining £100m.

Now consider a smaller company who make £2m a year from twenty thousand customers each paying £100 to be insured. This company pays out £1m to each customer who makes a claim, but the company only expects this to happen about once a year. This company collects £2m from customers, but shells out about £1m to the customer who claims insurance, meaning that they pocket the remaining £1m.

Both of these companies are expecting to make back the same amount of their investment (i.e. the money that they are paying back to claimers). The first company invests £100m in claims and pockets £100m, whilst the second company invests £1m and pockets £1m. Despite the fact that they both stand to make a healthy sum of money, consider the increased risk that faces the smaller company. For the big company, suppose that one-hundred and ten people have to be given £1m each instead of the one hundred customers that they expected. The big company now shells out £110m in claims, and is left with a slightly smaller sum of £90m for themselves. Now consider a handful more people claim money back from the smaller company. If just three people (two more than the one that was expected) need to have their insurance fulfilled, the small company would need to pay £3m out. This would leave the company in £2m worth of debt.

The fact that the big company have so many more customers means that they are less subjected to variance. They can handle a bit of bad luck, whereas the small company cannot afford any bad luck. Ergodicity is inextricably linked to sample size; the less data you have at your disposal, the less accurately you can make predictions.

Addressing this problem is particularly tricky. The only real way to deal with small sample sizes is to collect more data. Had Hennessey played the same number of minutes as the top goalkeepers in the blogger's sample, we could have more accurately assessed his ability. Until that point, it is hard to tell whether he really is a top class goalkeeper, or simply had a handful of good performances due to chance. All we can really do is maintain a healthy scepticism of such data, in an attempt to prevent being fooled by variance and randomness.

BLACK SWANS

We can say with a fair degree of confidence that the sun will rise tomorrow morning, because it has done so every morning of our existence so far. We have a large sample size to draw from, allowing us to make an assured prediction. Nevertheless, this doesn't mean that we can be absolutely sure that the sun will rise tomorrow, as the sample is not yet fully complete.

Nassim Nicholas Taleb, a Lebanese-American statistician, essayist and risk analyst, presents it like this: every swan that you have ever seen is probably white. Does that mean that there are no black swans? Of course not. For you to be absolutely sure that there are no black swans, you will have had to have seen *every* swan that exists. You can never be truly sure that there isn't a black swan hiding somewhere you haven't looked. Thus, it is impossible to say with complete certainty that there are no black swans, or that the sun will definitely rise tomorrow morning.

A major flaw with the human system of inference is that we take our past experiences as the only possible experiences that could have happened. We believe, because we have never seen a black swan, that they cease to exist. This idiosyncrasy in the wiring of humans is especially problematic for those whose livelihoods depend on successful prediction making, like professional gamblers or city traders. A large number of traders believe that their system is fool-proof because they have been using it for a couple of years and have consistently made money. They believe that every possible eventuality which could have upset their way of operating must have occurred during this short time period. They do not prepare themselves for a random, yet devastating, incident which has little probability of occurring, but carries dire consequences when it does come about. These rare and devastating events often cause traders to blow up, as they are not at all prepared for their occurrence. This trader will lose everything, simply because he did not protect himself from encountering a rare event. The recession in 2008 is another example of a black swan. No one expected the housing bubble to burst, simply because it had never done so before.

An event which is extremely uncommon but carries destructive circumstances has been come to be defined as a "black swan". An example outside of the trading world would be the sudden death of a close family member. No one wakes up in the morning expecting to encounter a black swan. Humans are naturally unprepared for such occasions. We are prone to dismiss unlikely events, despite the large negative impacts they could have on us. This stems from our subconscious, and incorrect, belief that the amount of information (the sample size) that we have collected is always sufficient.

A footballing example of a black swan occurring is Leicester City winning the Premier League in 2016. For the bookmakers, this was a devastating event. Most of the leading bookies had set the odds of the Foxes winning the Premier League at 5000/1, assigning them a 0.0002% chance of triumphing. Whilst it is true that such an upset had never occurred before in the history of the English game, it is also true that the English League football had only been played for little over a century at the time that the bookmakers made this prediction. There was not a large enough sample size of previous seasons for the bookmakers to assume that Leicester winning the league was as unlikely as they made it out to be. Just like the people who believe there are no black swans because they have never set eyes on one, or those traders who believe their system is fool-proof because it hasn't failed them yet, the bookies believed that such an incredible occurrence would almost certainly not take place. The bookmakers lost millions of pounds due to this particular black swan. At least they seemed to learn their lesson; the longest odds that they gave out the next season for a team to win the league was Hull City at 2000/1.

Out of Sample

It is clear that basing a prediction on a limited sized sample of data can be incredibly hazardous. A mistake even more damning would be to use data from outside of the correct sample to make forecasts. We sometimes unconsciously use irrelevant information in order to confirm what we believe to be true. This mistake can be made in many walks of life, and can have costly effects.

For example, let's say you have been drinking at a party. You're well over the limit, but you drove to the venue and don't want to have to leave your car there. You may try to convince yourself that it will be fine to drive home. After all, you have made thousands of journeys before and have only had one or two minor incidents. This proves that you are a good driver, and therefore it's highly unlikely that you will get into a crash, despite your inebriated state. However, the prediction that you will almost certainly be fine has been founded on data that was out of sample. The previous thousands of journeys that you have based your forecast on occurred when you were sober. The fact that you are not in a sober state for this journey renders the other thousands of journeys irrelevant. The sample of data which you should base your projection on is the number of journeys that you have made whilst drunk.

Mistaking out of sample data for useful information can be equally as hazardous in the world of sport. Before their Euro 2012 quarter-final with Italy, Roy Hodgson stepped up England's penalty-taking practice. England have a history of exiting international competitions through the ordeal of a penalty shoot-out. The nation crashed out of major tournaments on spot-kicks on five occasions in the twenty-two years prior to the 2012 quarter-final, a run that dated back to a devastating World Cup semi-final defeat to Germany in 1990.

Hodgson recognised the need to place particular emphasis on penalty-taking. Having a side confident from the spot meant that if England were on the back foot during the match then they could sit back and attempt to contain the Italians. Ensuring that his side were good from twelve yards gave Hodgson a tactical advantage. Indeed, the quarter-final did end up going to penalties. England sensed the opportunity to progress to the semi-finals by putting all their hours of hard training into practice. However, in typically English fashion, two penalties were missed and the Italians triumphed 4-2 in the shoot-out.

There were several reasons for England's shoot-out disappointment. Luck, of course, played a massive part. A sample size of four penalties is too small to assess England's penalty taking ability with absolute accuracy. There is no doubt that luck played a part in England's undoing.

Nevertheless, it is easy to argue that Hodgson made crucial mistakes. In preparing for the penalty shoot-out, Hodgson made players take several penalties against Joe Hart whilst the rest of the players, waiting for their turn, just stood around the edge of the box watching. This is a classic example of out of sample data in action. It is impossible to replicate the pressure that a penalty-taker feels when he steps up to take his spot-kick in front of a worldwide audience in the quarter-final of the European Championships. Taking a penalty on a training pitch with nothing depending on the outcome is very different to taking a penalty which decides the result of your national football team. However, there are ways in which you can come closer to replicating that pressure. Hodgson could have lined his players up on the halfway line, as they would in the actual match. He could have made them take the long, lonely walk from the centre of the pitch to the penalty box, as they would do in the shoot-out. If he was being totally thorough, he could have made them collect the ball themselves and place it on the spot, rather than having a coach kick it to them before their attempt, further replicating the conditions of an actual penalty shoot-out.

The training regime which Hodgson set up to prepare for a penalty shoot-out was drastically out of sample. It would have been impossible to exactly imitate the environment of the actual shoot-out, but he could have taken extra measures to ensure that the preparation was more closely matched to the real thing. Just like our example of drunk driving, Hodgson fooled himself into thinking that England were penalty-taking specialists because he based his judgement on data which was irrelevant.

EXPECTED VALUE

Expected value is possibly the most useful tool that can be used to make predictions. It is utilised in almost every financial realm, and is an incredibly important concept to comprehend. As we will see in the latter chapters, Matthew Benham has founded his success on this metric. An understanding of expected value is absolutely imperative if we wish to understand how the professional gambler made his millions.

The expected value of a variable is the long-run average value of repetitions of the experiment it represents. For instance, the expected value of a roll of a normal six-sided dice is 3.5, because this is the average of all the numbers which come up after a large number of rolls. Of course, it is impossible for us to roll a 3.5, but this is the average value that we would expect to come up if we rolled our dice, say, one million times. Likewise, the average person might expect to own 4.5 cars over the course of their lifetime. Obviously, it is impossible for anyone to own 4.5 cars, as it is impossible to break whole vehicles down into fractions. This figure simply reflects how many cars the average person might *expect* to own.

Expected value is used frequently in financial settings. For example, if you wanted to work out whether or not to purchase a lottery ticket, you could work out the amount of money that you could expect to make back from it. Suppose that a lottery is selling one thousand tickets for £2 each. Only one ticket can win the jackpot, which is set at £1,500. You want to work out whether it is worthwhile investing £2 of your money on a ticket. Expected value can help you do this, as it will tell you how much money you can expect the ticket to win over the long run.

The equation for working out expected value is very simple. Simply multiply the probability of each outcome occurring by the amount of money that you would make if it did occur, before adding all of these outcomes together. For example, in the lottery example given above, there are only two possible outcomes: either you win the £1,500 jackpot or you don't. Thus, in order to work out the expected value of a lottery ticket we must carry out the following equation:

(Chance of winning x Winning amount) + (Chance of losing + Losing amount)
(1/1000 x £1,500) + (999/1000 x £0) = Expected value of ticket
£1.50 + £0 = £1.50

Using this simple equation, we can work out that the expected value of a ticket for this lottery is £1.50. *This is what the lottery ticket is worth.* If we entered this lottery on hundreds of thousands of occasions, we would expect to make back an average of £1.50 each time. (Remember, just as we cannot actually own 4.5 cars in our lifetime, we cannot actually win £1.50 on any occasion. This is simply the amount that we can expect to win each time over the long run). Seeing as we know that the value of each ticket for this lottery is £1.50, we can now decide whether or not to purchase one. Clearly, paying £2 for a ticket that is only worth £1.50 is a bad idea. If someone offered to swap their pen worth £1.50 in exchange for your pen worth £2, you wouldn't take the deal. When there is a negative expected value, as in our lottery example, you should never stake your involvement.

The equation for expected value can also help us when there are more than two outcomes possible. Our prior example was simple; of the one thousand people who entered the lottery, one person won the jackpot and nine-hundred and ninety-nine people walked away empty-handed. What happens when we introduce a couple more possible outcomes? Suppose that the lottery still sold one thousand tickets at £2 each, but this time the prize for the winning ticket is £500, the second-place and third-place tickets win £300 and the fourth-placed, fifth placed and sixth placed tickets win £100. Now there are four different outcomes possible: you win £500, you win £300, you win £100 or you win nothing. Each of these outcomes has a different probability of occurring. The equation remains inherently the same, just with the updated variables:

(Chance of first-placed ticket x First-placed winnings) + (Chance of second or third-placed ticket x Second or third-placed winnings) + (Chance of fourth, fifth or sixth-placed ticket x Fourth, fifth or sixth-placed winnings)
(1/1000 x £500) + (2/1000 x £300) + (3/1000 x £100) = Expected value
*£0.5 + £0.6 + £0.3 = **£1.40***

The expected value of a ticket for this particular lottery is £1.40. Seeing that one of the one thousand tickets will win £500, two of the one thousand tickets will win £300, three of the one thousand tickets will win £100 and nine-hundred and ninety-four tickets will win nothing, we could expect each random ticket to be worth £1.40 before the draw is made. Again, this means that each ticket offers us negative value when they are being priced at £2. If each ticket only cost £1, there would a positive expectation and it would be worth investing our money.

A strong grasp of expected value is crucial to success in any financial industry. Bookmakers, casinos, lotteries and mutual fund managers all make fortunes by offering negative expected value deals to unassuming customers. Each bet placed at a bookmaker, each lottery ticket purchased at a corner shop and each staked wagered at a casino tends to have negative expectation. Over the long run, we will always lose money when dealing with these institutions. Bettors and gamblers are essentially buying products for less money that they are worth. They are paying £2 for commodities worth £1.50. In the latter chapters, we will study how to turn the odds on such establishments.

Before we leave expected value for the time being, let me share with you a particular experience where I found it useful. I was in a bar with some friends when someone proposed that we buy a round of drinks. However, instead of each paying for our own drinks, we were to each give our debit cards to the bartender to randomly pick one person to pay for the whole round. Some of the group opted out, worried they would have to pay for the entirety of the hefty bill. Others were keen to take part, focusing on the likelihood of obtaining free drinks. To make my decision, I quickly worked out the expected value of partaking in the game. There were six of us each wanting £8 worth of drinks. This meant that the unlucky individual who lost the game had to pay for the entire £48 worth of drinks (a loss of £40 because they still got to drink the £8 worth of alcohol that they spent on themselves), whilst the five who won were gifted £8 worth of drinks for free. Here was the equation which needed working out:

(Chance of my card being drawn x Losses) + (Chance of my card not being drawn x Winnings)
(1/6 x -£40) + (5/6 x £8) = Expected value
-£6.67 + £6.67 = £0

The expected value of entering the wager was £0. This makes sense when you think about it: when each individual has an equal chance of winning the same amount of drink, there is neither a negative nor positive expectation to be obtained. Over the long run, entering into the game would pay out the same amount as buying drinks for yourself. I decided that the social value of taking part tipped the decision in favour of placing my stake in the wager. On that particular occasion, the reader will be pleased to learn that the bartender did not select my card and I got £8 worth of drinks paid for by an unlucky friend.

THE SCIENCE OF PENALTIES

Looking at an aspect of the sport as statistically exposed as penalties reveals the usefulness of utilising data in football. The taking of spot-kicks is the one area of the beautiful game isolated enough to be analysed as thoroughly as other sports. A penalty is a single action. Much like a pitch in baseball, a sport which allows much more confident conclusions to be drawn from the data it supplies, a penalty involves two primary individuals: the penalty taker, who is trying to kick the ball into the goal, and the goalkeeper, who is trying to save the shot. In baseball, the pitcher is trying to throw the ball so that it evades the batsman, whilst the hitter is trying to smack it out of the park. Despite residing in completely different sports, the two scenarios are actually very similar.

Before matches, goalkeepers will often analyse data on which direction certain players tend to put their penalties. In 2011, Matthew Benham, the analytical hero of this book, watched from the stands as Brentford's Richard Lee saved three penalties in a row in a penalty shoot-out against Charlton Athletic. This was no coincidence; Lee had studied the penalty-taking tendencies of each of Charlton's players. This simple analysis was the difference between victory and defeat for Brentford on that particular evening.

We can utilise data from past penalties to determine the best ways of scoring from twelve yards. When Marcello Trotta stepped up to take the defining penalty of the 2012/13 Championship season, he elected to put his foot through the ball and blast it at goal, a tactic which resulted in the ball smashing into the crossbar. Was this a flawed philosophy? Should he have instead chosen to pick his spot and place the ball in the corner? Does it make a difference whether a player takes a long or short run up? Several studies have been conducted into the art of penalty-taking, and some of the results are truly fascinating.

Research headed by Michael Bar-Eli at the Ben-Gurion University in Israel analysed the video of 286 penalty kicks from professional leagues in Europe and South America as well as from the European Championships and World Cup competitions. The researchers coded each penalty kick into one of three vertical (high, middle or low) and horizontal (right, centre or left) sections of the goal. They also coded goalkeeper movements (dive right, dive left or stay central) and whether or not they stopped the shot. Efforts which missed the target were not included.

85% of the penalties were successful, over half of which were placed in the bottom third of the goal. These low attempts were successful around four out of five times. Comparatively, only 13% of shots were placed in the upper third of the goal. However, every single one of these efforts resulted in the penalty being converted. Almost every study that has been conducted in the field of penalty-taking has concluded that if the taker places a penalty in the top third of the goal, he has almost a 100% chance of scoring. It is incredibly hard for a goalkeeper to save a penalty that is above shoulder height.

A study conducted by the BBC into every penalty ever taken in a World Cup shoot-out supports this theory. 144 of the 204 penalties in the sample have been successfully converted, leaving us with a success rate of 70.6%. The vast majority of penalties are placed low and in the corner of the goal. Few are placed in the upper third, but those that are generally tend to beat the goalkeeper. In fact, of the thirty-seven penalties which were on target above shoulder height of the average goalkeeper, only one has ever been saved in a World Cup shoot-out.

The natural question that follows this conclusion is why doesn't every penalty-taker hit the ball into the top third of the goal? The answer lies literally outside of the box, or rather, the goal. We have not accounted for the penalties which miss the target completely. The BBC's analysis shows that thirteen of the two-hundred and four penalties ever taken in a World Cup shoot-out either hit the bar or went over. If we add these off-target penalties to the one's which are on-target and above shoulder height, we end up with a success rate of just 72%, substantially lower than the rate of 97.3% that we end up with when we don't incorporate the missed penalties. This is only marginally better than the 70.6% general success rate of all the penalties in the sample.

If a player can master the art of blasting a penalty high and on target, the stats show they can greatly increase their conversion rate. However, this is a difficult ability for even the best football players. Additionally, players are far more afraid of missing the target altogether than they are of having a penalty saved. There is no shame in having a penalty saved if it is placed low and in the bottom corner. If a player goes for the marginally more rewarding tactic of blasting the ball high and ends up missing the target altogether he is more likely to be ostracised by the fans, players and his manager. Statistically speaking, however, a player must insulate himself from this fear. Going for broke and shooting high into the goalmouth will give him the greatest probability of scoring.

The analytical revolution which is beginning to take place in the world of football means that most Premier League goalkeepers are able to study a penalty-taker's past spot-kicks. However, such profound analysis is not widely practiced lower down the Football League ladder. Neil Sullivan, the Doncaster goalkeeper who was tasked with saving Marcello Trotta's 2012/13 League One season-deciding penalty, hadn't the faintest idea of where the Italian would place his kick. What should a goalkeeper do if he has to rely simply on his gut instinct?

The answer can also be found in Bar-Eli's research. He discovered that slightly more shots were placed to the goalkeeper's right side compared to the centre or left. Most penalty takers choose to shoot across their body. As most footballers are right-footed it follows that most penalties are aimed to the goalkeeper's right. Of the three vertical thirds, kickers were most successful when shooting at the centre of the goal. Shots aimed down the middle were converted 87% of the time compared to an 83% success rate for shots placed either to the right or the left-hand sides of the goal.

This leads to an interesting conclusion. One would assume, because goalkeepers stand in the middle of the goal before the ball is struck, that this is the most likely place for the ball to be saved. However, the study shows that goalkeepers commit themselves to diving to one side or the other 94% of the time. This means penalties which are fired straight down the middle are more likely to find the net than those which are aimed for the corners. The reason why most players don't do this is the same reason why most players choose not to shoot high into the goal; fear of embarrassment. If a player aims for the middle of the goal and the goalkeeper saves it, the player will be rebuked for taking a poor penalty.

A good penalty-taker will realise that it doesn't matter how a penalty goes in. All that matters is that it *does* go in. Statistically speaking, a penalty has the highest chance of success if it is placed either in the top third of the goal or in the central third of the goal. If a player can master the art of placing penalties in these positions, and try to filter out the fear of embarrassment if he misses the target or has a penalty saved, then he and his team will benefit over the long-run.

DATA COLLECTION

There are two steps to making a successful prediction. The first step is collecting the data, a task which anyone can do provided they have the right equipment and a clear idea of what they are looking for. The second is knowing what to do with it and how to look at it. Both of these tasks are incredibly hard to achieve when it comes to football. Ever since the beautiful game was formed, we have been trying to understand how it works, how it should be played and, ultimately, how to account for the role of luck within the sport. The most sensible method of doing this is to collect as much information as possible, before searching through that information for the answers. This is what tens of thousands of analysts have been doing throughout the history of the sport.

One of the first men to master the art of collecting data in football was Charles Reep. Reep, born in Cornwall in 1904, trained as an accountant before becoming one of the first ever football analysts. He would keep track of games by using a pencil and a notebook, and developed shorthand codes for events such as passes, shots and turnovers. The detail which Reep went into with his collating of data was extraordinary. Reep stated that "each pass in the game [was] classified and recorded by its length, direction, height and outcome, as well as the positions on the pitch where the pass originated and ended". Over the course of his career, Reep's appetite for analysis led him to annotate more than 2,200 fixtures. Each match would take eighty hours to fully scrutinise.

The technology that we have today has revolutionised our ability to collect stats. Gone are the days of analysts sitting in the cold with a pen, notebook and flashlight. Football data companies employ analysts who reside in offices with highly intelligent equipment. However, collecting football data is still a laborious task, even with modern technology. There is no shortcut to the task of logging every single action in a match. Opta Sports are currently the leading company in this field, and their analysts will testify to the hours of dedication that go into recording information.

Opta was founded in the 1990s by a group of management consultants who felt the need to create a player performance index in football. They began collecting data on every player in the top division of English football with the aim of producing a reliable and informative index of each of these players' performances. Initially, the aim was to increase the brand of their company by gaining exposure through media outlets such as Sky Sports and *The Observer* newspaper. However, they soon discovered that the data they were collecting was far more valuable than the exposure they were gaining. Media outlets were desperate to buy stats from them, as were English football clubs themselves. The data revolution of football had begun.

Initially, the methods that Opta used were nothing special. Like Reep, they had to make do with a pen and paper. The stats that they were recording were as basic as shots, saves and passes. The matches were recorded on a video camera, before analysts spent hours stopping and starting the footage as they collected the data. The number of actions which took place in each game tended to be between 2,500 and 3,000, meaning each match took about four hours to fully code. Opta collect a huge amount of information; every header, every kick, every save. In order to demonstrate how an Opta analyst collects this data, let's focus on just one action, from one football match.

In 2010, Andres Iniesta scored a dramatic late winner for Spain in front of a live attendance exceeding 84,000, and a worldwide television audience of tens of millions. Iniesta's drilled shot won Spain the World Cup for the first time, and condemned the Netherlands to their third defeat in the final of the competition. The Spanish were jubilant at their extra time winner, the Dutch incensed that they hadn't been awarded a corner just moments before Iniesta's strike.

Thousands of miles away, one of the most significant footballing actions of the decade was being coded in an office by Opta analysts. To these analysts, Iniesta's goal was merely a series of numbers on a computer screen.

Figure 1-2: Iniesta's World Cup Final Goal in Opta's Code

game_id (World Cup Final 2010)	31804
event_id (Spain's 1196th event)	1196
id (Unique ID)	287890550
period_id (Extra Time, 2nd Half)	4
period_minute (Minute of the game)	115
event_type_id (Code for "Goal")	16
player_id (Andres Iniesta)	11237
team_id (Spain)	118

Figure 1-2 shows just some of the ways in which Opta's analysts code each event. Every action which takes place in each match that Opta analyse is given the same set of codes: which match it happens in, the period, minute and second of the game in which the event takes place, the number of the action for the respective team (e.g. Iniesta's goal was Spain's 1196th event of the 2010 World Cup final). Most crucial, however, is what is known as the "event_type_id". This number denotes what action took place.

Every event which happens in a match, whether it be a yellow card, a save, a clearance, an interception, a substitution, or any other action that could take place, is represented by a different number. For Opta's analysts, sixteen is the magic number; the number which signifies the event of a goal. Other notable numerals include the digits one, three and thirteen, which denote a pass, a dribble and a miss respectively. Analysts who work for the company say that, following hours of assigning numbers to actions, they have come to associate certain digits with certain events.

One particular Opta employee says that whenever he sees a house number marked sixteen, he instantly thinks "Goal!".

Opta also record the position on the pitch where each action happened. To do this they log the pitch axis and co-ordinates, as if measuring longitude and latitude on a map. The length of the pitch (the touchline along the side of the pitch) is seen as the X-axis, whereas the width of the pitch (the by-line which runs across the goal-mouth from one corner flag to the other) is defined as the Y-axis. Given the two co-ordinates, an Opta analyst can tell you the exact location of an event on the field of play. In the case of Andres Iniesta's goal, the X co-ordinates read 9.0 whilst the Y co-ordinates read 63.3. This tells us that he took the shot from just inside the box, and to the right-hand side of the goal.

Figure 1-3: Andres Iniesta's Shot Details in Opta's Code

X	9.0
Y	63.3
Goal Mouth Z Co-ordinate	5.6
Goal Mouth Y Co-ordinate	47.57
qualifier_id (Intentional assist)	154
qualifier_id (One bounce)	118
qualifier_id (Right foot)	20

Similar co-ordinates are given to the face of the goal itself. This enables the analysts to correctly locate the position of the goal where the ball crossed the line. Iniesta's winner went low into the bottom right-hand corner from the goalkeeper's perspective. The exact co-ordinates that Opta's analysts gave were 5.6 for the Z axis, and 47.57 for the Y axis.

Opta use even more specific codes to describe the nature of the goal in detail. This is done through what appears on the computer screen as a series of "qualifier_ids". For example, the goal was intentionally assisted by one of Iniesta's own teammates, meaning that Opta used the "qualifier_id" of 154. The ball bounced once before crossing the line, signified by the "qualifier_id" of 118. The "qualifier_id" of 20 signifies that the Spanish midfielder struck the ball with his right foot. Each goal is granted a series of these signals, specifying the type of build-up play, whether the goalkeeper got a touch or not, if the shot was a volley, half-volley, and so on. By looking at a series of numbers, an analyst could describe in perfect detail any goal that has ever been scored, without having ever actually seen the goal. A goal is no longer just a goal, it is a set of codes on a computer screen, from which an extraordinary amount of information can be gleamed.

Opta collate this type of information on thousands of teams and players. This data can tell you the aerial abilities of any central defender, the passing percentage of any midfielder or the shot-to-goal ratio of any forward. Opta possess a huge amount of information, and in a world where predictive success is both hard to achieve and vital to success, information is power.

Opta have mastered the first stage of prediction-making: data collection. The second step requires real genius to successfully master. How do you utilise, scrutinise and analyse the data in order to achieve predictive triumph? It is down to the football clubs and media outlets that buy Opta's data to interpret the information correctly.

Most teams use the stats to assess upcoming opponents, as well as to scrutinise their own team. The craving for data within football seems insatiable. Managers require the information to develop training sessions, improve tactics and sign players. Journalists, players, coaches, fans, executives, and even football academics all desire access to the most accurate and plentiful statistical resources. Companies who can supply such material reap great rewards.

As technology continues to progress, so does the means with which we can collect stats. A lot of clubs are now using chips located in their players' football boots to track their movements in training matches. It might not be too long until these devices are used in real fixtures. The ability to track the speed and location of all twenty-two players on a football pitch at any one time could revolutionise footballing data. This information could reveal aspects of the game that we cannot currently comprehend. The possibility of inserting similar tracking chips into the football itself has been suggested. This would remove the need for goal-line technology altogether, and grant us an even more profound insight into the game. The curvature of crosses, the power of shots, and the distance of passes could all be accurately measured if we could precisely measure the ball's location. We have barely scratched the surface as far as data collection in football is concerned.

Much of the technology is already available to us, but football is very embedded in its ways. Sports such as rugby and cricket have embraced the introduction of referee referrals, whereas football – possibly the sport most in need of such a change, has rejected the idea. Football is romantic in the sense that it hasn't changed all that much since its formation well over a century ago. But with that lack of change has come a lack of progress.

Despite the fact that collecting a greater quantity of match data will inevitably lead us to make more accurate footballing predictions, an even more prosperous methodology might be to collect a better *quality* of information. Matthew Benham and his team at Smartodds have not developed a supercomputer that gets fed stats and churns out the true ability of a team. What they have developed is a new way of looking at football, a smarter means of collecting data. These innovative methods are what made Benham millions through professional gambling, before allowing him to achieve success with Brentford and Midtjylland. Benham and his analysts don't bother collecting data on actions like passes, possession or shots. The way they analyse games is surprisingly simple; so simple, in fact, that it can be done with just a pen and paper. As we will see at a later point, these are the only tools that one needs to deploy Benham's ground-breaking means of data collection.

SENTIMENTS ARE DETRIMENTS

JOSÉ MOURINHO'S FALL FROM GRACE during his second spell as Chelsea manager is one of the most dramatic stories of English football history. In May of 2015, John Terry lifted the Premier League trophy to mark Chelsea as runaway Champions of the top division. The self-proclaimed "Special One" had returned to Stamford Bridge and delivered the silverware that owner Roman Abramovich craved. In August, as the 2015/16 Premier League season was about to get underway, Mourinho put pen to paper on a new four-year contract.

However, little over four months later Mourinho found himself sacked as manager, with Chelsea sitting perilously close to the relegation zone. Mounting the worst title defence in modern history (trumped only by Leicester's woeful effort the following season), and having amounted just fifteen points from their first sixteen games, Chelsea had completed a tragic fall that William Shakespeare would have been proud of. Having played little under half of their thirty-six game season, Chelsea had a goal difference of minus eight and sat just one point above the relegation zone. Fans, journalists and pundits frantically went about trying to decipher what had been the cause of this unheard of collapse.

Mourinho's hopes of a smooth transition into Chelsea's title defence were derailed from the opening game against Swansea City. A disagreement with team doctor Eva Carneiro provided a discordant start to the season. Mourinho was furious that, with Chelsea already down to ten men, Carneiro had rushed on to treat Eden Hazard. Protocol demands that any player who receives treatment must leave the field for a brief period. The medics' decision was declared "impulsive and naïve" by Mourinho, who was angry that his side were temporarily reduced to nine men whilst his player received medical attention. Carneiro was demoted within the club, leading to a backlash from the Football Medics Association. There were ensuing court cases against both the club and Mourinho on the grounds of constructive dismissal. The Eva Carneiro debacle was the beginning of the end for Mourinho.

The former Real Madrid manager had several run-ins with the authorities early on in the 2015/16 season. Mourinho's arrogance, defiance and brashness, the cornerstones of his personality, are what made him so popular with the media. However, as Chelsea began to decline, many suggested that the manager had entered a stage of delusion. Following Chelsea's 3-0 defeat at the hands of Manchester City in the second game of the season, Mourinho suggested to the media that the result was "fake" and that his team deserved more from the game. This was met by complete bemusement from both sets of supporters, with many suggesting the scoreline should have been even more one-sided.

Mourinho was then sent off at half-time in a loss at West Ham. The referee, Jon Moss, had invited Mourinho into his changing room at half-time in order to calm him down. According to the referee's report: "At this point Mr Mourinho became very aggressive. He shouted that you [expletive] referees are weak… Wenger is right about you… you are [expletive] weak."

Mourinho had, in fact, made errors before the season had even started. Whilst his rivals were busy adding to their squads, Mourinho chose to trust the team that had delivered him the title with ease the season beforehand. Manchester City's response to losing the title was to bring in stellar signings, such as £49m Raheem Sterling from Liverpool, £55m

Kevin de Bruyne from Wolfsburg and £32m defender Nicolas Otamendi from Valencia. Chelsea made a few low-key signings, but their squad was not significantly strengthened. In football, those who spend the most will win the most. Mourinho had the resources, but complacency had set in.

In the realms of football, it is the manager who is most heavily relied upon to make successful predictions. It is he who is entrusted with the power to sign or release players, the ability to tailor training sessions and develop tactics, and the authority to make substitutions when the battle is raging most fiercely. All of these decisions involve predictions as to what will leave the team with the greatest probability of achieving success. Mourinho was hailed as the master of prediction. What led to his sudden, unprecedented fall from grace?

MANAGERIAL BLINDNESS
Football is one of the most emotive sports in existence. A fan can feel a whole spectrum of emotions in a single afternoon. It is the infrequency and randomness of goals that inspires such passion, whether it be jubilance or despondency, from the fans that witness them. These emotions are part-and-parcel of the game. However, these sentiments can blur our vision and ultimately lead to catastrophic predictions.

Few football fans will be familiar with the intricacies of Sir Arthur Conan Doyle's short stories revolved around the character of Sherlock Holmes. A London-based "consulting detective" whose abilities border on the fantastic, Holmes is known for his astute logical reasoning, his ability to adopt almost any disguise, and his use of forensic science to solve difficult cases. The success of the fictional character's work is grounded in his outstanding predictive talent.

A budding forecaster can learn a lot from the adventures of Sherlock Holmes. The detective encourages probabilistic thinking, a cornerstone of prediction-making that radiates strongly in the world of gambling. His astonishing observation skills means that he is an expert in the field of what a football analyst might call "data collection". He sees what normal people would overlook, allowing him an all-important edge. Once he has the information, he skillfully examines and scrutinises it, a process which involves a series of deductions. He eliminates all of the impossible elements, he claims, leaving himself with what must be the truth. Several similarities can be drawn between the detective, searching for truth amongst the noise, and a football analyst attempting to make accurate judgements.

One of the most important lessons that can be learnt from Doyle's tales is that emotion causes inner conflict, preventing us from making correct forecasts. Holmes describes love, perhaps the strongest and most volatile emotion, as leading to "human error" when it comes to decision-making. Sentiment makes it impossible for someone to be objective and analyse information effectively. Sherlock Holmes, were he able to assess modern-day football, would wonder how a fan can make rational assessments of the team he supports.

Maintaining an objective view and to separating yourself from all biases is essential. José Mourinho is the perfect example of a manager who was unable to do this. In frequent interviews during his side's decline at the end of 2015 he would make bizarre and outlandish claims that led to many tagging him "the deluded one". After the defending Champions' defeat to Southampton, he declared that referees were "afraid to give decisions to Chelsea". This accusation came just months after he suggested that there was a media campaign against the Blues. Such comments signaled Mourinho's inability to separate his judgements from his emotions. He had allowed his sentiments to distort what he was seeing.

Judgement and prediction go hand in hand. Opinions shape the way we think, and our adjudications are what we found forecasts on. There is a widespread failure within football for fans to see their team in an unbiased manner. If you were to sit in the stands of any ground in the country this weekend, you would be guaranteed to hear unrestrained, discriminatory sledging of the referee in charge of the match. The man controlling the game undoubtedly has the hardest job in football. A referee can never win. Some of the decisions that need to be made are very ambiguous; there are always going to be fifty-fifty rulings to make. The fans and players of the team who end up on the wrong side of such decisions are going to feel understandably hard done by. Supporters will always look to blame someone. In reality, their anger should be directed at lady luck, but it is much easier to hurl abuse at a referee.

That being said, human error is one of the biggest chance inducing qualities in football. A lot of the randomness that plagues the sport is facilitated by the officials. If the referee has a bad day and ends up unfairly awarding a crucial decision or two in the opposition's favour, then your chances of winning are drastically reduced. Several of the most pivotal moments in sporting history have balanced on the mistakes of a referee. Of course, no official is purposefully biased. There seems no reason for him to favour one side or the other, especially as his livelihood depends on neutrality. His job is to be impartial, and if his superiors deem that he has made too many mistakes then he can be dismissed. This fact offers little consolation to fans whose teams are undone by refereeing blunders.

The randomness that such errors produce blurs our vision of the truth, distorts the league tables and corrupts our predictions. In a game with such fine margins as football, in a sport where goals are so rare and have such high value, even one refereeing mistake can have drastic consequences for the team that it goes against. However, whilst it is true that wrong decisions are going to be made, it is also likely that luck will even out over time. A team is going to get roughly the same number of wrong decisions given in their favour as they are going to get given against them. The main problem is when a wrong decision is given in a match that has a lot riding on it, such as in a cup final or a "six-pointer"[4]. There are fixtures that carry more weight than others, where you really don't want bad luck to upset your chance of victory.

---

4 A "six-pointer" is a term used to describe a league match which occurs between two teams near each other in the table, such as if first were playing second. Not only does winning earn you three points, but it also ensures that you close rivals drop three points. Thus, a six-point swing is achieved in your favour.

Many have called for the introduction of technology to combat this problem. Goal-line technology has recently been introduced at the top level of English football after years of campaigning. This has reduced any doubt over whether the whole ball has crossed the line, in the process removing some of the chance from the game. Some have called for a review system to be introduced to football, as it has been in rugby and cricket. Under such a system, each team would be allowed to make two reviews during the match. The referee would ask a fourth (or fifth) official to study video evidence and determine whether the original decision should be upheld or overturned. Having such a system in place would all but eliminate controversial red cards, penalties and off-sides. Refereeing mistakes are random occurrences, making it harder for us to make accurate predictions.

MEAN REGRESSION

The term *regression to the mean* suggests that luck tends to even out over time. This is a common phenomenon in statistics, and an important one to understand when we are trying to fight our own biases. Regression to the mean is prevalent in all sports, not least in football. A striker who has an incredible season, scoring thirty goals throughout the campaign, is probably not going to do as well in the next season. Equally, a team who goes on an extraordinarily poor run of form, losing several games in a row, will probably have their form revert back to normal eventually. This is because, whenever a series of unexpected events take place, the likelihood is that they will always revert back to the norm eventually. They will regress to the mean.

Extreme events can be both good, such as the player who has a very high scoring season, but can also be bad, like the team who go on a long losing streak. In these situations, it is common for people to overreact. This is what makes clubs pay far too much money for a striker who appears to be the next best player. One of the many inefficiencies of the transfer market is that strikers are drastically overpriced compared to their contribution on the field of play, whilst goalkeepers and defenders tend to be undervalued. For one thing, defenders and, in particular, goalkeepers tend to operate at a high level of performance for much longer than strikers. It is common to see goalkeepers still playing at the top level in their late thirties.

The other reason that strikers are often overvalued is because they tend to be judged wholly on the number of goals that they score. A striker's ability to hit the back of the net is easy to measure, whereas a defender's ability to prevent goals is hard to gauge. Whilst scoring a goal is seen as an individual activity, conceding a goal is seen as a failure of the collective. A *player* scores a goal; a *team* concedes a goal.

Smartodds, Matthew Benham's football analytics company, consider attacking as a shared duty when analysing matches. The attacking threat of a team does not depend solely on the ability of one striker, but on the capability of all the forward-thinking players in the side. We will see this reflected in Benham's thinking when we outline his philosophy in more specific terms. Because strikers are judged solely on the number of goals they score, an average forward can become massively overvalued should he go on an incredible (and lucky) run of form. This leads to a misidentification of luck for skill. Some of the most incredible transfer flops in footballing history have come as a result of this phenomenon.

A perfect example of a player regressing to the mean is ex-Swansea player Michu, who became something of a deity back in 2012. He arrived in Wales for just £2million from cash-strapped La Liga side Rayo Vallecano. The striker was unheard of in English football before his arrival. He announced himself on his debut against QPR, scoring two goals and assisting another.

Michu scored twenty-two goals in the 2012/13 season[5]. His performances at Swansea even led to him being capped by the Spanish na-

---

5 Eighteen in the Premier League, one in the FA Cup and three in Swansea League Cup campaign (Including one in the final at Wembley, where Swansea defeated Bradford).

tional side. Following his break-through campaign, Michu was linked with a move to some of the giants of the sport. Arsenal were linked with a £25million swoop for the forward, whilst Liverpool submitted an enquiry. However, Swansea refused to accept any offer for less than £30million, a price that no club were willing to match.

His second season with Swansea started less well. He was hit by an ankle injury after only a handful of mediocre performances. When he returned to the field he couldn't replicate the form that he had shown in the 2012/13 campaign. He was loaned out to Napoli, where he flopped. The Siren's Song, one of Napoli's most popular blogs, describe Michu as "just plain bad". Michu wasn't an awful player, he had simply regressed to the mean. The Spaniard was an average forward who had had one incredibly lucky season.

Even when he was playing for Swansea, Michu wasn't a dazzling performer. His work-rate off the ball was poor, and he amassed very few assists. It turned out that Michu was just an ordinary player who had had an extraordinary season. Clubs such as Arsenal and Liverpool had dodged a bullet by not agreeing to sign him. There was no way that he was worth the £30million that Swansea were demanding. Besides, at the age of twenty-seven his abilities were always likely to decline from that point anyway.

Looking at data of the top scorers from every Premier league season from 2004/05 to 2014/15 shows regression to the mean in action. Let's take every player who scored fifteen goals or more in one season and compare it to the number he scored in his next campaign. There are sixty-one players' seasons where more than fourteen goals were scored[6]. Six of the players left the Premier League after their free scoring 15+ season, meaning their data is not included in the findings. Simply for your interest, the full list of players is printed on the following page.

---

6 There are less than sixty-one players in the sample, due to the fact that the likes of Wayne Rooney have scored 15+ goals in more than one season.

Figure 2-1: Net Goals Scored Between 15+ Season and the Next (2004/05-2014/15)

Player	Season	Goals	Next Season	Goals	Net Difference
Thierry Henry	2004/05	25	2005/06	27	2
Andy Johnson	2004/05	21	2005/06	N/A	N/A
Thierry Henry	2005/06	27	2006/07	10	-17
Darren Bent	2005/06	18	2006/07	13	-5
Robbie Keane	2005/06	16	2006/07	11	-5
Frank Lampard	2005/06	16	2006/07	11	-5
Wayne Rooney	2005/06	16	2006/07	14	-2
Didier Drogba	2006/07	20	2007/08	8	-12
Benni McCarthy	2006/07	18	2007/08	8	-10
Cristiano Ronaldo	2006/07	17	2007/08	31	14
Cristiano Ronaldo	2007/08	31	2008/09	18	-13
Fernando Torres	2007/08	24	2008/09	14	-10
Emmanuel Adebayor	2007/08	24	2008/09	10	-14
Roque Santa Cruz	2007/08	19	2008/09	4	-15
Robbie Keane	2007/08	15	2008/09	10	-5
Benjani Mwaruwari	2007/08	15	2008/09	1	-14
Aiyegbeni Yakubu	2007/08	15	2008/09	4	-11
Dimitar Barbatov	2007/08	15	2008/09	9	-6
Nicolas Anelka	2008/09	19	2009/10	11	-8
Cristiano Ronaldo	2008/09	18	2009/10	N/A	N/A
Steven Gerrard	2008/09	16	2009/10	9	-7
Didier Drogba	2009/10	29	2010/11	11	-18
Wayne Rooney	2009/10	26	2010/11	11	-15
Darren Bent	2009/10	24	2010/11	17	-7
Carlos Tevez	2009/10	23	2010/11	20	-3
Frank Lampard	2009/10	22	2010/11	10	-12
Jermaine Defoe	2009/10	18	2010/11	4	-14
Fernando Torres	2009/10	18	2010/11	10	-8
Francesc Fabregas	2009/10	15	2010/11	3	-12
Dimitar Barbatov	2010/11	20	2011/12	7	-13
Carlos Tevez	2010/11	20	2011/12	4	-16
Robin Van Persie	2010/11	18	2011/12	30	12
Darren Bent	2010/11	17	2011/12	9	-8
Peter Odemwingie	2010/11	15	2011/12	10	-5
Robin Van Persie	2011/12	30	2012/13	26	-4
Wayne Rooney	2011/12	27	2012/13	12	-15
Sergio Aguero	2011/12	23	2012/13	12	-11
Clint Dempsey	2011/12	17	2012/13	7	-10
Emmanuel Adebayor	2011/12	17	2012/13	5	-12
Aiyegbeni Yakubu	2011/12	17	2012/13	N/A	N/A
Demba Ba	2011/12	16	2012/13	15	-1
Grant Holt	2011/12	15	2012/13	8	-7
Robin Van Persie	2012/13	26	2013/14	12	-14
Luis Suarez	2012/13	23	2013/14	31	8
Gareth Bale	2012/13	21	2013/14	N/A	N/A
Christian Benteke	2012/13	19	2013/14	10	-9
Michu	2012/13	18	2013/14	2	-16
Romelu Lukaku	2012/13	17	2013/14	15	-2
Ricky Lambert	2012/13	15	2013/14	13	-2
Dimitar Barbatov	2012/13	15	2013/14	4	-11
Demba Ba	2012/13	15	2013/14	5	-10
Frank Lampard	2012/13	15	2013/14	6	-9
Luis Suarez	2013/14	31	2014/15	N/A	N/A
Daniel Sturridge	2013/14	21	2014/15	4	-17
Yaya Toure	2013/14	20	2014/15	10	-10
Sergio Aguero	2013/14	17	2014/15	26	9
Wayne Rooney	2013/14	17	2014/15	12	-5
Olivier Giroud	2013/14	16	2014/15	14	-2
Edin Dzeko	2013/14	16	2014/15	4	-12
Wilfried Bony	2013/14	16	2014/15	11	-5
Romelu Lukaku	2013/14	15	2014/15	10	-5
Jay Rodriguez	2013/14	15	2014/15	N/A	N/A

As you can see from the net goal difference column on the right-hand side, a large proportion regressed to the mean. Any player who has scored fifteen or more goals in one season has had an extraordinary campaign. The likelihood is that they will follow it up with a more ordinary one. The exceptions are players such as Cristiano Ronaldo and Wayne Rooney, who appear more than once in the table. Any player who is consistently performing at an extraordinary level is an extraordinary player. The saying goes that form is temporary, but class is permanent. This quotation perfectly sums up regression to the mean.

Mean Regression - Premier League Top Scorers

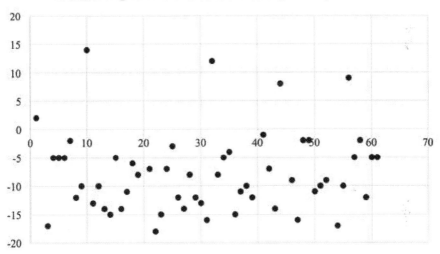

The above graph shows the net amount of goals the players scored the season after their 15+ campaign. The vertical axis shows the net goals, whilst the horizontal axis shows the players' rank out of sixty-one as they appear in the above table. Let's use the example of Thierry Henry. He was the top scorer of the 2004/05 season with 25 goals, meaning that he is "1" on the horizontal axis (as he is the first player listed on the table). He ended the 2005/06 season with 27 goals, two more than he had amounted in the previous campaign. Thus, his net goal difference is +2. Henry improved on his previous season, but in this respect he is in the minority.

Of the fifty-five footballers, only five went on to improve on their previous campaign. The other fifty regressed to the mean, indicating that chance had played a large part in their spectacular 15+ scoring season. The vast majority of players find themselves in the negative realms of net goal difference, with many scoring over ten goals less the season after they hit the heights as one of the league's top scorers. The average net goal difference of all the players was -7.75. This means if a player scored fifteen or more goals in a campaign, he would score an average of almost eight less the following season.

These numbers show how a striker can become severely overvalued after a good season. When a club buys a striker who has just scored upwards of fifteen goals in a campaign, they expect him to do the same for his new club. This means they are willing to pay big money for him, like the £25million that Arsenal were allegedly prepared to spend on Michu. However, the likelihood is that he will score significantly less the next season.

The key for clubs looking to be successful in the transfer market is to realise when one of your players is drastically overvalued, and sell him. Selling your best players is key to progressing as a football club, even though it may seem counterintuitive. Buying undervalued commodities and selling overvalued commodities is the key to upgrading in wealth. Matthew Benham has used this thinking to establish himself as a master investor. Benham's secret formula, to be revealed in the latter sections, is what allows him to identify undervalued players. However, it is his wily knowledge of how to play the market that allows him to keep improving his squads. When a player becomes overvalued, you should sell him. Michu had become significantly overpriced, and Swansea should have traded him before his performances regressed to the mean.

Andre Gray is a classic example of Benham's philosophy in action. Benham's algorithms spotted Gray when he was playing in the fifth tier of English football for Luton Town. Gray was performing at the level of a good Championship striker according to Benham's calculations. No one in the higher leagues were willing to gamble on the forward, but Benham sensed an investment opportunity. He brought Gray to Brentford for £500k. Gray thrived in the second tier of English football, scoring sixteen league goals in his first season at Brentford.

Benham had spotted an undervalued talent, but his cunning didn't stop there. When the transfer window came around, Benham realised that Gray was likely to be overvalued by other clubs. The striker had had an extraordinary season and was likely to regress to the mean next campaign. Gray was sold to Burnley for a fee eventually rising to £9million, eighteen times what Brentford had spent on him a year earlier. Benham's understanding of how to exploit inefficiencies in the transfer market has allowed Brentford FC to continuously punch above its financial weight. One such inefficiency is a failure to understand that players will always regress to the mean.

Regression to the mean works both ways. It can also have negative impacts on a player, team or manager. When a decent team goes on an extraordinarily poor run of form, it often leaves the owner with a very important prediction to make. Will sacking the manager have a positive effect on results?

In the modern age of football, the lifespan of a manager is incredibly short. When English football resumed after World War Two, the average length that a manager spent at a club was around 2,500 days, the equivalent of 6.8 years. In 2014, the average managerial tenure was about 20% of that. The average manager in England can now expect to serve for roughly 500 days, less than a year and a half. Over the last 60 or so years, the time which managers spend at football clubs has been gradually decreasing. If the current trend continues then by the late 2020s we can expect the average managerial tenure to be less than a year.

The sense of urgency that surrounds football creates a big problem for those attempting to make accurate predictions. Fans are notoriously short-sighted, and have an inability to understand long-term plans. When one of their teams' best players is sold, fans don't see a wise investment being cashed in. They don't see the potential for that money to be re-invested to ensure the sustainability of their club. Instead, all they see is a gaping hole left in the starting line-up. This short-sightedness must be avoided by the managers and owners who run football clubs. These men require clear long-term plans in order to achieve success. The stability that managers such as Arsène Wenger and Sir Alex Ferguson have provided shows how valuable continuity can be to football clubs.

Benham has removed some of the problems surrounding the unremitting urgency in football by taking power away from his managers. He has realised that the exposable nature of head coaches is detrimental to football clubs. Benham has decided upon a solution that is becoming more and more popular: the appointment of a director of football. This is a common move in European football, as it ensures that power is taken out of the hands of the manager. Brentford's model could be likened to a clock: the head coach is responsible for the second hand (day-to-day strategy); the directors of football (Rasmus Ankersen and Phil Giles, who has a Ph.D. in statistics) are responsible for the minute hand (medium-term strategy, focused on transfers and player replacement); and the board, including Benham, responsible for the hour hand (long-term strategy and objectives).

In fact, Benham has gone several steps further. At Brentford, Benham has also employed a Head of Football Philosophy, who ensures that the brand of football played by the club remains the same from the youth team up to the first team. Thus, the style of football adopted by the club is continuous, regardless of new managers who might come and go in quick succession. It is dangerous for such managers to implement their own brand of football, signing players that adhere to such a style and releasing those who don't, before leaving the club. This can leave the next manager with players that don't suit *his* particular style. Managers like to sign players who fit with their particular tactical preferences. This costs clubs a lot of money, as managers are turned over so regularly. Having a Head of Football Philosophy counters such problems by ensuring that the same style is maintained at the club.

Benham has also taken the power of vetoing transfers out of the hands of the manager, preferring to consult a transfer committee when deciding whether or not to sign a player. This methodology will be studied in more depth later on.

In the modern day, video games such as *Football Manager* do not help the reputation of men who run football clubs. *Football Manager*, a game that began being produced in the 1990s as *Championship Manager*, gives the gamer an incredibly realistic simulation of what it would be like to manage a club. From dealing with players' agents to developing in-depth tactics, the game is known for being highly addictive. In fact, the average amount of time consumers spent playing *Football Manager 2015* was 250 hours; the equivalent to ten days straight. The director of Sports Interactive, Miles Jacobson, claims that there are some individuals who have played it for over 3,000 hours. Over twenty million copies have been sold on PC, Mac and smartphone. Those who play the game tend to be football fanatics who demand the highest level of accuracy. When a fan of Portsmouth FC plays *Football Manager*, he expects each of the players in the game to display the same attributes as when he visits Fratton Park every other Saturday.

Sports Interactive, the developer of the game, has spent the last two decades building its own network of "scouts" to ensure absolute authenticity. These scouts are dedicated *Football Manager* fans who attend real-life matches and training sessions. Just like the scouts who are employed by professional football clubs, they report back to their authorities, who in turn ensure that the game's database remains realistic. Some scouts watch a single team, others a whole league, and all remain in regular contact with the development studio, whilst swapping tips and experiences on the company's buzzing forums. It is little surprise that the game predicted Lionel Messi would become the best player in the world when he was just seventeen years old.

The game provides data on the ability of 300,000 players; from shooting to heading, from positional sense to aggression, from determination to flair. It's an enormous resource. Indeed, in 2008, Everton signed an official deal to use the Football Manager database to search for players and staff. The game is a classic example of the two stages of analysis. The data is collected and supplied by Sports Interactive, but it is up to the gamer to scrutinise the data and draw conclusions from it.

However, just like any video game, it is all run through a series of algorithms and equations. The more you play the game, the better you become at adhering to the procedures that the game puts you through. The realism of *Football Manager* tricks you into thinking that it would be this simple to *actually* run a football club. Thus, real managers come under scrutiny for underperforming, when in fact their job is much harder than the public perceive.

When a football team is underperforming, it's a lot easier for fans to blame the individual manager than the collective group of players. From an owner's point of view, it is infinitely easier to fire the manager than the entirety of the playing staff. Many have suggested that the players were at fault for Chelsea's decline in 2015, but it would have been impossible for Abramovich to sack the whole squad. It was much simpler to get rid of Mourinho.

The advancement of social media means that fans can now become even more vocal in their disapproval of head coaches. Twitter is a breeding ground for impatience, petulance and frustration when it comes to underperforming managers. Owners feel the need to bow down to the whims of fans, who bay for the blood of the manager when their team goes on a bad run of form. The executives believe that making a change will reverse the fortune of the club.

This is a flawed philosophy. Whilst it is true that a team's form normally improves after a new manager is put in place, this is not necessarily due to the change of regime. The upturn in form can be attributed to a regression to the mean. After a certain amount of time, extraordinary events have to revert back to being ordinary. By definition, if an unusual incident keeps taking place then it is no longer unusual. A team who has an abnormally bad run of results will naturally have their form revert back to normal, whether the manager is sacked or not.

Ensuring a manager that he will have a long reign gives him job security, stops him from overspending on transfers, and certifies stability at the football club. Long-serving managers such as Alex Ferguson or Arsène Wenger prove that patience serves dividends. It is well documented that Ferguson came under pressure at the beginning of his United career. However, the owners stuck with him and he went on to create a dynasty at the club. Wenger has also been intensely scrutinised at various points in his Arsenal career. However, on each occasion that the North London club's form dropped, it eventually reverted back to normal and the owners were left thankful that they stuck with the Frenchman. Making a snap decision based on short-term success (or failure) will almost always lead to failed predictions. A team who are performing extraordinarily badly will regress back to their average level of performance over time.

Economist Dr Bas ter Weel was one of the first men to prove this. Ter Weel examined managerial turnover across eighteen seasons (1986-2004) of the Eredivisie, the top tier of Dutch football. What he found was that a team's form tended to improve immediately after they sacked their manager. This verdict is exactly what you would expect to find. Owners of football clubs theorise that a change in personnel will benefit the team. They see it as a case of if it *is* broken, then *do* fix it. However, before sacking their manager, owners should consider the result of the other course of action. Ter Weel found that *clubs that don't sack their manager experience the exact same upturn in form.*

Ter Weel found that clubs who stuck by their manager whilst going through a bad slump ended up reversing the trend in an identical fashion to the clubs who did sack their head coaches. The performances of the teams regressed to their natural mean position without the club having to take the drastic action of sacking their boss. A club's form will tend to right itself at exactly the same pace, whether or not they fire their manager. Ter Weel is keen to note that this phenomenon occurs throughout world football, not just the Eredivisie. The data suggests that you should think twice before calling for your manager's head when your team next hits a bumpy patch of form.

These findings imply that managers actually have very little impact on the success of their sides. The position of a team in the league table is generally affected more by the wealth and luck than by the man in charge. I would wholeheartedly argue that the strength of the playing staff is several times more vital than the manager in charge. Brian Clough once said that "players lose you games, not tactics. There's so much crap talked about tactics by people who barely know how to win at dominoes". If it is players that lose you games, it is players that also win you games. In other words, the most crucial role of the manager is to bring the best playing staff possible to their football club. Tactics have minimal effect, especially if you do not have players good enough to deploy them. Of course, the ability of a team's playing staff is largely determined by the wealth of the club, not by the ability of the manager. Thus, it follows, the manager has very little impact over whether his team succeeds or not. Moreover, what little influence the manager does have over proceedings is not enough to be able set him apart from other professional managers. It would be interesting to put a great manager, such as Pep Guardiola, in charge of a struggling League Two side and see if he could bring them success. Conversely, if you put a lower division manager in charge of a club with the wealth of Manchester City, would that team perform much differently?

The fact that managers perform so inconsistently also leads us to doubt the impact that they have on their clubs. The top players may have bad games, but over the long run they are consistently excellent. Managers, on the other hand, struggle to find a constancy to their performances. Mourinho, the self-acclaimed "special one", was hailed as one of the best managers in the world. However, his gargantuan flop at Chelsea in 2015 showed that even he could not control bad luck. Conversely, Claudio Ranieri was considered an average head coach when he was appointed by Leicester in 2015. Despite a career in management that spanned twenty-eight years and fourteen different sides, Ranieri had never won a top flight trophy. Then in 2015/16, despite all the odds, Leicester won the league and the Italian was named PFA Manager of the year. Surely Ranieri hadn't suddenly become an incredible manager overnight? This type of inconsistency is typical of football managers, as further indicated by the fact that Ranieri was actually sacked by Leicester the following season.

Incredibly, the five managers that won the Premier League between the years 2012 and 2016 all left their sides before the following season had finished (Mancini with Manchester City in 2012, Ferguson with Manchester United in 2013, Pellegrini with Manchester City in 2014, Mourinho with Chelsea in 2015 and Ranieri with Leicester in 2016). Alex Ferguson retired from football, but the other four coaches were all sacked by their clubs. They were fired because their teams had had an extraordinary title-winning season, and they were blamed when their sides' performances regressed to the mean the following season.

Perhaps the head coach simply serves as a figurehead of the team, someone to blame when things are going badly and someone to glorify when success is brought to the club. Some might argue that there are things managers can do to set themselves apart from their peers. A manager who successfully motivates his team, governs his players and, in particular, exploits the inefficiencies in the transfer market can certainly give his team a slightly better chance of success than one who doesn't. In football, a sport heavily governed by luck, it is important to gain whatever advantage you can over your opposition. Ultimately, however, we often mistake luck for skill when it comes to the ability of managers.

CORRELATION DOESN'T ALWAYS MEAN CAUSATION

The findings of Ter Weel also highlight another important thing that we must note when attempting to make successful predictions; correlation doesn't always imply causation. When we see that two things correlate we tend to believe there must be a link between the two. More often than not there is no connection between them, they just happen to correlate. Just because you sack your manager and then your form improves, it doesn't mean that you form improved *because* you sacked your manager.

Let's take a non-football example. In winter people tend to wear scarves more often to keep themselves warm. In this same season, more ponds tend to freeze over. If one were to look at a graph showing the frequency of people wearing scarves and the frequency of ponds freezing over, both would show dramatic spikes during the winter period. The two things correlate. However, just because they correlate doesn't mean they have a causal effect on each other. Ponds don't freeze over *because* people wear scarves, both just happen to occur at the same time of year.

A second example: the proportion of male babies born in Hospital A is 53%, whilst the same figure in Hospital B is 44%. Should a couple who want a boy chose to have their baby delivered at Hospital A rather than Hospital B? Of course not! The fact that more boy babies were born in Hospital A is a coincidence. There is no causal relationship between the two factors, and the couple should not take notice of the correlation when making their decision of which hospital to go to.

This all seems obvious enough, but in football correlation is constantly mistaken for causation – or at least it is suggested that correlation equals causation. Manchester City's captain and main central defender Vincent Kompany was injured for much of the start of the 2015/16 campaign. In situations like this, media outlets tend to use data showing how the team performs with and without that player. They look for interesting stats which correlates with popular belief. For example, because Kompany was City's strongest central defender and he has been missing from the line-up, one would expect the Sky Blues to be weaker defensively as a result. If they can find evidence for this, the media can claim to have proved this theory.

The stats at the beginning of 2016 seemed to tell the full story. In the 12 games Kompany had been involved in, City had kept seven clean sheets. In the 19 other matches, Manuel Pellegrini's side had kept just two. This is the exact kind of stat that media outlets love. It seems to tell the full story; when Vincent Kompany doesn't player Manchester City's defence is significantly weakened. Whilst this may be the case, we should always approach these types of statistics with caution. Just because the figures *correlate*, it does not mean that they are *causal*. There are a whole host of reasons that City's defence might have performed poorly besides that fact that Kompany was injured. It is possible that City played against stronger opponents whilst he was missing, or that City simply entered a bad patch of form over this period.

When attempting to predict the outcome of events, we naturally look to the past in search of indicators. It is important that we try to understand why outcomes are taking place, and we naturally get excited when we see a pattern forming. However, we must be careful not to mistake correlation for causation. Just because two entities seem to be bound by the same cause, doesn't mean that they are. Carrying out a birth at a particular hospital will not increase your chances of having a boy. An injury to a centre-back will not always be the cause of a drastic inundation of goals. The form of a club will not necessarily improve *because* of the sacking of their manager.

THE AVAILABILITY HEURISTIC

José Mourinho was wrong to point to refereeing decisions when trying to excuse Chelsea's failing form on the pitch, just as Abramovich was possibly wrong to sack Mourinho. Both men failed to take into account the fact that extraordinary results always regress to the mean. Mourinho should have realised that, even if a few decisions had gone against Chelsea, their luck would eventually revert to the norm. Similarly, although Chelsea's form was extraordinarily poor, Abramovich should have realised that it was always going to regress to the mean. Their extraordinarily bad run of form was likely to right itself naturally, whether he sacked Mourinho or not.

Perhaps the most significant reason for Mourinho's extreme downturn in fortune was his own human error. The Chelsea manager spent too much time reflecting on what had gone wrong, as opposed to trying put it right. When he made accusations against the referees, the media, and his own staff, the Portuguese fell victim to a phenomenon known as the *"availability heuristic"*.

A heuristic is an approach to decision-making that employs a practical methodology not guaranteed to be optimal or perfect, but sufficient for immediate goals. It is a sort of mental short-cut. The availability heuristic suggests that we remember information that is most available to us and most relevant to our circumstances. It would be more beneficial to remember every piece of information that we are told, but our brains cannot handle such copious amounts of data. Therefore, we tend to only remember what is significant to us, and what is significant to us tends to be information which aligns with our own beliefs.

The human brain is also flawed in that it remembers spectacular moments far more easily than ordinary ones. This can have negative impacts on our powers of prediction. For example, many England fans will remember Rob Green's howler in the 2010 World Cup. Clint Dempsey of the USA took a shot from outside the box which Green looked like he'd gather with ease. The ball trundled towards the England goalkeeper, slipped through his palms and ended up rolling agonizingly slowly over the line. It was a classic goalkeeping catastrophe, performed in front of a worldwide audience. The game ended in a stalemate, meaning England ended up with a harder draw in the next round.

Rob Green was not a particularly bad goalkeeper. However, throughout the rest of his career he was defined by that moment. If the howler had happened in some obscure Premier League game against lowly opposition, the public would have forgotten about it in a matter of days. The fact that the incident happened for the national team on a global stage meant it was much more memorable. Unfortunately for Green, the availability heuristic meant this event stayed in the minds of England fans for many years.

A lot of what our brains remember is information that conforms to our views on something. This is very dangerous; if we *want* to believe something, we will subconsciously look for signals that adhere to those beliefs. To take an example from football, a fan may make a judgement that a new signing isn't very good. Every time the player makes a mistake, whether it be a misplaced pass or a sliced shot, the fan will subconsciously place the incident to the forefront of his memory, as it conforms to his original belief. This can result in the fan holding a particularly harsh view of the player, in the same way that many fans dismissed Green as a poor goal-keeper because of his one incredibly memorable error.

Approaching data with the agenda of reaching a particular conclusion is very dangerous. Consider an aging player who is trying to convince his club to offer him a new deal. The club might be unwilling to do so, due to the player's declining ability. The player may turn to data to try and prove to the club that he is still valuable. He would do this by cherry-picking the stats which make him look best. Clearly, this will form an inaccurate analysis of his ability. His agenda will have undermined his evaluation.

José Mourinho *wanted* to believe that Chelsea's downfall was out of his control. He clung to any piece of evidence that conformed to that view. It probably wasn't true that Chelsea were extraordinarily unlucky when it came to refereeing decisions, and it certainly wasn't true that there was a media campaign against the Blues. Just like the fan who makes a pre-diction about the future success of a player, Mourinho's judgement was skewed by his bias. He was searching for facts that suggested the decline was neither his nor his team's fault, leading him to mistake noise for signal.

We must always be aware of the effects that various heuristics play on our judgement. Put simply, heuristics are cognitive short-cuts which the human brain takes to avoid short-wiring. We use heuristics with the knowledge that there is a better way of doing something, but that that way would be inefficient for our immediate needs. Another way of think-ing about heuristics is this: imagine if you theorised over *every* idea that came into your head. We would spend so much time doting on trivial matters that it would not be worth our time to get out of bed in the morning. Thus, we must prioritise certain thoughts and feelings, whilst neglecting others to the back of our brain.

I like to think that heuristics are to our actions what an editor is to a newspaper publication. An editor could spend hours and hours reviewing and revising each edition of his newspaper, making each sentence per-fect in an attempt to craft a faultless publication. However, this process would be incredibly time-consuming and inefficient. It would take far too long to actually publish any material, as he would constantly be picking tiny holes in the writing. As such, the editor must accept that there will be slight mistakes, or some aspects that could be done better. For the sake of effectiveness, he must attempt to reach a standard of quality which is not perfect, but suffices nevertheless. Our brain does the same thing; it cannot ponder on every slight problem, so must sometimes disregard information. Heuristics are a necessity for us to function, but they can also be potential pitfalls when making predictions.

DON'T JUDGE A BOOK BY ITS COVER

Another prevalent shortcoming of the human brain is that it makes judgements based on irrelevant or artificial factors. We tell ourselves to not judge a book by its cover, yet we subconsciously do this the whole time. Appearances can be misleading. Managers and scouts should not rely solely on their eyes when it comes to assessing matters such as player performance. The cover of the book does not tell the whole story.

Billy Beane was able to exploit this inefficiency within the game of baseball. Whilst other general managers would immediately disregard certain pitchers because of their unusual throwing action, Beane preferred to assess players by consulting his statistical model. The other clubs let irrelevant external biases dictate whether or not they signed a player, creating an inefficiency which Beane could exploit. Beane's analytical gauges of player performance allowed him to see things that other clubs couldn't. This meant he could purchase good pitchers on the cheap, as they were undervalued by other teams. The Oakland A's competed with much bigger clubs on the back of this methodology.

Football seems to be more efficient than baseball in this regard. Broadly speaking, all footballers have the same techniques and styles. There aren't many unusual ways to kick a ball. However, some players still have strange external factors which don't necessarily mean that they perform worse, but put coaches and scouts off signing them. One Brentford player who fits this category is a young midfielder called Ryan Woods. He was brought to the club in 2015 by Matthew Benham, purchased from

League Two Shrewsbury Town for around £1million. Woods had an unusual gait; the way he ran and walked around the football pitch was quite peculiar. This would deter some managers, but Benham's stats showed he was an excellent player despite the external incongruity. Woods has gone on to become a very successful Championship player, winning Brentford's Players' Player of the Year Award 2016/17.

In a sense, the visual biases which dissuade coaches from signing players are a form of discrimination. Any form of unfair discrimination which occurs creates an inefficiency. For instance, small players are often discriminated against because scouts choose to prefer stronger, more athletic players. This means that smaller players, despite sometimes being just as effective as larger players, are overlooked (no pun intended). In the Summer of 2015, N'Golo Kante was on the radar of several Premier League clubs. Many of these teams quickly disregarded him, believing that his height of 5ft 6in was too small for a combative midfielder. Leicester chose to trust Kante's impressive stats over the irrelevant prejudice, signing him for around £5.6m. The midfielder was sold to Chelsea a season later for £32m and won the PFA Player of the Year 2017.

The most obvious form of discrimination which has been apparent in football is racism. Fortunately, racism has receded in the sport, but in the recent past black players would often be unfairly marginalised. Even as recently as the 1980's and 1990's, some clubs (notably Liverpool and Everton) refused to play black players. This created an enormous inefficiency within the game. In order to get a place in a starting line-up, a black player had to be considerably better than his white counter-part. This meant that black players were drastically undervalued. A club could buy a black footballer with much more talent than a white footballer for a lot less money. If a team were to have realised this inefficiency at the time, they could have built a title winning team of black players for very little money at all.

Eventually, as racism slowly regressed from the sport, black players were given equal opportunities to white players. Nowadays, it is safe to assume that if there is a black footballer with the same ability as a white footballer, they would be given an equal chance to succeed. In the modern game, those who are not good enough will be replaced, no matter what skin colour they have. The infiltration of data into football means that there is nowhere to hide.

Just as our superfluous beliefs can trick us into undervaluing players, they can also lead us to overvalue the ability of a player. When scouts attend youth team matches, they are faced with the difficult task of keeping tabs on twenty-two players at once. When faced with such a large number of similar objects to focus on, discerning between them can be difficult. The brain tends to focus on things that stand out. For example, a player with shiny pink boots may feature more prominently in the mind. Equally, a player with bright ginger hair will stick out, making him more likely to be recommended when the scout files his report back to his seniors.

Visual biases certainly take place on the field of play, but it is also true that they occur behind the scenes. There is still an alarmingly small number of black managers in English football; the average figure for the last decade being around five at the ninety-two clubs at any one period. The market for determining good managers is much less efficient than it is for players. Whilst players perform in front of the crowds, much of what a manager does is behind the scenes. Thus, it is easy to determine who are the best players, but it is a lot harder to discern who are the best managers. When we struggle to clearly define who is the best, our visual biases start to take precedence. Just like the scout who notices the player with the bright red hair, owners who are appointing a new head coach tend to base their decision on the appearance of the candidates. Most managers follow the same set of guidelines: they are almost always either white, conservative in appearance or former players. More often than not they are all three.

Being white does not make one candidate a better manager than another. Just like the racism towards players in past decades, discrimination still occurs against black managers. It will take longer for managers to achieve the same equal opportunities as players now receive. For white players there is nowhere to hide, as it is obvious if you are worse than your black counter-part. White managers, on the other hand, can take sanctuary in the fact that it is less apparent whether they are underperforming.

Similarly, football maintains a deluded notion that in order to be a manger you have to have played the game at a high level. Owners are won over by the argument that playing football well automatically translates into managing football well. Obviously the theory that you don't understand the game if you weren't a player is ridiculous. Managers such as José Mourinho, Brendan Rodgers and Roy Hodgson disprove the argument entirely.

Football is something of a cult, in which appearances and superfluous exteriors are extremely important. There are criteria which are considered acceptable within the inner circle of football. For example, one can be confident of being granted access to the exclusive club if you already have a family member on the inside. Football, like all social circles, is about connections. Having a relative in a position of power inside the game grants you access to the inner circle. Many would argue that Nigel Clough, son of the legendary Brian Clough, is not a particularly good manager. Despite this, Nigel has been given several managerial opportunities, in part because of his father's renowned reputation. The same could be said for Darren Ferguson, son of Alex Ferguson. A preference for well-known names occurs with players as well. The Schmeichels, Wright-Phillips[7], Hazards, Nevilles, Ferdinands, Lampards, Rooneys and countless others are all examples of familial bonds within football. Whilst there is certainly something to be said for genes playing a role, if you rock up to a trial with the surname Beckham you will be likely to provoke a favorable reaction.

On the other hand, people will tend to reject what they perceive to be unfamiliar or unusual. One ex-player tells the story of when the club he captained appointed a new, foreign manager. The player was skeptical of the decision to appoint the previously unheard-of coach. He dismissed the ability of his new boss simply because he didn't *look* like a Premier League manager. The spectacles he wore made him appear more like a

---

7 Shaun and Bradley were both sons of Ian Wright.

philosophy professor. His instincts told him that the man could not be a good manager, *simply because he didn't look like a good manager*. This is a prime example of an individual being met with opposition from the inner ranks of football because of irrelevant external factors. The manager in that particular story was Arsène Wenger, who went on to become one of the most successful Premier League managers of all-time.

This goes some way to explaining why there has been a reluctance within football to trust statistical modelling. Nerds and statisticians look funny and use big words, all the while sitting behind a computer running through complicated algorithms. They are perceived to not truly understand football. They've never played the game. Thus, they are denied access to the prominent positions within the sport. Only in recent years have clubs started turning more attention to statistical analysis. The irony is that using cold hard data is the most sure-fire way of cutting out our unfair discriminations, but the analysts who are capable of utilising this data are themselves unfairly discriminated against.

The ultimate result of all of these prejudices is that football remains behind the times, outdated and inefficient. Most of the people on the inside of the game, the players, coaches and pundits, tend to be less educated than the average person. In order to be a professional footballer, one must dedicate all of their time to training. This means education takes a back seat. Many clubs do have some type of schooling system set up, but usually the players take a flimsy course in tourism and just about scrape a pass. This is hardly a decent learning experience, but becoming a professional footballer is an incredibly hard task. It is necessary that young players focus their attention towards training, rather than studying Shakespeare or Pythagoras.

As we have seen, most other professions within football – be it managing, coaching or punditry, are made up of ex-players. Consequently, these vocations are filled by the men who gave up education early to pursue a career as a footballer. Of course, they tend to be considered experts with regards to the playing side of the game. However, it means that football remains unintelligent when it comes to other aspects of the sport. Arsène Wenger was able to exploit this. The Frenchman has a degree in economics and has used this knowledge to succeed in the transfer market. Similarly, Matthew Benham has a background in investment banking, which he has used to develop his innovative philosophy.

If you recall, at the beginning of the book we examined the stories of Billy Beane and Matthew Benham. These two men have both developed ground-breaking methods of analysing their respective sports. Beane led the statistical revolution in baseball, utilising the statistic of on-base percentage in particular. Benham has done the same in football, using a revolutionary metric called Expected Goals which will be outlined in the latter chapters. Both these men have achieved extraordinary success with their respective teams. However, both these men have also faced opposition to their methods. In part, this is because traditional coaches and managers are inclined to feel threatened by new means of operating. Either that, or they simply don't *understand* the mathematical systems used by Beane and Benham.

External factors, though, are a large reason behind the blind rejection of these statistical gurus, particularly in the case of Benham. Beane played baseball professionally, and although he never reached the heights that were expected of him, he was already considered as being on the "inside" of the sport. Benham, on the other hand, has never played football. He has had to work his way into the game by using the money he accumulated through betting on the sport.

When he bought Danish side FC Midtjylland, Benham's approach was met with skepticism. Some of the players and fans rejected the notion that this outsider could successfully run their football club. Had Midtjylland not been bankrupt and in desperate need of investment, Benham never would have got the chance to implement his data-driven methods. Benham's is a rare case; a man who has been able to change his status from an "outsider" to an "insider".

SURVIVORSHIP BIAS

Humans seem to naturally undervalue the effect that chance plays in life, whilst at the same time overvaluing the role that skill plays. This misevaluation is rampant in politics, economics and broader society, but perhaps even more so in the world of sport. Those who have attained the greatest success are presumed to have done so because they possess the highest level of ability. We assume that someone who is at the top of their field must have got to that position through merit. This misinterpretation of luck for skill is called "survivorship bias".

Consider an example. Cast your mind back a couple of millennia to Roman times. Thousands of people used to flock to Colosseums to watch gladiators fight to death. This sport was the football of that age. Now imagine that television companies broadcasted these gladiatorial battles around the globe. Imagine that pundits would sit and assess each fighter before and after each contest. They would, like in the modern game of football, offer their views on who will win, who will lose, and offer complex strategic reasons for why each result takes place. These pundits will serve as our victims of survivorship bias.

Now imagine that the biggest tournament (the FA Gladiators Cup, if you will) consists of 256 different gladiators, each fighting one another individually with the hope of progressing to the next round. This format resembles the modern day knock-out competition. However, let's add one non-variable to the tournament; each gladiator has a 50% chance of winning against any other fighter. In other words, every single gladiator is of equal ability, and the victor of each duel will be down to chance alone. Which gladiator progresses through each round might as well be decided through the toss of a coin. Each of the 256 competitors has an equal chance of emerging victorious against one another, and thus an equal chance of winning the overall tournament.

After six rounds of fighting, 252 of the participants have been defeated. This leaves just four gladiators left in the competition. They have each overpowered six opponents to reach this stage, and are unanimously named the best challengers in the land. Very few would disagree with the assertion that these four fighters are icons of the gladiatorial world. After all, the chance of any one gladiator progressing to the final four at the beginning of the tournament was only 1.6%. The pundits go into detail explaining what has given these elite fighters the edge over their vanquished opponents. They study the physique, the fighting style and the weapons used by of each of the four conquerors, looking to find the reasons behind their success.

However, as we established at the beginning of the tournament, each of these gladiators has the same amount of ability as any of the 252 who were vanquished. If we bring back to life a gladiator who was defeated in the first round, and pitted him against one of the four who had won all six of his fights, who would be more likely to win? Were you to ask one of the pundits, he would tell you that the gladiator from the elite four would win easily. He might cite that there was a 98.4% chance that these gladiators would be defeated before this point, meaning the gladiators must have been incredibly skilled to beat the odds.

However, in reality, each of the elite four would still only have a 50% chance of emerging victorious if pitted against one of the already-defeated fighters. The pundit will have fallen victim to survivorship bias, which tells us that the gladiators must have achieved success on merit. We are fooled to believe that the survivors are more skillful than the deceased, despite the fact that they are of equal ability. This misinterpretation of luck for skill is criminal.

Additionally, the remaining four fighters, whose survival has been down to nothing more than chance, will become overconfident in their ability. Remember that humans will look for patterns in data which conform to their opinions. The gladiators naturally want to believe that they are the best, and will assume that an extraordinary record of six wins and no losses validates this belief. These individuals are perhaps the biggest victims of survivorship bias.

The modern day football manager is perhaps one of the greatest fools of such a fallacy. In previous sections, we have raised questions as to the actual impact that managers have on the success of their football clubs.

There is a growing consensus within football that the record of a manager is down to luck more than anything else. The team he inherits, the funds he is able to work with, and the random nature of football all have more of an impact on the success of a manager than the skill of the individual. Despite this, a head coach with a great record will often attribute this to the incredible talent that he possesses. A manager who has had a string of poor results will blame bad luck, whilst a manager who has had a run of good results will put it down to his own ability.

There is no finer example than José Mourinho. When he arrived at Stamford Bridge for his first stint as Chelsea manager, the Portuguese had just won the Champions League with Porto. He notoriously claimed in his first press conference that he thought he was "special". Mourinho insinuated that Porto's success had been down to his managerial brilliance. However, one could easily argue that luck was the main reason for Mourinho's achievements at his former club. If one were looking to discredit the Portuguese's rise to prominence, they could point to a number of things which happened to swing his way earlier on in his career. For example, had Mourinho's Porto not scored a last minute goal against Alex Ferguson's Manchester United in the Round of Sixteen of that famous Champions League campaign, they would have been knocked out before the Quarter-finals and Mourinho never would have been made Chelsea manager. That last-gasp goal was one of many hugely influential moments that happened to swing Mourinho's way in his 2004 Champions League triumph, the defining moment of his career. Just like the four gladiators considered better than the rest, Porto were incredibly lucky to win the competition. If the tournament were to be replayed from the beginning, with the exact same squads in the exact same groups, Mourinho's Porto would have next to no chance of overall victory.

Fast-forward a couple of years to his second stint at Chelsea, and the evidence that Mourinho's success has been facilitated largely by chance begins to stack up. Chelsea mounted the worst title defence that the Premier League has ever seen in 2015/16, leading to the sacking of Mourinho before Christmas. Unsurprisingly, the manager, who a couple of years beforehand had accredited Porto's unrivalled success to his own supreme ability, blamed the unrivalled decline of Chelsea on anybody but himself. He criticised the referees, the Chelsea staff (both playing and non-playing) and even the fans for the regression of the West London club.

Most importantly, the Portuguese blamed bad luck. In actuality, Mourinho was quite right to blame misfortune for Chelsea's decline. Football is a sport littered with randomness. We assume that it is deterministic, that all teams get what they deserve and that those with the most skill will prosper, but this is not the case. Chelsea's manager made some severe errors, but the main cause for their decline was simply bad luck. Mourinho was right to recognise this but, as aforementioned, it is very easy to blame misfortune when things are going badly. In 2004, when claiming that his ability was "special", Mourinho should have noted that his success up to that point had largely been down to *good* luck. This natural tendency of humans to blame failure on bad luck whilst crediting success to their own personal skill is known as attribution bias.

There are two main reasons that Mourinho is one of the most highly regarded managers in the game. Firstly, he has been very lucky, particularly in finding himself in the top jobs in the first place. Secondly, his incredible charisma has made him a media sensation; fans everywhere either love him, or love to hate him. His hard work and natural ability play some part, although a much smaller part than we are inclined to believe. Survivorship bias has led us to overrate his ability. Of course, no one overrates his ability more so than himself.

PROBLEMATIC ELIMINATION PROCESSES

Cup competitions, whilst hugely entertaining, are bad at defining who the best teams actually are. The winners of such competitions are often not the most skilled teams, but the luckiest. Take the FA Cup, for example. Whilst the probability of each team progressing is not necessarily the clear-cut 50% that we gave to each of the gladiators in our previous example, the odds will very rarely exceed 70% in favour of one team. In recent times, big clubs have often fielded much weakened sides against smaller clubs, thus levelling the playing field even further.

The luck involved in winning such a competition is revealed when you compute the odds that a high quality team has of triumphing before the tournament gets underway. Let's say that a team has a 70% chance of progressing through each round of the FA Cup, and they enter at the Third Round stage. It is highly unlikely that any team would have such a great chance of progressing through each round, but we'll use this exaggerated probability to prove the point. There are six matches that the team must win in order to lift the trophy, meaning they have an 11.8% chance of winning the tournament overall. That means that a side with a 70% chance of progressing through every round would still have just over a one in ten chance of overall victory. Such is the luck that is needed to win the trophy. "The magic of the cup" is a phrase which unintentionally depicts the inherent randomness that exists in knock-out tournaments.

A league table may not perfectly reflect the ability of teams (there is still a lot of luck involved), but it does give a much more accurate assessment than a cup competition. The increased sample size of matches, rational assignment of points and, most crucially, the fact that no team is ever eliminated on the basis of one result, means that each club is given a fairer chance to demonstrate their ability. In normal life, however, the devising of a league table is often unmanageable. There are many areas in which a process of elimination is more practical, despite the obvious flaws with this type of system.

Here are a couple of example from the worlds of business and politics. *The Apprentice* is a television show in which candidates compete to win a large investment from a business tycoon, and a chance to start their own business under their stewardship. The UK version of the programme stars Lord Alan Sugar as the potential investor, the man who decides which candidates remain in the process and which get fired. The lay-out of the show dictates that one (or more) candidates are removed from the process each weak. This is a similar elimination process to a knock-out tournament.

Say that twelve candidates of roughly equal ability enter the process, and one is fired each week. This means that each one has an 11/12 (92%) chance of surviving the first week, a 10/11 (91%) chance of surviving the second week, a 9/10 (90%) chance of surviving the third week, and so on and so forth. This continues until the final week, when the two surviving candidates each have a 50% chance of claiming the investment.

Of course, these probabilities assume that all the candidates have an equal level of ability. Whilst it is reasonable to assume that the general skill of each candidate is similar to that of each other candidate (the pro-gramme claims to have gathered the best business minds in the country – surely there can't be that much difference towards the very top end?), some will undeniably be better contestants than others. Thus, in the first week, the best candidates may have close to a 96% chance of survival, whilst the less skilled will verge more towards 85%. Nevertheless, the problem with such a system persists. The simple fact is that, for a candidate of average ability, the odds of progressing to the next round are always above 49.9%. Even when it gets down to the final three, a candidate whose skill is no different to the other two has a healthy 66% chance of progressing. Let's say that two candidates have greater ability than the other one, that less skilled contestant may still only have a 50% chance of being eliminated, whilst the other two each only have a 25% chance.

We can see how there is large potential for unskilled candidates to make it to the latter stages of the process. Even if they do not win the investment, they can still clock up more screen-time which could go a long way to furthering their careers. Meanwhile, a highly skilled candidate could unluckily be eliminated in the first round. A much more insightful way to run the process would be to install a league ranking system. Each candidate would win a certain number of points each round, and the candidate with the highest tally of points at the end of the process would win. However, this structure would be hard to manage and less exciting for viewers to watch. Whilst it would be the most efficient way of deciphering who the most skillful candidates are, it would not be the most convenient.

A more advanced example of a flawed elimination process is the Labour Party leadership election. This process is fairly complex. Essentially, the leader of the Labour Party is elected through an Alternative Voting (AV) system. In this system, a number of candidates stand to become elected, but no candidate can win with under 50% of the vote. Voters can vote for their first preference and second preference choice. A series of rounds are conducted, after each of which the candidate with the least amount of first preference votes is eliminated. The eliminated candidates' second preference votes are then distributed accordingly to the remaining candidates.

For example, say that the votes are counted up in the first round, and no candidate has attained over 50% of the vote. The candidate with the least amount of votes is eliminated, and their second preference votes get distributed appropriately to the remaining candidates. If there is still no candidate with over 50% of the vote, then the next remaining candidate with the fewest number of votes is eliminated, and their second preference votes are distributed accordingly. This process of elimination is continued until a candidate obtains over 50% of the vote.

The AV Voting system that Labour use was heavily criticised in 2010 after Ed Miliband was nudged over the line by Union voters. He had been second in every round of elimination to his brother David, but the second preference votes that he obtained in the final round meant that he emerged victorious. Despite receiving less votes than his brother from the other two sections of the party, the Labour MPs and full party members, Ed was elected as leader. It is not difficult to conclude that Ed Miliband was elected more by the role of chance induced by the flawed voting system than by his skill as a politician.

Elimination processes occur regularly throughout many walks of life. Whenever we compete with a number of other potential candidates, whether it be in the world of finance, sport, or simply biological evolution, we must always recognise the role that randomness plays. The richest men and women in the world are often cited as role models who we should aspire to be like. What we don't consider is that these people all got to where they are with a strong boost from chance. We only see the success stories. We don't see the hundreds of thousands of people with the exact same skills and attributes who failed in making it large.

Bill Gates is probably amongst the most cited role models. He is one of the wealthiest men in the world, to the point where if he dropped a $100 note, it literally wouldn't be worth his time to pick it up. In the time that it would take him to scoop up the note, he would have made in excess of its worth. Many admire him, and read books on how to achieve the type of "millionaire mindset" that men like him have used to achieve success. What we don't consider is the people with the exact same mindset, but who have failed in their business endeavors.

Suppose that one hundred people all came up with a business model that had a 5% chance of achieving great success, but a 95% chance of completely failing. A book could be written about the five people who end up succeeding, insinuating that we should all adopt such a business model because it made these five people extremely wealthy. What the book will have failed to mention, however, was the other ninety-five people who failed. Just like the imaginary pundits who praised the four surviving gladiators, the readers of the "millionaire mindset" book will have fallen victim to survivorship bias.

STICKING WITH THE HERD

In many walks of life, we are forced to compete with others. Football managers contend with one another to make the best decisions. Professional gamblers compete with bookmakers to see who can make the most accurate predictions. Even players will study the techniques of their rivals in order to improve their own game. The aim of sport is to outdo your competitors. The same is true for areas such as politics, business and law.

When competing with others, we naturally tend to pay attention to their methods. This can sometimes compromise our own decisions and predictions. It is for this reason that owners are inherently reluctant to appoint black managers, and why analytical methods are rejected by football. Traditionally, clubs haven't used statistical modelling to define their recruitment and their style of play. Similarly, black managers are very rarely appointed at football clubs. Owners are afraid that if they go against the norm and end up failing, they will be ostracised. If they stick to what has always been done and it fails, they can put it down to bad luck. Thus, owners and managers tend to stick with the herd.

To further explain the process of herding, let's look at Matthew Benham's decision to implicate his mathematical philosophy at FC Midtjylland[8]. In truth, Benham was always going to introduce his methods at Midtjylland. He wanted to use the Danish club as a laboratory for his radical ideas. For the sake of this example, however, let's suppose that he bought the club and *then* made the decision whether to overhaul its structure or not. When he became the owner of Midtjylland he had two choices. He could follow the herd and stick with the traditional means of operating. Conversely, he could change the entire structure of the club in order to accommodate his untested analytical methods.

Consider the possible outcomes if he chooses the first option, and decides to follow the traditional scouting methods which are used throughout European football:

- **FC Midtjylland Succeeds**: In this scenario the football club flourishes in both league and cup. Benham is thanked for his investment and reaps the rewards of owning a modestly successful football club.
- **FC Midtjylland Fails**: The club doesn't achieve any form of glory, and may end up fighting against relegation. Benham doesn't receive any media coverage, and perhaps regrets his decision to invest in the club.

---

8 Benham used his radical methods to some extent at Brentford when he took them over in 2012. When he bought FC Midtjylland in 2014, he wanted to test what would happen if he took these methods to the logical extreme. They turned out to work successfully, and one year later he instigated them fully at Brentford.

These are the scenarios that most football clubs face. If they outperform expectations then they get to enjoy more money, greater fame and all the rewards that come with success. The opposite applies if they fail, but they can blame their demise on bad luck. Now consider the consequences if Benham goes for the second option and implements his radical philosophy:

- **FC Midtjylland Succeeds**: Benham's gamble has paid off and he has gained an edge on all of his rivals. He receives a lot of favourable media coverage, labelling him the pioneer who changed the way football is thought about.
- **FC Midtjylland Fails**: Benham is ostracised as an ignorant fool who tried to go against the generally accepted way in which football should be played. He is ridiculed by the media, who laugh him out of town for trying to change a sport that had been played in the same way for over a century.

Clearly, the stakes are much higher when you go against the general consensus. There are much greater rewards if you succeed, but if you fail you're humiliated. Choosing which path to take will depend on how confident you are in your own predictive abilities. Certain personalities will choose to take the risk, but when your whole career is on the line it is sensible to conclude that you would follow the herd.

The same process applies when owners are deciding whether to appoint black, female, or "outsider" managers. Should it pay off, they reap the rewards of their successful prediction. If it fails, they are scorned for going against tradition and trying to outsmart the system. The vast majority of people will choose to stick with the herd. Thus, the minorities struggle to get jobs as managers and innovative ideas tend to take a back seat.

Benham chose to gamble. He implemented his radical ideas at FC Midtjylland, who won their first ever Danish Superliga title within a year of Benham taking charge. Brentford have now started to make their mark on English football, following the same unique philosophy that Benham introduced to Midtjylland. Benham's decision not to let the movement of the herd dictate his own destination paid off.

COMBATTING VISUAL BIAS

When making predictions, visual and preferential biases are noise which distract us from the truth. Good forecasters will take measures to make sure that they don't fall victim to these prejudices.

One of the most overbearing visual biases that fans can fall victim to is that of "attractive football". Nothing in football is more beautiful than a slick attacking move, involving many players making one-touch passes and cutting through the opposition with precision. Barcelona are an example of a club who have mastered such an approach. Teams who can implement this style of play are revered in the footballing world. On the other end of the spectrum you find teams who play "ugly football". Stoke City became famous for their unattractiveness under their long-serving manager Tony Pulis. Their philosophy followed the principle that you could only score if you were near the opposition's goal. Therefore, the most efficient way of playing football was to get the ball into the opposition's final third as quickly as possible. Stoke utilised what is known as direct football, the long-ball tactic, or, put simply, "hoofing it". This brand of football is commonly associated with the lower tiers of English football. The theory goes that such sides don't have good enough players to pass the ball well, and their solution is to lump it up the pitch. The football connoisseurs look down on this style of play with disgust.

This is an example of visual bias getting in the way of the truth. Stoke have competed in the Premier League for many years on a shoe-string budget. Based on the club's finances, they should have been relegated years ago. The Potters have far exceeded expectations by retaining their top-flight status with relative ease. Their ugly style of play has no doubt helped them achieve this. If Stoke tried to play beautiful passing football like many of the other Premier League teams, they would have surely been relegated. They realised that David is destined to lose when he fights with the same tools as Goliath. Instead, they developed a physical style of play that effectively combatted the passing football played by teams with better, more expensive players.

Stoke fans would have undoubtedly liked to see their team further towards the Barcelona end of the scale. However, they would be letting their visual biases get the better of them. The truth is that Stoke were better off playing ugly football. Indeed, now that the Potters have played in the Premier League for nearly a decade, they have accumulated enough money to bring in better players and adopt a more attractive style of play.

Matthew Benham has taken several steps to counter the problems created by our natural biases. The Brentford and Midtjylland owner has implemented some unusual changes at his clubs with the aim of reducing the deficiencies caused by human preconceptions.

Firstly, Benham has deployed a more mathematical approach to the game. His philosophy is very much geared towards statistics. Data is the antidote to the disease of natural human bias. Our own judgements can be misguided, but cold, hard facts don't lie. As we will see in the final chapters, Benham's approach, though relatively simple and easy to conduct, relies heavily on data and stats.

Benham realised that head coaches often fall victim to their biases in half-time team talks. It is natural for managers to get caught up in the emotion of a match. We have already seen José Mourinho's rants about referees, physios and almost anything else that could be blamed. Bias judgements can distract the men in charge from what is important: the actuality of what is happening on the pitch. The half-time team talk is the manager's one chance to clearly communicate his ideas, thoughts and tactics to his team during a match. Thus, it is of vital importance that conflicting biases and emotions are prevented from misguiding the team talk.

Brentford and FC Midtjylland, Matthew Benham's two football clubs, have developed ways of getting around this problem. The coaches are sent texts to their phones at half-time outlining the key stats from the first half. The information which they are sent is based around innovative data which Benham collects. This gives the manager an outline for his team talk. It tells him whether the team are over-performing or underperforming, and in which areas they need to improve.

Rasmus Ankersen, Benham's right-hand man, was the man who recommended that Benham buy FC Midtjylland. The Dane is now the chairman of Midtjylland and a director of football at Brentford. Ankersen has explained how the texts which are sent at half-time outline how the team are measuring up to certain key metrics: "These effective key performance indicators give a more accurate message to the players". This reliance on facts removes the ability for human emotions to get in the way of the truth, and ensures that the manager's half-time team talk is always accurate.

Another way in which Benham's clubs remove the emotional bias of a manager is to equip him with a team of analysts, who talk to the head coach through an ear-piece during matches. These analysts usually sit with half a dozen laptops adjacent to the media section inside the stadium. Their main job is to recommend which substitutions the manager should make, as well as when to make them, based on data that is being collected during the game. As a result, the most important in-match changes that the team makes are data-driven, rather than being based on gut-feeling.

The argument for stats to be prioritised over gut-feeling is one which runs throughout this book. The traditionalists will argue that *you cannot use data to judge the size of a player's heart*. I have seen it written that *'football is poetry, not mathematics'*. This line of argument can easily be dismembered by looking at the *Moneyball* revolution in baseball. Billy Beane would remind the data sceptics that the people who get thrown out of casinos are the card counters, not those gambling based on gut-feeling.

Brentford and Midtjylland's analysts are able to separate themselves from the emotion of the game, something that a manager cannot do. Managers are too involved to make clear and concise judgements. When making substitutions they may let the extremities of their emotions take the better of them. Whether it be fury at a refereeing decision or euphoria at a goal being scored, a coach's emotions can blind him from making rational decisions. The analysts can offer objective advice, supported by data, suggesting what tactical decisions will give the team the best chance of victory.

Benham has also taken the power of vetoing transfers out of the manager's hands. The manager doesn't have final say on who the club signs. Benham has teams of analysts, experts and coaches who make up a transfer committee. When his models highlight a player who Brentford or Midtjylland should sign, the committee discuss it.

The manager, as a member of the committee, does have some say in each signing. The clubs would rarely sign a player whom the head coach doesn't like. However, the manager cannot sign a player without first consulting the committee. If the player ranks poorly in Benham's statistical models, there is very little chance of the club signing him. This 'cabinet' style of working is similar to how the senior members of the British parliament convene to discuss matters of the state. Benham's managers operate within a democracy, not a dictatorship.

The idea is that personal biases are quashed by the decision of the collective. In the traditional recruitment methods, if a manager sees a player that he likes then he signs him. Conversely, he can easily disregard any player who he doesn't like. This means that his own personal biases and beliefs may hold him back. For example, if a manager believes that small players hold little value because they are weak, there will be no one there to correct his mistake[9]. His team will suffer because of a personal prejudice that he holds.

Using a transfer committee combats this by eliminating individual biases. One manager will have quite a lot of wrongly informed beliefs. By having several people all contribute their ideas and opinions, you are

---

9 Such a belief used to be common in football. Scouts were told to look for strong, physical athletes. In reality, small players' low centre of gravity gives them an advantage, with their agility being a particularly dangerous attacking weapon.

increasing the sample size of information that you can use. The individual flaws of each person are cancelled out by the shared experience of the collective. Whilst transfer committees may not be an inimitable innovation, what makes Benham's so unique is their reliance on the statistical methods that will be laid out in the latter chapters.

Liverpool are probably the most notable club to have used such a structure in recent years. Their approach has achieved moderate success. The committee realised that Fernando Torres was starting to decline in ability around the same time that Chelsea became interested in him. The committee decided to sell him to the London side for £50m. Surely enough, Torres' form deteriorated just as the committee had predicted. Had Liverpool left the decision down to one manager, he probably wouldn't have spotted the trend.

Another example of the wisdom of the collective working at Liverpool was their capture of a young Uruguayan forward back in 2010. They spotted him playing for Ajax in the Eredivisie. Although Luis Suarez had a decent goal scoring record, the Dutch league was considered significantly weaker than the Premier League. Liverpool's transfer committee decided to take a £22.8m gamble on the forward, who left the Reds for more than three times that amount just over three years later. An individual manager might not have been willing to back the signing of Suarez.

Looking to the future, it wouldn't be surprising to see more clubs drift away from the traditional managerial structure and towards systems with transfer committees in place. Losing the power to sign players and make substitutions of their own free will may be hard to take for some managers. Indeed, Mark Warburton refused to work under Benham's system when his power of vetoing transfers was removed[10]. However, there is a positive aspect to this change for head coaches. In existing structures, the great power of the manager makes them an easy scapegoat. They come under a great amount of criticism when their team isn't performing

---

10 We will discuss the Warburton saga at a greater length later on in this book. In short, Warburton was a well-respected manager who left Brentford very suddenly and mysteriously. Some fans turned against Benham, not understanding why such a successful manager had been "sacked" by the owner. Again, more on this later.

well. A poor run of form will often result in the manager losing his job. A shift to a more collective and democratic system, such as the one's at Brentford and Midtjylland (and to some extent at Liverpool), will make the role of the manager more stable. It will become harder to sack the man in charge, leading to a greater job security for managers. This stability can surely only be a good thing for both the managers and the football clubs that they run.

THE FLAWED WORLD
OF PUNDITRY

In 1995, WHEN DISCUSSING ALEX Ferguson's Manchester United on Match of the Day, Alan Hansen famously said that "you can't win anything with kids". Hansen was speaking after Ferguson's side had lost by two goals to Aston Villa on the opening day of the 1995-96 season. The line has gone down in footballing folklore as one of the worst predictions in footballing history. Manchester United went on to win both the Premier League and FA Cup that season. As Ferguson's team became one of English football's most successful ever sides, Hansen's forecast went on to become one of the English football's worst ever predictions.

As the sport has evolved to the changing landscape of television broadcasting, so too has the art of football punditry. Sky Sports have led this change, with BT Sport following more recently. The broadcasts of Premier League games are often preceded by a lengthy preview of the match. These build-ups will normally feature three or four ex-professional footballers assessing the skill of the teams in question.

The art of prediction inevitably becomes tied up in this. The pundits will try to spot young, bright talent who they tip to become future superstars. They will offer their forecasts as to where in the table certain teams will finish the season. They will predict the outcome of the match they are previewing. These television build-ups provide some valuable context to the matches. However, the predictions made by pundits during these previews are often extraordinarily unsuccessful. By looking at the flawed predictive tendencies of these "experts", we can further our own forecasting abilities.

MANCHESTER CITY OR SALFORD CITY?

In 2008 Manchester City were bought by billionaire Sheikh Mansour. Mansour is one of football's wealthiest owners, worth at least £17bn. He bought Manchester City for £210m and has since accumulated well over half a billion pounds in annual losses, excluding approximately £200m on facility upgrades. The value of the club has soared nearly fivefold from £210m in 2010 to £900m in 2015. Almost overnight, the Manchester side were transformed from an average top division outfit into a side glistening with superstars. Their transfer spending ascended from just £2.4m in the 2006/07 season to around £127.7m in the 2008/09 campaign. In 2012 they won the Premier League thanks to "that" last-gasp Sergio Aguero goal against QPR. Manchester City's success is a testament to the influence of money in football.

The correlation between the success of a football club and the expense of their wage bill is extremely strong. The amount that City spent on player wages increased enormously after they were taken over by their new Abu Dhabi owners. In the space of two years they brought in stars such as Robinho, Carlos Tevez, Nigel De Jong, Jo, Roque Santa Cruz, Joleon Lescott, Kolo Toure and Emmanuel Adebayor, each of whom cost in excess of £15million. Success naturally followed this influx of superstars, even though many of them turned out to be flops.

Under five miles down the road from Manchester City lies a football club which draws several unlikely parallels with the Sky Blues. Salford City have spent the entirety of their history competing in non-league football. Recently they have been competing in the Northern Premier League Division One (North), the eighth tier of the English pyramid and four divisions below League Two. They were as contextually unremarkable as Manchester City – never exceeding expectations but consistently performing to their anticipated ability. Just like Manchester City, the club was taken over by owners who were comparatively extraordinarily wealthy.

In 2014, Salford City were purchased by five ex-Manchester United legends; Gary Neville, Phil Neville, Ryan Giggs, Paul Scholes and Nicky Butt. The quintet aimed to guide the club to new heights, with the goal of reaching the Championship within fifteen years. This would mean taking the club from the eighth tier to the second tier of English football. Although they did not directly manage the team, the owners employed a very hands-on approach in their guiding of the club. They even helped coach the side and develop tactics.

We can use this case study to the test the generally accepted premise that ex-footballers are the most qualified to run a football club. Gary Neville was also one of the most prominent pundits in England, appearing regularly alongside Jamie Carragher on Sky Sports. One would assume that if pundits really are experts, they would also make good managers. Assessing Neville's failed reigns at Salford and Valencia may help us understand why pundits are actually incredibly bad at making predictions.

It might be useful at this point to note that Salford City players don't lead a stereotypical footballer's lifestyle. The players are part-timers who have other jobs besides football. The wages that Salford pay is nowhere near enough to support a household. The average attendance of a Salford match was under one hundred people before the new owners took over. The players even wash their own kit. Away from the glitz and glamour of the Premier League, there are thousands of clubs around England just like Salford City.

Soon after purchasing the club, the new owners brought in a striker named Gary Seddon. He was a massive coup for Salford, having recently dropped down from the Football League. He was to Salford City what Robinho was to Manchester City. There were three reasons why Salford were able to attract such a comparatively high-profile player. Firstly, the BBC programme that featured the take-over of Salford City by the five Manchester United legends would no doubt heavily focus on him. This television exposure would no doubt help Seddon's modelling career, a vocation that he maintained alongside football. Secondly, the chance to work with footballing icons such as Gary Neville and Ryan Giggs was an opportunity which the forward would find hard to refuse. Thirdly, and most importantly, the nouveaux-rich Salford City could offer Seddon wages which exceeded any other club that would want him.

This is a prime example of a club being able to lure in top players because they have the resources to pay in excess of what they were worth. Whether you are Manchester City in the Premier League, or Salford City in the eighth tier, being able to outspend your opposition is a huge advantage. The lucrative salary that Salford were able to pay Seddon probably didn't reflect his ability as a footballer. The club overspent on the striker. However, when you have a budget which is significantly larger than your nearest competition, there is no need to find a smart means of operating. Salford City, just like Manchester City, wanted big name transfers and were willing to pay excessive money to make them happen.

Indeed, Gary Seddon became a success. He was scoring goals and Salford were thriving in their lowly division. Despite a performance dip in the middle stages of the season, during which their manager was sacked and replaced by two of the top coaches at that level, Salford City ended up achieving promotion. Whilst the campaign was undoubtedly successful in comparison to their recent history, this does not mean that the owners were effective in how they ran the club. In fact, they were far from it. Gary Neville was the main owner pulling the strings at Salford City, with help from his brother Phil Neville. The other three ex-Manchester United legends offered the odd piece of advice, but mainly served as window dressing for the BBC programme.

Salford City had been successful compared to previous seasons, but in previous seasons they hadn't had such vast amounts money ploughed into the club. The mid-season dip ensured that the club only just achieved promotion, when in fact they should have run away with the league title. In fact, Gary Neville even had to call upon a billionaire friend of his to inject a very healthy sum of money into the club in order to improve its facilities and pay for the contracts of the two new managers. Neville asked Singapore-based billionaire Peter Lim, who also owned Valencia, to buy a 50% stake in the club midway through the season.

The BBC programme made out the club's rise as some incredible, romantic story. The truth is, with the kind of money that was pumped into Salford City, any club could be taken over by almost anyone and achieve success. Few people would call Manchester City's rise to prominence a romantic tale. It is not necessarily a bad thing that wealthy owners are buying football clubs and splashing the cash to achieve success, but we should not find ourselves surprised when a club that spends far more than its rivals achieves greater success. Whether you are Manchester City or Salford City, money talks. Those who possess it have a great advantage, and those who don't have it are forced to find new ways of competing.

NEVILLE-ENCIA

Gary Neville is a notoriously busy man. Between offering expert punditry for Sky Sports and almost single-handedly running Salford City, the ex-Manchester United full-back managed to find the time to take another job. In late 2015, shortly after the end of his first season at Salford, Neville became manager of La Liga side Valencia. He was hired by the aforementioned Peter Lim, who owned the Spanish club. Phil Neville had already been appointed as assistant manager by Lim, whom both the Neville brothers had been friends with for a number of years.

Looking at Valencia's success under Gary Neville offers a thought-provoking insight into how being a successful football pundit doesn't necessarily translate into being a successful manager. It took Neville nine matches to achieve his first win, with his Valencia side losing a staggering seven-nil to Barcelona. The five points they picked up over this spell left them with a miserable average of just 0.56 points per game, the worst record in the *whole* of La Liga.

The appointment of both Gary and Phil Neville is a prime example of the exclusivity that operates within football. Gary is the perfect template of what owners look for when hiring a head coach. A white, conservative looking, ex-professional footballer is always going to win in managerial top trumps. Furthermore, the Nevilles were not hired for their inherent managerial skill, but because they were friends with the owner. Gary Neville was almost certainly not the best manager that Lim could have hired. However, someone with the appearance and profile of Neville is a very safe choice for an owner, and one that he can easily justify if it ends up not working out. There was probably a manager out there who was black who would have been better than Neville. There was probably a manager out there who had never played football professionally who would have been better than Neville. There was probably a nerdy-looking analyst out there who would have been better than Neville. Despite the fact that hiring any of these people over Neville would have increased Valencia's chance of success, football chooses to favour the white, conservative-looking, ex-professional player.

Returning to the main point, Gary Neville's managerial record seems to suggest that pundits aren't as clued up as we'd expect them to be. He failed to reach the level expected of him at both Salford and at Valencia. How was it possible that one of the most highly regarded football pundits of this generation failed so spectacularly when handed his own clubs to manage?

The Hedgehog and the Fox

Many football fans will be unfamiliar with the works of social theorist Isaiah Berlin. In 1953, the philosopher wrote an essay which divided writers and thinkers into two categories. There were hedgehogs, who view the world through the lens of a single defining idea (examples include Plato, Dante, Nietzsche and Ibsen). Then there were foxes, who draw on a wide variety of experiences (examples include Aristotle, Shakespeare and Montaigne). This gave birth to the concept of the hedgehog and the fox. The two terms have come to offer opposing definitions of the human character. In simple terms, a person can be fox-like or hedgehog-like in their approach to prediction-making. Berlin's work can grant us a great insight into the characteristics of pundits, managers and gamblers when applied to football.

A hedgehog lives their life by broad, all-encompassing principles. They are inflexible when it comes to changing their standpoint, and will generally defend their beliefs stubbornly. An example of a hedgehog is someone like Karl Marx, the father of communism. Marx believed that communism was the inevitable conclusion to human society. He viewed the world in terms of class; there were those who were rich and exploitative of the working classes, and those who poor and were exploited by the aristocracy. The aristocracy was made up of a few very wealthy people, whilst the masses were forced to suffer under their dominion. The theory went that the rich bourgeoisie were inherently greedy, and would continue to exploit the working class until breaking point. Eventually the working class would revolt against the aristocracy, leading to a 'dictatorship of the proletariat'. Control of government would be seized by the working class. Eventually all power would erode away, leaving in its place a utopian society in which everyone is equal. There would be one single class, with everyone pulling together and contributing to the best of their abilities.

This theory is obviously severely misguided. Despite contemporary critics of Marxism, the revolutionary socialist stuck to his belief and lived his life by these broad, overbearing principles. His prediction that the poor would rise up against the rich, resulting in the emergence of a single class, has clearly not come to fruition. The fact that he was unwilling to change his forecast under any circumstance makes Karl Marx the archetypal hedgehog.

A fox-like person, on the other hand, constantly updates and revises their predictions as they go along. This wily creature reacts to changing circumstances as they develop. A fox will also be more cautious in their predictions. They will think probabilistically, and will understand the role that chance can play in any undecided outcome.

Figure 3-1: Differences Between Hedgehogs and Foxes

Hedgehogs	Foxes
Unwilling to admit they might be wrong	Do not tend to shift the blame
Will often approach the views of outsiders with skepticism	Open to new ideas from any available source
Often very rigid in their ways, unwilling to adapt their model	Can adapt to different methods
Arrogant in their predictions, deploy an "all-in" approach	Understand the importance of caution
Tend to look no further than "Yes" or "No" predictions	Good knowledge of the rules of probability
Place reliance on ideas or notions	Look to hard facts to validate theories

Foxes make for the better forecasters. Their ability to think rationally allows them to make more successful predictions. Bookmakers are incredibly foxy in the way they go about making calculations. They set odds governed by probability, and they are willing to update their predictions based on new information. These fox-like principles are outlined in a relatively new form of gambling: in-play betting. Certain bookmakers offer this feature on their apps, allowing the bettor to stake wagers whilst the match is taking place. This forces both the gambler and the bookmakers to be constantly updating their predictions. The odds will change as a match progresses. If either party is not flexible in their approach to in-play betting, they will lose a lot of money. A gambler must be fox-like in order to succeed.

When Isaiah Berlin wrote his essay, he had much less literal implications in mind. Marx was a hedgehog who refused to change his beliefs about human nature, failing to take on board criticism from other circles. Perhaps communism would have survived longer if he had altered his predictions to adapt to changing political circumstances, or if his thinking had reached a compromise with other ideologies. Instead, his fixed and unremitting forecast that the bourgeoisie would fall of its own accord became a failed prediction. Karl Marx would not have been very good at in-play betting.

Hedgehogs live their lives by following broad principles, but these do not necessarily have to be such intellectually astute philosophies as that of communism. For example, a friend of mine holds a theory that everyone on the planet looks like either a rat or a pig. Granted, this is a slightly ridiculous example, but you may be surprised at how valid the theory becomes when you begin to adopt it. Indeed, when you look out for it, most people do look a little bit like either a rat or a pig. I, myself, am happy to admit that I look like a rat, whilst that same friend of mine considers themselves a pig.

However, if one were to live their life by this principle, they might one day come across someone who looks nothing like either a rat or a pig (perhaps they look like a frog). Thus, their assumption that everyone looks like one of these animals is deemed incorrect. They must become fox-like and update their judgement, or else their theory will be outdated and incorrect. Broad and overreaching principles tend to have exceptions. Accepting new information and updating our beliefs accordingly is essential if one is to become a fox.

HEDGEHOG PUNDITRY

Whilst prosperous bettors are fox-like, the reverse can be said for successful pundits. Generally speaking, television personalities and sports pundits tend to act like hedgehogs. They are inclined make bold and outlandish predictions with the hope that some of their long-shot forecasts will come to fruition. They seldom take into account the role of probability. Television pundits don't like to deal with uncertainty, meaning they make overconfident predictions. In order to make their point seem more commanding, the pundit generally doesn't bother assessing both sides of the argument.

An example of this happening is when Alan Hansen made his cata-strophic prediction that Alex Ferguson "[couldn't] win anything with kids". A fox would have assessed the situation; perhaps stating that it is *unlikely* that you could win a trophy with such a young team. By allowing Ferguson no chance of success, Hansen thought that he was making his theory sound more valid. However, despite the fact that he made his argument sound stronger through his confident use of language, the prediction was no more accurate as a result. Pundits tend to see uncertainty as a weakness when, in reality, football is shrouded in uncertainty. The so-called "experts" dilute the sport with their hedgehog-like judgements and predictions.

The clip of Hansen's disastrous forecast is available to watch on-line. The assurance with which he dismisses Ferguson's side is striking. "They've got problems… the trick to winning the championship is to have strength in depth and they just haven't got it". In truth, Hansen probably knew that Ferguson had at least a small chance of winning a trophy that year. Why, then, did Hansen make a prediction that he knew would prob-ably fail? Why did he allow himself to act like a massive hedgehog?

There are several reasons why hedgehogs make for entertaining tele-vision pundits, even though they are bad at making predictions. Firstly, an audacious prediction-maker is a lot more exciting than a rational one. Like every business, television companies want to keep their consumers happy. Having an Alan Hansen on your show makes for much more inter-esting viewing than having some analyst who has worked out the exact probabilities that Manchester United will win a trophy. Even if a hedgehog like Hansen makes a prediction which is clearly not going to come to frui-tion, a viewer can take a certain pleasure in disagreeing with the pundit. Fans often like to criticise managers and players, claiming that they could do a better job. The same principle applies with pundits. Supporters like to think that they are the experts of the sport. Hansen's "you can't win anything with kids" comment may not have been a successful predic-tion, but it did receive a great deal of publicity. The clip has been viewed hundreds of thousands of times online. The BBC and Match of the Day won't care that one of their pundits was disastrously wrong, but they will care about the increase in ratings that the prediction attracted.

Another point to make is that pundits don't have any checks on them. There is no inherent *need* for them to be right. It doesn't matter if a pundit makes a handful of failed predictions, they will still be offered more punditry jobs. Alan Hansen didn't get sacked because of his disastrous forecast – if anything, his increased publicity would have gotten him even more job offers. Punditry isn't like betting. If a gambler makes a catastrophic prediction, he can lose thousands of pounds. This forces him to strive to be as accurate as possible. A pundit has no such checks in place.

If we want pundits to become foxier, we must *give them a reason to be right*. Holding pundits accountable for their predictions will force them to try and make those predictions as accurate as possible. The majority of hedgehog-like pundits are never penalised for their misjudgements. If we hold them liable for their mistakes, they will be forced to stop making them. The predictive success of pundits will improve if we force them to put something on the line. In other words, encourage them to place bets on their predictions. Giving them a stake in the matter would prompt them to try and get as many forecasts as possible correct.

Gary Lineker stated just over halfway through the 2015/16 season that if Leicester City won the Premier League title, he would do the first Match of the Day broadcast of the next season in his underwear. Lineker obviously meant this as a bit of a joke, but in making this assertion he was being unassumingly foxy. By putting something on the line (the embarrassment of having to present a TV programme half naked) he showed his full confidence in the prediction.

We would undoubtedly end up with more successful predictions if other pundits were willing to *prove* their confidence in their forecasts. In an ideal world, any disagreement between two parties would end in one of two ways. Firstly, the two parties would attempt to revise their predictions and reach a compromise. Failing this, however, they would be forced to place a wager on the outcome of the event. If they both truly have full confidence in their calculations, then they should be eager to do this.

Here's an example; suppose we were discussing who was going to win the Merseyside derby. I think that Liverpool have the best chance of victory, but you are adamant that Everton are the favourites for the tie. There is a clear disagreement in our standpoints. We must now reach one of the two aforementioned conclusions. We can attempt to reach a compromise. Perhaps we both revise our predictions and concede that a draw is the most likely result? Maybe I decide to join your side of the argument, or vice versa? If it is clear that neither of us is willing to concede ground in our respective beliefs, the alternative outcome is necessary. We should place a wager on the outcome of the event. Seeing that we both hold differing and unshifting opinions, it is in our best interests to exploit the situation for monetary rewards.

This is essentially how betting markets work. Bookmakers serve as the devil's advocate, being willing to bet against any outcome that you choose. If I thought that Liverpool would win the derby, I could place a bet with any bookmakers. Equally, if you thought that Everton would emerge victorious, then you could place a wager on this outcome. The bookmakers are willing to challenge any opinion that you have, but in turn they pay out slightly less than is "fair" if you do win. In the same way that the house takes a cut of the winnings in poker, bookmakers take a commission for providing you with the service. That's why it is so hard to consistently make money on sports betting.

Differences in opinion may come about not only in the outcome of certain events, but also in the *probabilities* of event outcomes. Reverting back to the Merseyside derby example, it is possible that you and I both agree that Liverpool are the more likely side to emerge triumphant. However, I may think the Reds have a 60 percent chance of victory, whilst you speculate that they have a 40 percent of winning. In this scenario the same process should take place, as there is still a fundamental disagreement in our two standpoints.

It is obviously impractical for this process to be repeated every time we encounter a disagreement in our lives. Despite ensuring that people attempt to make the most accurate forecasts possible, it is unreasonable to expect them to place a wager every time they encounter a differing view. In a world like this, where everyone would have to prove their confidence in their predictions, the foxes would rule over the hedgehogs. Marx, Plato and Alan Hansen would all lose money quickly, whilst those who understand the rules of prediction set out in this book would prosper.

Pundits will always maintain hedgehog tendencies. Despite the fact that their predictions may be inaccurate, their outlandish judgements do provide some form of entertainment value. We must simply be aware that, whilst these forecasts may be what is required of pundits to have successful careers in the media, we must not succumb to the same hedgehog tendencies in our own prediction-making endeavours. In order to achieve the greatest prophetic success in life, we must adopt a more fox-like way of thinking.

Football Media's Forecasting Failures

For decades, football clubs have faced the problem of putting a price on the actual goods they are selling. What makes the sport such an addictive entity isn't the buying of merchandise, team shirts or anything else you can find in a club's superstore. To a certain extent, the enjoyment doesn't even come from attending matches, or from sitting in the stand with a piping hot chicken balti pie. These are the things that fans spend money on, but none of these purchases are essential for a fan to enjoy football. In fact, the vast majority of fans probably don't spend any money on these things. Most fans are what could be described as "armchair fans". They follow their team's results online and watch them on television from the comfort of their own homes. This means that football clubs don't make any money from the majority of their supporters, besides from television income. Anyone can be a fan free of charge. With the technology that now exists it is possible to obsessively support a club without ever seeing

the stadium or players in real life. There is a huge community of passion-
ate Manchester United fans in Asia, many of whom wouldn't be able to
point out where Manchester is on a map of the world.

The thing that football offers its fans is an unrivalled sense of community. No club could ever charge its supporters for thinking, talking or
sharing in the glory of the sport. This is what really makes football worthwhile, and it is free. Whether it be discussing the latest results, gossiping
over transfer rumours, or evaluating whether a particular manager should
be sacked, football's followers can't get enough of the constant drama
provided by the sport. There are heroes and there are villains, there are
success stories and there are tragedies. Crucially, there is a sense of unpredictability. Clubs can put a price on a matchday ticket, on the cost of
a scarf or a cup of tea at half-time, but they can never put a price on the
sense of belonging that a supporter attains by sharing a mutual interest
with millions of other people across the globe.

The fan is caught in a weird sort of limbo. Whilst being unable to influence the game in the way that those inside the sport can, they are linked
to their respective clubs through hours of dedication. Ordinary fans cannot claim to be a part of the exclusive inside realms of the sport, occupied
by owners, managers, pundits and the like. However, the service to their
clubs, the hours of following their side up and down the country, and the
ever-increasing money that they spend on tickets, certainly links them to
the team in some capacity. Supporters are caught in a peculiar position
– they are consumers of the incessant hyper-active media that surrounds
football, but are unable to influence events directly.

The fact that the fan is neither on the inside nor the outside of the
sport makes the role of sports media crucial. Television broadcasters,
newspapers and websites tend to be the ones who profit from football's
addictive nature. They cash in on the enormous hype that surrounds the
beautiful game by enabling information from clubs to reach the fans. If
you want to hear about a possible new signing, you would tend to look
towards social media or a reliable sports channel. The club's official website is probably the last place you would look. Football has become more

and more secretive, with an increasing number of transfers being "undisclosed". The people on the inside naturally hide information from the fans on the outside.

Media outlets prosper from this. The market of football media has become over-saturated. Just as football clubs strive to find an edge over the competition, so too do newspapers, websites and TV channels strive to outdo each other and gain the attention of consumers. This can create a lot of unhelpful noise. Websites tend to exaggerate information or twist facts in order to gain more page views. The more traffic that flows through a site, the more money that site will gain through advertising. These sites need to attract as many consumers as possible. The easiest way to do this is to post engaging titles which draw readers in and to fill their site with "shocking" or "incredible" stories. The problem is that the stories are either heavily exaggerated or, in some cases, completely made up. Credibility is becoming increasingly compromised as media outlets clamber for the attention of consumers.

This is particularly true when it comes to transfer speculation. Football clubs are understandably reluctant to reveal who they wish to sign. If other clubs were to find out that a club is interested in a player, they might too become interested, which would decrease the chance of the original club successfully completing the signing. In recent years, Matthew Benham's recruitment of players to Brentford FC has been exceptional. Several players have been brought to the club for small fees, and sold on a couple of seasons later for much larger sums of money. As a result, some clubs now monitor Brentford's transfer activity and will look to swoop for any players that the Bees appear to be paying attention to. Thus, it is in the club's interest to hide their interest in a player until he has officially signed.

This can become frustrating for the fans. Much of the information that they receive is speculation. Gossip columns have become incredibly popular in recent years. Social media, too, has birthed a whole new monster when it comes to potential transfers. One tweet from an anonymous account about a player's potential movement can give rise to great excitement from supporters. Any slight sign of an impending transfer can be exaggerated by websites looking for more hits. Noise can easily be mistaken for the truth when the media report on football. People love to read about big signings that might occur, or the potential sacking of managers. It is no wonder that the word "saga" is often attributed to an ongoing story involving a player's potential transfer.

FIRED OR EXPIRED?

In the February of 2015, Brentford fans were in dreamland. Matthew Benham's innovative and secret statistical methods had led the club to their highest league position in many decades. With just a few months left in the season, the Bees had a decent chance of securing promotion to the Premier League for the first time in their history. In the process, they would achieve the rare feat of acquiring back-to-back promotions from the third division. Brentford, despite having one of the smallest budgets in the Championship, were within touching distance of Premier League football.

Then an unexpected bombshell dropped. Mark Warburton, the beloved manager who had steered Brentford to promotion from League One the previous season, was to leave the club at the end of the campaign. Warburton had the best win ratio of any Brentford manager in the entire history of the club. He was softly spoken, honest, and had a fantastic relationship with the players.

Warburton, like Benham, was a former city trader. One day he decided that he had made enough money to retire from finance, and took a 90% pay-cut to pursue a career in football, his one true passion. He worked in the youth ranks at Watford before becoming a part of Brentford's back-room staff. When Bees manager Uwe Rösler got poached by Wigan, with Brentford wallowing in the depths of League One, Warburton got his big break. Benham hired Warburton as manager and the former Enfield player guided Brentford to the second tier for the first time in twenty years. Warburton's winning habit didn't stop once the Bees entered the

Championship. When the February of 2015 came around the fans were dreaming of Premier League football being played at Griffin Park, a stadium with a capacity of just 12,000. So why was Warburton being "sacked" halfway through Brentford's most successful season since the 1970s?

There was a media frenzy. Matthew Benham was portrayed as an ignorant, tyrannical owner. He was compared to the likes of Massimo Cellino and Vincent Tan, club owners who had made incredibly poor decisions in preceding years. Tan had chosen to change Cardiff's traditional blue kit to red. He felt that red strip would resonate better with the Welsh supporters, whose national team also played in that colour, but was forced to change it back to blue after a violent backlash from the fans.

Cellino was an even more oppressive owner. The Italian had an inherent distrust of the number seventeen, which prompted him to remove every seat number seventeen in the stadium of his former club, Cagliari, replacing them with '16b'. He was known not to attend any Leeds matches which took place on the seventeenth day of a month. When the Whites played their seventeenth home game of the 2015/16 Championship campaign, the official matchday programme was given the issue number of '16b'. He distrusted the number seventeen to such an extent that when he took over the club he instructed the Leeds manager, Dave Hockaday, to drop Paddy Kenny on the basis that he was born on 17th May. The goalkeeper was the second highest earner of the Leeds playing staff, but was told he would never play for the club again. Cellino believed that Kenny was bad luck, and in football the rich get what they want. Incidentally, the Italian also has a distrust of the colour purple.

These men were brainless tyrants at their respective football clubs. However, their reputations have wider ranging implications; it means that football owners are easily dismissed as moronic dictators who know nothing about the sport. When news broke that Brentford were planning to fire the most successful manager in their history, many lumped Benham into the same pot.

The problem with the story of Mark Warburton's departure was that no one knew anything with certainty. Even the official club statement was incredibly vague. In fact, Brentford's media team have been a bit of a running joke in the years since the infamous Warburton announcement. Amongst many bizarre claims, the statement compared football to a "village". This dancing around the issue caused confusion amongst fans and the media alike.

The secrecy that surrounds football means that people often mistake noise for signal, as they desperately try to use the little information that they receive to make judgements. Because no one really knew what was behind Warburton's mysterious departure, most people made this mistake. It *looked* as though the most likely explanation was that Benham was a deluded owner. This theory would adhere to trends set by other owners of football clubs in recent years. The media reports that Benham had sacked Warburton were incorrect. However, news outlets aren't necessarily concerned with what is truthful, they are concerned with running the most interesting version of a story that they can get away with.

There were two major mistakes that almost everybody who reported the story made. The first was that they claimed Warburton had been fired, when in fact he had simply not had his contract renewed. The second, and arguably more important point, was that Warburton had actually chosen to leave. Here's what really happened at Brentford in the opening months of 2015.

Since he had bought the majority shareholding in the club back in 2012, Benham had been gradually implementing his innovative statistical methods into the way the club operated. His system had been producing excellent results in a limited capacity at Brentford and at its logical extreme at FC Midtjylland, the other football club that Benham owns. In 2014, he had revolutionised the whole structure of Midtjylland, basing their entire approach around mathematical modelling. This overhauling of the club's structure guided them to a first Danish Superliga title win in their history. With Brentford flying high in the Championship, and the model seeming to be working successfully in England as well as Denmark, Benham decided to replicate the overhauling of Midtjylland's structure at Brentford.

The main way that Benham utilises his data is in player recruitment. We have already looked into the transfer committee that Brentford use. Benham wanted the head coach to have a strong input into the signing of players, but take away the prerogative of an absolute veto from the manager. This meant that Warburton would no longer have the final say when it came to buying or selling players. As we have seen, taking power away from the manager eliminates the impact of his individual biases. However, Warburton didn't feel comfortable with the changes. Adhering to a traditionalist line of thought, he was sceptical of Benham's radical alterations to the structure of the club.

After lengthy discussions it became apparent that Benham and Warburton weren't going to reach a compromise. The owner wanted to go all in with his pioneering and radical structure changes, but the manager simply wasn't willing to give up his power to veto transfers. As a result of this, the two decided that it was in the interest of both parties to go their separate ways when Warburton's contract expired at the end of the season.

None of this was known by the media or the general public. Brentford's statement gave "a difference in footballing philosophies" as the main reason for Warburton's departure. To the Brentford fans this didn't go a long way to clarifying why such a successful and beloved manager had been "sacked". Most people assumed that the relationship between the two men had deteriorated when, in fact, they parted on pretty good terms. Most people took Warburton's side, thinking he was an innocent manager who had been hounded out of the club by a ruthless owner. Others pointed out that Benham had been a fan of the club since 1979, and that every decision he made was in the best interests of Brentford. They argued that he had been caught in between a rock and a hard place. He could keep his well-liked manager[11] and abandon the innovative footballing philosophy that had won him millions of pounds as a professional

---

11 Until a bigger club swooped in and poached Warburton for themselves, of course. The likelihood was that another side would have offered him more lucrative wages at some point in the near future, luring him away from Griffin Park whether Benham wanted him to stay or not.

bettor. Conversely, he could allow Warburton to find a new club and continue with his analytical quest.

The following quote from Benham himself, extracted from the Brentford club statement over Warburton's departure, outlines the decision that he made:

"Innovation, not increased funding, can be the only route to success for clubs such as ours, and I fully accept that innovation is never without risk. We are continuing to build a strong base for the future."

It is made clear that modernisation mattered more to Benham than the managerial ability of Warburton. As a professional gambler, Benham is keenly aware of how to deal with risk and reward. He concluded that taking the risk of letting Warburton leave would pay out for Brentford in the future, should they continue to utilise the methods that he had already fully installed at FC Midtjylland.

So, Warburton was allowed to leave and media outlets ran the story that Benham had sacked Brentford's most successful ever manager. The truth is that the Brentford owner would have probably preferred to be made out as a tyrant than to have journalists delve further into his ground-breaking methods. The secrets to his "footballing philosophy" are well guarded. If other clubs were to have discovered how effective and relatively simple Benham's processes were, any edge that Benham had would have been lost. When a gambler knows who will win a particular sporting fixture, he doesn't go around telling everyone his inside information. Instead, he places a bet on that team. This is why there are very few, if any, reliable tipsters. Anyone who is able to make money through gambling doesn't post tips online, they use the information to make themselves rich. Benham's system is his most prized possession; if other teams knew it then Brentford and Midtjylland wouldn't be able to gain an edge. In the world of betting, as in the world of football, those who speak don't know, and those who know don't speak.

The type of misreporting that occurred during the Warburton saga is prevalent within the world of sport. You will probably have noticed the fact that the media coverage of football tends to foster the tendencies of hedgehogs. Several parallels can be drawn between the judgements of the pundits that we looked at earlier in the chapter and the news outlets that produce coverage on the beautiful game.

First and foremost, there is little room for rationality in football media. A truly rational outlet would have reported the facts, whilst also stressing that nothing was truly certain and a lot was going on behind the scenes. This would have been accurate and logical, but it also would have been perceived as flimsy and insubstantial journalism. Readers want to read confident and affirmed news stories. They don't want to read about "known unknowns", the things that we know we don't know. In an attempt to please their consumers, media outlets tend to turn everything into "known knowns". Even when they know that they don't know something, they must speculate so as to prevent any sense of doubt creeping into their story. The media didn't know much about why Warburton left Brentford, but they *assumed* that he must have been sacked. They knew that the story of Benham firing Warburton, though it hadn't been confirmed by any reliable source, would get a lot of reads from consumers.

This unwillingness to admit any sort of doubt resonates throughout punditry and journalism. The media's running of the Mark Warburton saga is comparable to Alan Hansen making his Manchester United prediction. Both made it seem as though they knew exactly what was going on, when in fact neither had it right at all. Both allowed no room for reservation or rationality. Both were massive hedgehogs. This unwillingness to acknowledge uncertainty can be dangerous in one of the most secretive sports of them all.

WHO WANTS TO BE A MANAGER?

Pundits have nothing to lose when making predictions. They don't have a stake in the outcome of the event, which means that other agendas can take precedence. If this is the case, perhaps the reverse could also be true. It seems natural that the people who have the biggest stake in a result would make the most accurate predictions. In football, this tends to be the fans. Fans pay extortionate prices to go and watch their team. Fans devote days of their lives to following their side up and down the country. Fans have the most riding on the outcome of their teams' games[12]. Players, coaches and owners come and go, but a fan can stick by one club for the entirety of their lifetime.

If we assume that supporters have the most stake in the outcome of a match, would it also be safe to assume that they would make the most accurate predictions about matters concerning the club? In other words, would allowing the fans to collectively manage a team have a positive impact on the club? This is exactly what Will Brooks, a former football journalist, wanted to find out when he set up MyFootballClub.

Brooks' aim was to find 50,000 football enthusiasts from around the world to purchase a club in England. The central premise of MyFootballClub was to allow these paid members to control the club through a democratic voting process conducted online. The idea was that the members would essentially run the club. They would be able to vote on things like which players to sign, whether to sack the manager and even what type of food to serve at the stadium. Every decision that could possibly be made would be done so collectively through an online vote available to every member. This would remove the dictatorial powers of the manager, allowing the wisdom of the collective to prevail.

MyFootballClub's membership reached over 53,000 in August 2007, just a few months after Brooks began his search. In January 2008, MyFC opened a poll to their members online asking whether or not they would be in favour of taking over National League side Ebbsfleet United. 96 per cent of the members voted in favour of purchasing a controlling stake in the club.

---

12 You could argue that the players and management have more riding on the outcome of each match. This is certainly true in terms of monetary gains, but fans tend to have much more emotional investment in the result.

There was a mixed reaction in the world of football to the announcement that Ebbsfleet would be run by fans. The traditionalists opposed the idea, arguing that a club needed a strong figurehead in charge. The autocratic manager is an intrinsic part of football. Having an omnipotent coach steering the club allows for decisions to made swiftly and with conviction. Opening the decision-making process up to the public, who generally have little knowledge of the sport, was a foolish thing to do.

Conversely, there were some who responded positively to the idea. A more democratic approach to running a football club would mean that the wisdom of the collective could be utilised. The biases and misinformed opinions of one man may be enough to hamper the progress of a team, but when over 50,000 people are voting on a decision then the individual irrationalities tend to be drowned out by the noise of the collective. A representative of Brentford FC, not yet owned by Matthew Benham, told CNN that the deal was "a very positive move for football because the club is owned by people who have real passion for it."

Ebbsfleet were successful in their first season at the hands of MyFC. In 2008, the team won the FA Trophy, lifting the cup at Wembley stadium and giving the project a large publicity boost. However, questions still remained about the premise of an internet society running a football club. Originally it was the prerogative of the fans to make every decision both on and off the pitch, including who should be named in the starting line-up before each match. However, following a vote of MyFC's members, it was decided that selection issues should be left to head coach Liam Daish. It was concluded that, as the fans didn't get the chance to watch training sessions, they could not assess either the mentality or fitness of the players in the same way that Daish could.

Following this vote, the structure at Ebbsfleet closely resembled that of the British parliament. The founding idea of democracy is that everyone should have an equal say in the running of the country – or, in the case of MyFootballClub, the running of Ebbsfleet United. However, the notion of direct democracy, where every member of a society is involved in the decision-making process, is flawed. Due to the logistical struggles that it involves, direct democracy can only occur in very small states. Ancient Athens were able to operate under such a system, where every citizen voted on every important debate. In these types of municipals, everyone in society would air their opinion on every contentious matter. Clearly the construction of a House of Commons that fits all sixty-five million British citizens inside is unrealistic. Not *everyone* can vote on *every* single issue that is raised.

The solution that British politics provides? Elect representatives to vote on behalf of a group of people. In Britain we have 650 members of parliament who each represent a geographical area of the state, which is known as a constituency. These MPs are entrusted to reflect the views of tens of thousands of people each. Of course, this means that some people's opinions will not be heard, but it is the job of the government to try and bring the greatest happiness to the greatest number. In essence, the same system was in place at Ebbsfleet. The fans realised that they didn't have the time or knowledge to assess the squad effectively. It made logistical sense to allow the manager to represent their decision. This sole individual could dedicate all of his time and energy into channeling the views of the fans and deciding upon the best course of action.

In August 2008, the members of MyFC were asked to make their first vote of real significance. Usually it is the privilege of the manager to decide whether or not to accept a transfer offer for a player. When Ebbsfleet received an offer of £140,000 for striker John Akinde from Bristol City, the decision was opened up to the members of MyFC. The MyFC members voted to accept the transfer offer with more than an 82% majority. This was a historic moment in football; for the first time ever the fans had been allowed to make a major decision on behalf of the club. The people who cared the most about the team were being allowed to run it as they pleased.

Membership in MyFootballClub dwindled after their early success, and they eventually had to sell Ebbsfleet after running into serious financial trouble. Despite this, the project has not been viewed as a failure. The National League is a very turbulent division of English football. Ebbsfleet were competing with several much larger clubs, including teams like Luton Town who received higher attendances than some League One sides. The fact that they held their own in the division is an achievement within itself.

Several other projects have sprung up in other countries with the same aims of MyFootballClub. Brazil, Denmark, France, Germany, Italy, Spain and the USA are amongst nations within which fan-run clubs have appeared. The degrees of success have been varied, but the idea of the democratic running of a football club has fascinated people worldwide. The most accurate predictions possible are made when something is at stake, as was the case for the fans running Ebbsfleet. Surely there can be no harm in utilising the power of modern technology to open up online votes to loyal fans. To some extent, many clubs already do this; supporters are often able to vote for their man of the match on the club website after each game. If a club were to open up similar polls for other decisions, they might better be able to understand the thoughts and feelings of their fanbase. Fans are essentially scouts who pay to watch their team, and managers who realise this could utilise these thousands of opinions to improve their own predictions.

Clearly, in some cases, it wouldn't be in the interest of the club to open a decision up to its supporters. As aforementioned, clubs are notoriously opaque when it comes to financial affairs. Transfer signings are becoming increasingly "undisclosed". A club might not want to divulge its financial details to the general public, which would allow other clubs to take advantage of the information. However, even by including the fans very slightly in decision-making processes, clubs might begin to break down the barrier that currently exists between themselves and their fanbases. This void between the two parties is currently filled by the media, who often misreport or misinterpret news stories. A more democratic approach to the running of football clubs might just be the way forward.

A RESULTS BASED BUSINESS

One of the greatest failings within football is that the result dictates the narrative. We place too much emphasis on what the scoreline reads at full time, often neglecting what *actually* happened during the ninety minutes. Fans are so keen to see their team climb the league table or progress to the next round of the cup that all they really care about is the result of the match. The performance and, more importantly, the ability of the sides is often neglected.

This is a great inefficiency within football. It means that a run of bad luck often results in a sacking. A key injury or a poor refereeing decision can be the difference between a manager losing or keeping his job. Context often goes out the window; all that owners and fans tend to care about is how many points a team can accumulate. This a dangerous attitude to take when assessing a sport with so much noise surrounding it. Because goals occur so rarely, there is a huge deal of luck involved in football. This means that results don't accurately reflect the ability of teams. Sides can perform well and lose, whilst others can play poorly and emerge triumphant.

Examples of the result dictating the narrative occur every week. Suppose a team goes into half-time with a one goal advantage. In the second half they decide to sit deep and defend in an attempt to conserve their lead. They theorise that mounting a rear guard action will give them the best chance of winning. In the last minute, the other team hits the crossbar and the ball bounces clear. The team ends up winning the game, meaning the post-match verdict will probably highlight the tactical genius displayed by the manager. The team will be praised for their resilient defending and there will be several positives for them to take away.

Now consider what would have happened if the ball had hit the crossbar and gone in. The team would have drawn the game, conceding in the last minute. Now the post-match verdict looks very different. The pundits will say that the team were naïve to spend the whole of the second half sitting deep, as it invited pressure onto their defence. The fans will be extremely disappointed that their team has not won the game. They will probably look for a scapegoat, usually the manager. The final ruling of the match will be that two points were dropped.

The width of the crossbar will have decided whether the manager was a tactical genius or incredibly naïve. This makes little sense. Surely the holistic performance of a football team in a particular match cannot be decided by pure chance.

The same example could be made using Marcelo Trotta's penalty miss that was described in the opening chapter. Had Trotta scored the spot-kick, he would have secured Brentford's first promotion to the Championship for nineteen years and would've become a legend at the club. However, his penalty hit the underside of the crossbar and bounced away to safety. As a result, many fans turned on him and blamed him for ruining the Bees' season. The difference of a couple of inches ultimately decided whether Trotta was a hero or villain.

In football, just as failure turns bad luck into stupidity, success turns good luck into genius. As we saw when assessing survivorship bias in an earlier section, the role of chance is absolutely crucial to how we are perceived. Midway through FC Midtjyland's 2014/15 title winning season, Matthew Benham's Danish side ran out two-one victors against the side bottom of the league. Rasmus Ankersen, chairman of the club and Benham's right-hand man, received congratulations from those around him after the match. However, Ankersen later revealed that Benham's models indicated Midtjylland were lucky to win the game. They had actually been outperformed by the team who were bottom of the league. Lady luck had decided to favour Midtjylland that afternoon, and if football was a fair game then they would have lost. The fans rejoiced at the result, when in fact they should have been concerned about the performance.

In that instance, Benham and Ankersen were fortunate that football is a results based business. Not only can this true in the case of a team, but also in that of an individual player. Strikers are placed under enormous pressure to score. A significant goal drought will often result in a forward being left out of the side. Attackers are judged on how many goals they score, as opposed to their overall contribution to the team. It may be that a striker is taking defenders out of the game with cunning runs, thus creating space for other teammates to move into. Or, it may be that a forward is holding the ball up expertly, and taking part in the build-up play of most of his team's goals. However, these things are not easily spotted or measured, meaning that the forward will often not get credit for such contributions. Football's heavy dependence on results over performance means that it is vital for a striker to score goals.

Similarly, a forward may not be getting the required service. It would be a great mistake to think that a striker surrounded by a team of poor players should be able to score the same amount as one surrounded by world class talent. A good striker may be let down by the team around him, meaning his true ability isn't accurately reflected by the amount of goals he scores. Fans will normally point the finger at the strikers if their team aren't scoring enough goals, when it will probably be the case that the forwards simply aren't receiving good enough service from the midfield, or have been left isolated by the manager's chosen formation. Ultimately, we must assess strikers by their performances, not their goal tally. We must not let the result (of how often they score), dictate the narrative (of the performances they put in).

In football, the outcome certainly dictates the storyline. This would explain why the man of the match is almost always the top goal scorer in the game. The thinking behind this is that the man of the match should be the player who has had the most positive impact on the game. In this sense, it makes sense that the player who scores the most goals should be presented with the award. However, most goals are scored from simple chances, and every goal has a huge amount of luck associated with it. This means that the man of the match is decided more by fortune than anything else. A player who works tirelessly off the ball for ninety minutes is arguably more deserving than a player who does nothing but take one kick which finds the net. The problem is that it is harder to measure how hard a player works, or how his movement off the ball has benefitted his team. Individual player performance is incredibly difficult to gauge in football. However, it is very easy to measure whether a goal scorer has scored or not. Call it the incompetence of the people who choose the man of the match, or call it an inability to accurately measure the impact of each player on a game, but most man of the match decisions are unfair.

The salient point to understand is that we should try to make judgements based on performance rather than results. There is a crucial difference between the two. Results are inundated with noise, whereas performances reflect the *actual* ability of a team or player. The result often lies to us; teams frequently win football matches undeservedly. The ability of sides is assessed based on the final score, rather than on their actual performance. Forwards tend to be judged on how many goals they scored, rather than their actual contribution to their team. The idea that the sign of a good team is one who grinds out results when performing badly is nonsense. That is the sign of a *lucky* team.

Football is a sport where the lucky prevail, and the unlucky are left to console themselves with that very fact. The final scoreline often tells a different story to the narrative of the game. In order to better asses the ability of each team, we must create new ways of "keeping score" rather than just counting the number of goals that go in. This is that approach that Matthew Benham's success has been found on.

A Mug's Game

At the beginning of the 2015/16 Premier League season, Leicester City were touted by most bookies as 5000/1 outsiders to win the league. This equates to a 0.0002% chance of the Foxes lifting the trophy. To put it into perspective, the bookies believed that the following things were more likely to happen than Leicester winning the title: a woman to be appointed as the manager of a Premier League club in the next season; Elvis Presley to be found alive; the Loch Ness monster to surface in the River Clyde; David Cameron, Prime Minister at the time, to be appointed Aston Villa manager.

Leicester fan John Pryke decided to take a £20 gamble on his team to do the unthinkable. The potential £100k winnings seemed a long way off at the start of the season, but with just a handful of games to go Leicester sat three points clear at the summit of the Premier League table. It was at this point that Pryke lost his bottle and decided to cash out on his bet for £29k. He theorised that Leicester's title challenge was about to falter, and that £29k was a lot of money to win off a £20 bet. Pundits and fans alike had been waiting for the Foxes' fairy-tale story to come to an end for some time. Many would applaud Pryke for holding his nerve for as long as he did. Ladbrokes, the bookmakers with which Pryke had placed his ambitious wager, said that a total of forty-seven punters had placed the same bet at the start of the season. A representative from Ladbrokes encouraged Pryke's choice to cash out, stating that 'John's gut must be telling him to cash out' and that they 'don't blame him for making that decision'[13].

Leicester's incredible story won them the hearts of many neutrals. The bookmakers, on the other hand, were certainly not gunning for the Foxes. Sky Bet were forced to pay-out in excess of £5m due the Leicester's success. To put that into perspective, the previous season they had made a profit of just £150k as a result of Chelsea winning the Premier League. Bookmakers throughout England had never had to pay out such a large amount in the history of sports betting. What Leicester had achieved truly was a modern day miracle. The largest bet placed with an online bookmaker was a full £40, meaning that the bettor was due £200k in winnings.

Leicester City's 2015/16 Premier League victory was one that no one would have forecasted at the beginning of season. Any fan, analyst or pundit who would have made such a prediction would have been laughed out of town. The Foxes' wonder season can teach us a lot about how to gamble successfully.

A NATION OF GAMBLERS

So far in this book we have studied how not to make poor predictions. We have laid the foundations of predictive success by learning what mistakes to avoid making when forecasting the beautiful game. Hopefully, the remaining pages will act as a guide of what things we need to actually *do* in order to make accurate footballing assessments. Instead of looking at *why* we make poor predictions, we will look at *how* to make good ones.

The British seem to have an obsession with gambling that borders on the unhealthy. There are over 8,700 betting shops across the nation, whilst six out of ten Britons spend more than £50 per month on gambling in one form or another. The average household spends £2.49 on Saturday's lotto draw, money that an incredibly small proportion of the British public ever see come back again in the form of reasonable winnings. The National

---

13 The bookies will always encourage you to cash out your bet. We will see why shortly.

Lottery took in £3.42bn (after prizes were handed out) from April 2015 to March 2016. In this same time period, the total gross gambling yield in the UK was £13.6bn.

Gambling is certainly an addiction. Many of the best professional gamblers say that they originally didn't gamble to make money, they did so because they loved the rush they got from doing it. They realised that if they wanted to keep feeling that rush then they would have to become good at betting, otherwise they would lose all their money and have nothing left to bet with! Once they became good at gambling, they found out that doing it professionally could earn them a living.

Matthew Benham, the protagonist of this book, worked in the city before trying his hand at professional gambling. Many city traders will tell you that the rush you experience from the pressure of making million pound trades is somewhat equivocal to that of placing bets of a similar magnitude. Pressure, risk and money – the three key links between the worlds of football, betting and trading in the city. His time on the trading floor taught Benham the basic principles of risk and reward. He recognised the role that chance plays in the markets. He understood that every bet was a sort of investment on the future outcome of an event. He knew that if he could calculate the probability that a bookmakers were giving to something, as well as calculate his own probability of the event occurring, he could exploit any undervalued odds which the bookmakers provided. The system he uses to calculate his own odds is the secret that has been so closely guarded; his pioneering approach to the sport that allows him to make better forecasts than even the bookies.

If you weren't following all that, do not worry. The main principles to becoming a successful gambler will be uncovered in the following pages, and Benham's ground-breaking methods will be disclosed in the latter chapters. The point to grasp at this stage is that Benham was able to use his experience from the trading floors of investment banking in order to understand the key principles of betting.

He set about deploying this knowledge by founding a company called Smartodds. The company provides statistical modelling for professional gamblers, allowing them the best opportunity to make money. In return, the professional bettors – or "clients" – pay to access Smartodds' data. Just like Opta sell their match statistics to media outlets, Smartodds sell their innovative data to professional gamblers (who, incidentally, are required to sign confidentiality agreements which ensure that Benham's methods remain a secret). The company has been so successful that Benham has made enough money to buy two football clubs – Brentford FC in England and FC Midtjylland in Denmark.

Smartodds has taken on other additional responsibilities since Benham purchased his two football clubs. It is now also used for scouting and recruitment purposes. Brentford and Midtjylland use the company's statistical models to identify transfer targets. Additionally, the managers of these teams use the company's data when profiling upcoming opposition. We will study these functions of Smartodds in greater detail later on, once it has been revealed how the pioneering methods work.

There is no doubt that Benham is one of the greatest professional gamblers of all-time. Despite the fact that he is incredibly wary of talking to the media[14], Benham has built up a reputation within English football as the face of the analytical revolution. If you were to attend a Brentford away match and got chatting to fans of the host team, it is likely that one of the more knowledgeable opposition supporters would ask you about Brentford's *Moneyball* approach. Benham's success has been founded on his ability to reap the rewards of his predictive talent through betting on football matches.

A Bookies' Eye View

It is crucial for successful gamblers to understand how the bookmakers set their odds. When going to war, it is of equal importance to understand the

---

14 Benham only ever does interviews for obscure fansites that only Brentford or Midtjylland supporters follow. Rasmus Ankersen, Benham's right-hand man, has become the face of his revolutionary approach. If you scour the internet, you can find hints of how Benham's model works, but his exact system is a very closely guarded secret. I will reveal his previously undisclosed methods later on.

methods of your enemies as it is to develop your own tactics. When taking on the bookmakers, it is essential that we comprehend how they operate. The first step is to learn how to translate a set of odds into percentages.

Each set of odds that a bookmaker offers (e.g. 4/1, 12/5, 1/1, etc.) on the outcome of a football match – or any other sporting fixture for that matter, reflects a probability that the bookies have assigned to that outcome occurring. Gerolamo Cardano, a 16th Century mathematician, was the first person to developed the notion of odds, which outlines the ratio of favourable to unfavourable outcomes. For example, in a match between Bayern Munich and Borussia Dortmund, the odds may be set as the following:

Home win (Bayern): **11/10**

Draw: **5/2**

Away win (Dortmund): **11/4**

These numbers will mean little to the average bettor, other than representing how much money would be returned if a certain stake was placed. If you were to bet £10 on Bayern to win, the odds of 11/10 mean you receive £21 back if the hosts emerge victorious[15]. If you placed £10 on a draw to occur, the odds of 5/2 mean that you receive £35 back should the match end in a stalemate. £10 on an away win would mean a pay-out of £37.50, because of the 11/4 odds. This is all you really need to know in order to gamble. Congratulations, you are now as good at betting as most of the British public.

Having this knowledge allows you a small glimpse into the probabilities at play. It doesn't take a rocket scientist to work out that betting

---

15 In essence you would actually only be winning £11. Seeing as you placed a £10 stake, this would return to you should your bet be successful. Obviously if your bet is unsuccessful the bookies would keep the £10

£10 on Bayern will return less money than betting the same amount on Dortmund. It follows that Bayern must be favourites, as the bookies are willing to pay-out less money if they emerge victorious. Another thing you can gleam from this knowledge is vaguely by *how much* Bayern are favourites. If the bookies had set the odds on Dortmund to win at 10/1 then it is obvious that an away victory is highly unlikely, as the bookies are willing to pay-out a lot of money if this result occurs. The longer the odds, the less probable it is for that outcome to occur. The odds of 5000/1 that the bookies set for Leicester to win the 2015/16 Premier League title reflect the fact that it was a near impossible accomplishment.

In order to assess the bookmakers' predictions with the highest level of accuracy, we must convert their odds into exact probabilities. Being able to visualise the chance of an event occurring can help us determine whether we think the bookmakers are correct. As it turns out, there is a relatively easy formula for doing this. Here is how to calculate odds into percentages if the odds are A/B:

If the odds are A/B and the percentage that they reflect is X...
B / (A+B) = X

This may seem a little daunting, but once you understand how the formula works you will be able to calculate the percentage chance of any set of odds. Let's suppose that we wanted to work out the percentage chance of a draw occurring in our match between Bayern Munich and Borussia Dortmund. Here is what we would do, given that the odds of a stalemate are 5/2:

Given that A is 5, B is 2 and X is the percentage we want to work out,
B / (A+B) = X
2 / (5+2) = X
2/7 = X
X = 28.6%

It's as easy as that. You simply take the second number (the "stake" number), which in the case of "5/2" is simply "2". You then divide this number by the two numbers added together, which in this case is "2" plus "5". You are left with a fraction that reflects the chances of that event occurring. All that's left to do is translate that fraction into a percentage, something that you are taught how to do at the age of about twelve. At this point a calculator is often required. Two divided by seven leaves you with a percentage of 28.6%. This is the probability that the bookies have assigned to a draw occurring in our theoretical Bayern Munich match.

If we wanted to work out the percentage of an away win, we would use the same formula with the odds of 11/4. We would divide four by fifteen, leaving us with 26.7%. Translating the odds that the bookies set into percentages, thus allowing us to visualise the chance of events occurring, is the single most important task to perform when betting. It doesn't matter how much you know about the two teams playing each other if you cannot accurately gauge the position of the bookmakers.

It is staggering that the vast majority of bettors do not know how to translate odds into percentages. Even if you do not carry a pocket sized calculator with you everywhere you go (although most phones nowadays have calculators pre-installed), you can get a good idea of the chance the bookies have assigned to a result by working out the odds as a fraction. For instance, 4/15 is close to 5/15, which is obviously 33.3%. 4/15 is also close to 4/16, which is 25%. Thus, we can infer that 4/15 is just under 33.3% and just over 25% - a good estimation considering the true percentage is about 27%. You could do computations like this without any calculation device.

Additionally, many odds translate into fractions which are easily adapted into percentages. The odds of 1/1 (or "evens", as it is more commonly known) is obviously 50%. When you use $B/(A+B) = X$ to convert the odds into a fraction, you are left with one divided by two. Here are some other examples of odds which can easily be translated into percentages, without even needing to whip out the calculator:

Figure 4-1: Odds Which Easily Translate into Percentages

Odds	Fraction	Percentage
1/3	3/4	75%
1/2	2/3	66.7%
2/3	3/5	60%
3/2	2/5	40%
2/1	1/3	33.3%
3/1	1/4	25%

Additionally, there are only a finite number of odds which the bookmakers use. A draw usually occurs in a football match around 25-35% of the time, thus the bookmakers tend to reuse odds for this outcome[16]. Experienced bettors memorise the percentages for each set of odds over time, simply because they would have calculated these percentages on so many occasions. Seeing as the vast majority of readers won't be experienced bettors, and the task of going through every single set of odds and translating them into percentages is laborious, I thought I'd lend a helping hand by dedicating a page or two of this book entirely to showing the most commonly used odds as percentages. This gambling cheat sheet can be found at the end of the manuscript. You're welcome.

---

16 12/5 (29.4%) and 23/10 (30.3%) are probably the most common odds associated with a draw. I have encountered these odds hundreds of times when placing bets. If you were to look at the bookmakers' odds for this weekend's set of fixtures, I could almost guarantee that either of these odds would appear in at least one match.

Why the Bookies Always Win

You may think that, having learnt how to calculate odds into percentages, you are now ready to go and bash some bookies. You would be wrong. Unless you understand how the bookmakers actually make their money, you cannot realistically expect to be making any of your own. In order to explain the complexities of how bookmakers operate, let's revert back to our match between Bayern Munich and Dortmund. If you recall, we set the odds as the following:

Home win (Bayern): **11/10**

Draw: **5/2**

Away win (Dortmund): **11/4**

You will notice that something strange occurs when you add up the three percentages of each outcome occurring. *Figure 5-1* shows the likelihoods that the bookmakers have assigned each event.

Figure 5-1: Odds, Fractions and Percentages for Bayern Munich v Borussia Dortmund

	Odds	**Fraction**	**Percentage**
Home Win	11/10	10/21	47.6%
Draw	5/2	2/7	28.6%
Away Win	11/4	4/15	26.7%
Total	-	-	**102.9%**

As you can see, the bookies believe that a home win is the most likely result, followed by a draw and an away win on virtually equal footing. The incongruity occurs when you turn your attention to the bottom right-hand side of the table. The bookmakers must have made a mistake! There is no way that the chances of an event happening can add up to 102.9%, is there? Surely percentages must *always* be out of one hundred? After all, 'per cent' literally means 'out of one hundred'. Where has that extra 2.9% come from?

The answer is that all bookmakers always calculate their odds to over 100%. This is known as the bookies' *"overround"*. Usually if you were to add up the bookmakers' probabilities of a team winning, drawing and losing a match, the total would equate to 105-108%[17]. This is how the bookmakers make their money. By overestimating the chance of an event occurring, they allow themselves to pay out less than they really should be paying out. In casinos the house always takes a cut of the action, a sort of commission they incur for their services. The same principle applies with bookmakers, it's just that most bettors don't realise. The extra 2.9% means that if a total of £102,900 is bet on the Bayern Munich match, then the bookies will only expect to pay out around £100,000. The other £2,900 goes directly into their pockets.

The mathematics behind this process may seem confusing, but once you wrap your head around it it's actually very simple. A bookmaker who was completely fair would add the probabilities of each outcome occurring up to 100% every time. Over the long run, this bookmaker would neither gain nor lose money. They should theoretically break even.

A bookmaker who added their percentages up to 90% would lose money over the long run. They would pay out more generously than they realistically should. Given that 7/3 equates to 30%, bookmakers who set odds of 7/3 for a home win, 7/3 for a draw and 7/3 for an away win would always lose money because they would always have to pay out more than necessary.

A bookmaker who wanted to make lots and lots of money would add their percentages up to far more than 100% (say, 125%). This bookmaker

---

17 The figure depends on a range of variables: which bookies you use, which fixture you bet on, etc.

probably wouldn't receive much business, as bettors would become aware of such ungenerous odds. The bookies add their odds up to enough to make a sizeable profit, whilst still realising the need to compete with all the other bookmakers out there. Bookmakers who set their odds at much more than 110% would receive few customers. They are forced to find a balance between greed and pragmatism.

It is of vital importance for all bookmakers to calibrate their odds so that they overvalue the chance of an event occurring. When the bookies underestimate the probability of something happening, they tend to end up paying big dividends. For example, the bookies clearly underestimated the probability of Leicester winning the Premier League in 2016. They were forced to pay out big money as a result. The whole premise of betting is that bets on unlikely events are rarely successful, but make up for this by paying out greater amounts of money when they do come off.

As long as they calibrate their odds correctly, the bookmakers will always make money in the long run. Their overround ensures this. Of course, the bookmakers know that they will have to pay out on a certain number of bets. Similarly, professional gamblers know that they will lose a certain amount of bets. The trick for both parties is to win more money than they lose. This isn't to say that you must win more *often* than you lose. You if you place £1 on a 10/1 outcome five times, and it comes off once, you have still made money despite losing four of your five bets. The key to gambling is finding the *good value bets*.

A good example of how the bookmakers' process works can be found in the betting of cricket. Most bookmakers offer bettors the chance to place a wager on who will win the coin toss at the beginning of the match – effectively a bet on whether the coin will come up heads or tails. This type of betting perfectly demonstrates how the bookmakers make their money, and how the ignorance of some gamblers means that they end up out of pocket.

The chance of either team to win the flip of the coin is obviously 50%. You can study the coin tossing form of the two captains, you can look at the amount of times that this particular umpire has tossed a heads, but at the end of the day blind luck will dictate whether it's heads or tails. Suppose a completely fair bookmaker were to offer odds of 1/1 on either outcome occurring. Let's say that half of the bettors who take up this offer were to place a collective £1,000 on heads, whilst the other half of our group of bettors stake a total of £1,000 on tails. Seeing as it is a 50-50 bet, you would expect the total placed on each side of the bet to be roughly equal. Before the event has taken place the bookmaker has £2000 sitting in their bank account.

Now consider what happens after the coin toss occurs. If the odds are 1/1 (50%), then the bookmaker would have to pay out a total of £2,000 to the bettors who correctly predicted which side the coin would fall on. Those punters who incorrectly guessed whether it would be heads or tails would be due no winnings, meaning that the bookmaker would break even. They would have been forced to pay out the full £2,000 that they originally collected to the winning punters, and will have none left in the bank for themselves.

Of course, no bookmaker can be successful by offering completely fair odds. What they do instead is set the odds at 10/11 instead of at 1/1. Instead of offering a fifty percent chance of the coin coming up as either heads or tails, they are now offering a 52.4% chance of either event occurring. When both sets of odds are added together the final sum in 104.8%. This gives the bookmaker a 4.8% margin.

Now consider the same scenario as before, but with the odds set at 10/11 instead of at 1/1. The same group of punters bet £1,000 on heads, whilst the second group bet £1,000 of tails. The chances are still just as likely for heads to appear as it is for tails, meaning that the spread of the money will still be roughly equal. Before the event occurs, the bookmaker once again collects £2,000 worth of stake.

However, contemplate what now happens after the coin is tossed. Let's say that the coin comes up heads. The bookmaker must pay the punters who placed a wager on this occurring. The odds of 10/11 dictate that £1,909.09 should be paid out if £1,000 was placed on this outcome (£909.09 in winnings plus the original stake of £1,000). The winning bettors still rejoice that they have won the bet, whilst the losers commiserate that they have wasted their money on a losing wager.

But who are the real winners? As always, it is the bookmakers. They are left with a total of £90.91 in their bank account after paying out the winnings. Like some sort of magic trick, their overround has ensured that they made money. Most bettors do not even realise that they have been made to pay a sort of commission to the bookmakers. Gamblers don't tend to acknowledge the negative expected value in the bets they place, partly because they have not assessed the exact probabilities the bookmakers offer.

Whilst the winning bettors will have made money on that individual bet, over the long run they will lose money. Unless they have some inside tip as to whether the coin will come up heads or tails, they will die a slow monetary death at the hands of the bookies' overround. Consider what happens if you placed a £10 bet on the coin coming up heads with the bookmakers' usual odds of 10/11. The coin is flipped and lands on heads. You've won your bet, and collect your winnings of £19.09. You decide to place another £10 bet on the same result occurring next week. This time the coin comes up tails and you lose your £10. Now you are left with just £9.09.

You realise that the £10 that you started with has now been whittled down by £0.91. You decide it is worth another punt, and bet the £9.09 that you have remaining on heads. You win! You collect your winnings of £17.35 (the £8.26 that the odds dictate you win, plus your original stake of £9.09). Your balance now stands at £17.35, which is £7.35 more than you started with.

Wow, you're actually a really good bettor. You might as well place another bet on the coin coming up heads. You stake another £10 on this wager, but this time the coin comes up tails. Your balance now stands at £7.35. Wait! How did that happen? You started with £10, and you have placed two winning bets as well as two losing bets. You have been right as many times as you have been wrong. How can you now only be left with £7.35?

This is exactly why gambling is described as a tax on those who don't understand the laws of probability. The overround that the bookmakers add means that you will always have negative expectation on uninformed bets. In other words, unless you are able to more accurately assess the probabilities of events occurring than the bookmakers, you will always lose money over the long run.

The cycle that is described above is hard to break out of. *Gambling is addictive*. When you have made money, you convince yourself that you are an expert bettor. It can be difficult to walk away whilst you are up. Conversely, when you have lost money, you always feel the urge to chase your losses. A gambler who has lost £5 will always want to try and reclaim that money, inevitably leading to the gambler becoming further in debt. Attribution bias means we think we are skilled when we win, but unlucky when we lose. We attribute success to internal factors (i.e. our ability), and failure down to external factors (i.e. bad luck). We have already come across this bias earlier in the book, when looking at how managers denote success to their ability and failure to bad luck. Attribution bias is how gamblers get hooked, and how their bank accounts get drained by the bookmakers.

The toss of the coin that is used in our example is transferrable to every sporting event that takes place. The difference being that with most sporting events there are three outcomes, due to the fact that a draw is possible. Whilst the toss of a coin is clearly a 50/50 event, a sporting event is often a 45/30/25 event. The chance of the various outcomes can adjust and flex depending on which teams are playing. However, this doesn't change the bookmakers' methods. Whatever the chances are of a home win/draw/away win, the bookmakers can always inflate the percentage chance of an outcome occurring.

The only other difference between the coin tossing example and a match of football is that, whilst the toss of a coin is decided purely by chance, the outcome of a football match has an element of skill to it. If we perform a more accurate assessment of the ability of teams than the bookmakers, something that Matthew Benham has been able to do with his pioneering system, then we may be able to make some serious money.

OVERCONFIDENCE VERSUS UNCERTAINTY

Before we study the correct approach to gambling, let us briefly touch upon the mentality that any successful bettor must adopt. There is a vicious cycle that can easily result in a gambling addiction: when we are up we become overconfident in our ability, and when we are down we tend to chase our losses. Those who do not possess a sturdy mental strength can lose a lot of money. Knowing when and when not to place a bet according to our psychological state is just as important as knowing which bets to place in the first instance.

This section aims to ensure that we do not fall victim to the mind games that gambling can play. In order to successfully beat the bookies, a bettor must remain cool, composed and rational. We saw in the second chapter what implications await us when we become too emotionally involved in our predictions. José Mourinho became blinded by his sentiments, ultimately leading to his downfall at Chelsea. Studies show that there are two conflicting sides to the human brain. The first is slow, rational and thoughtful, whilst the second is impulsive, emotional and takes short-cuts (known as heuristics). When betting, we must try to pay attention to the former.

Overconfidence can be extremely hazardous to the success of our forecasts. It is easy to confuse luck for ability when we are on a run of good form. A bettor who has exceeded his monetary expectations may believe either that he has some divine ability to predict the future, or that he should take advantage of his current streak of good luck. It is at this point that he should adhere to the age old cliché that you should *quit whilst you're ahead*. His form is surely only going to regress to the mean, resulting in his losing of money to the bookies' commission. Additionally, a bettor is likely to feel less pressure to be correct when he has already made money. This can result in him taking less care with his forecasts. Or, the gambler might start placing more dangerous bets with the hope of winning even greater sums. Any professional gambler would tell you that becoming overconfident is ultimately destructive.

Paradoxically, uncertainty does not always fall into the same pot. Intuition would tell us that doubt is an even greater weakness than overconfidence. However, as long as we recognise when we do not know something, and account for the implications that this might hold, admitting that we are uncertain can be a much better choice than taking a wild stab in the dark.

Uncertainty can be divided into two categories: known unknowns and unknown unknowns. Known unknowns are the things that we know we don't know. An unknown unknown is something which we don't know that we don't know. We have no awareness that unknown unknowns even exist. These can be particularly threatening to the success of our predictions, as we have no way of incorporating their potential impact into our models.

Information is key for professional gamblers, who dedicate most of their time to researching form, injuries, stats, or anything else which might affect the outcome of a sporting event. They attempt to eliminate every possible unknown unknown that can exist. Known unknowns are less of a threat to the models of these bettors. They can attempt to find out more about them so that they become known knowns. If that proves impossible, they can at least incorporate the margin for variance into their predictions.

For example, an injury to a key player can affect a team's chances of winning. Suppose that Barcelona's Lionel Messi was injured in a warm up. A bettor who was trying to forecast the outcome of the match might give Barcelona a 60% chance of winning. The injury to Messi might mean that the *actual* chance of them winning is now reduced to 56%. If the injury to Messi is an unknown unknown (in other words, the bettor has no idea that anything has changed since he last calculated his odds), then his prediction is clearly overvaluing the chance of a Barcelona victory by 4%. If Messi's injury is a known unknown (let's say that the bettor has heard from word of mouth that an unidentified player was injured in the warm up), then the bettor can adjust his model so as to incorporate this new information. He may not know how big of an impact this will have on the game – after all, to his mind it might have been an insignificant substitute who was injured in the warm up. At least now he can modify his forecast to give it more room for error, or decide not to place a bet on the match at all.

Known unknowns embody risk, whilst unknown unknowns epitomise uncertainty. When faced with something that we know that we don't know, we can still attempt to quantify the risk to reward ratio that we are faced with. The bettor can decide whether he wants to opt out of his bet on Barcelona now that he knows that one of their players has been injured. On the other hand, unknown unknowns are extremely dangerous. The bettor is oblivious to the fact that new information has arisen, and has no way of changing his prediction accordingly.

Whilst overconfidence is a clear weakness, uncertainty isn't as black and white. As long as we recognise when we do not know the full story, and attempt to adopt a fox-like approach to incoming information, we can calibrate our predictions to give us the best chance of success.

How to Gamble Like a Professional

Let us now turn our attention to the specific methods we can use to beat the bookies. It is important to understand that gambling is essentially an investment on the future outcome of an event. This is why investment bankers so often become prosperous professional gamblers. When an investor looks to buy, they are searching for stocks which will rise in value. When a property developer hunts for a piece of housing to purchase, they look at which areas they think will be worth more in the future. When a manager tries to sign a player, he should be trying to identify a talent who is underrated by the rest of the footballing world. In every single one of these fields, the key is to exploit the *undervalued* prospects in the market. Buy commodities when they are undervalued, sell them when they are overvalued. Following this basic principle will increase your capital.

In every walk of life, we attempt to find value for money. If Supermarket A sells milk for £2.30 and Supermarket B sells the exact same product for £1.50, it's obvious which supermarket we will buy our milk from. Businesses constantly offer deals on their products in order to entice us to their stores. This is because they know that we will attempt to find value for money. Finding and developing undervalued commodities is the central theme of *Moneyball* – Michael Lewis' excellent book detailing the philosophy deployed by Oakland A's general manager Billy Beane. Beane sought to find baseball players that had been disregarded by other clubs, but who could actually bring a lot more value to his team than their price tag suggested. He did this by using statistical models, much in the same way that Matthew Benham is doing in football.

The hunting of undervalued products translates itself perfectly into sports betting. The key to betting on football fixtures isn't to place bets on who you think will win, but to place bets when you think that the bookmakers are underestimating the chance of a particular outcome occurring. In other words, if you think that a team has a greater chance of winning than the bookmakers are suggesting, put money on it!

Professional gamblers make their money by using the following system. The bettor will develop a model which works out the chances of Team A winning against Team B. The bettor will then translate into percentages the bookmakers' odds of Team A winning, a draw occurring, and Team B winning. Next, he will compare his own calculations to the bookmakers' calculations. If the bettor's model predicts that a team has a significantly greater chance of victory than the bookies are suggesting, he will place a bet on that team to win.

Let's add some context to this procedure. Suppose that our gambler is deciding whether to place a bet on the Bayern Munich match that we used as an example at the beginning of the chapter. The odds for the match were as follows:

Home win (Bayern): **11/10**

Draw: **5/2**

Away win (Dortmund): **11/4**

The bettor will want to visualise more clearly the probabilities that the bookmakers have assigned to each event occurring. He would do this by using the simple formula for translating odds into percentages – also described at the start of this chapter. He would calculate that the book-maker's odds suggest there is a 47.6% chance of a Bayern victory, a 28.6% chance of a draw occurring, and a 26.7% probability that Dortmund will emerge victorious.

The bettor would then consult his own model. A "model", in this instance, can be defined as a complex mathematical algorithm that one has developed, or simply as a rough mental estimation of which team will win. The ordinary bettor will not have devised an intricate formula which will tell him the exact probability of Bayern winning, but he will still have a good idea of their chances. Suppose he believes that Bayern have got a 55% chance of victory. In this instance, he should place a bet on a home win, as he estimates that Bayern have 7.4% more of a chance of winning than the bookies have declared. A professional gambler's model may be more intricate, spouting out a more precise prediction, but the basic principle remains the same.

If you think that the bookmakers have underestimated the chance of a particular result occurring, you should place a bet on it. This may seem counterintuitive. Suppose, for instance, that your model predicts a 35% probability of Dortmund winning. This suggests there is little over a third of a chance that the visitors will emerge victorious. You have calculated that the bookmakers believe there is only a 26.7% chance of an away win. Intuition tells you that you should not place a bet on this. For one thing, your model is telling you that Bayern Munich are much more likely to win. Given that your model is predicting a Dortmund defeat, surely it would be idiotic to place money on this outcome? *Your own model tells you there is a 65% chance that a bet on Dortmund will lose.* Surely you should place your money on the team that gives you the best chance of winning your bet?

In this instance, your intuition would be wrong. Gambling is all about finding the undervalued prospects, and exploiting them as often as possible. Whilst it is true that your bet only has a 35% chance of winning, given that your model is accurate, it is also true that *over the long run you will make money*. Betting on the outcome of sporting fixtures is no different to investing in other markets in the sense that you must always think long-term. You simply aren't going to win every bet you place, but it is important to find good value for your money when you do place a wager. Otherwise the bookmakers' overround will eat away at your funds.

A good way of explaining this concept is through using more manageable odds. Say that the bookies are offering 9/1 on Cristiano Ronaldo to score first in a match of football. These odds translate to 10%, meaning that the bookmakers have assigned Ronaldo a one in ten chance of opening the scoring. You then consult your own model, which predicts that there is a 20% chance of Ronaldo opening the scoring. This is good news. The bookmakers appear to have drastically undervalued the chance of Ronaldo scoring first. Nevertheless, your intuition tells you that you should not place a bet on this event occurring. After all, there is only a 20% chance that your bet will win. Four out of five times you will lose your money. The logical thing to do seems to not place the bet.

However, consider what happens if you place a £5 bet on this outcome one hundred times. If your model is correct – meaning that Ronaldo does indeed open the scoring 20% of the time, then 80% of the time your bet will lose. Ronaldo will not score the first goal of the match, meaning that you have lost your fiver. This accumulates to a combined loss of £400 (eighty £5 bets have been placed and lost). The other 20% of the time, however, Ronaldo does score first and your bet is won. These twenty bets each return £45 – the amount that the odds of 9/1 dictate you should win[18]. Twenty bets which each return £45 means that you have made a total of £900 in winnings. If you subtract your losses of £400 from your winnings of £900, you are left with a handsome £500.

In this scenario, by realising the potential of the undervalued outcome, you have managed to double your original stake. In reality, bookies rarely undervalue the odds of something happening so drastically. On the infrequent occasions that you spot a set of odds that seem to underestimate the probability of an event occurring, you should place a bet on it. Any undervalued set of odds will leave you with a positive expected value on the bet.

The trouble, as we discovered earlier on, is that the bookies always add an overround to ensure their backs are covered. Our advantage as bettors is that we can *choose* which bets to place. If we had to place a bet on every single match that the bookmakers offered odds for, we would almost certainly lose money. We have the advantage of only placing money on bets that we really think we can make money from. We can pick and choose which bets look fruitful to us, and look to capitalise on any mistakes that the bookmakers might make. Professional gamblers will generally have some sort of mathematical model which they will use to calculate their own odds. The ordinary bettor, on the other hand, will just use his instinct to identify the undervalued outcomes.

Natural human intuition often gets in the way when it comes to gambling. The average punter will bet on a team who he thinks has a good chance of winning. He will pay little attention to the bookmakers' own

---

18 Note that we do not include the £5 stake in this figure. Although £50 will be returned to you from each bet that you win, you haven't actually won that £5. You already had this money beforehand, and could have chosen not to bet with it in the first place.

predictions (reflected in the odds that they offer). This gambler is no better than those who place money on the result of a coin toss when the odds are set at 10/11. The only way to consistently make money betting on football is to calculate the bookmakers' odds into percentages, determine your own probabilities, and use this information to highlight the undervalued outcomes.

Don't Cash Out or Place Accumulators

There are two areas of sports betting which are widely misunderstood; the cashing out of bets and the placing of accumulators. Ordinary bettors think that these two "services" are there to assist gamblers in their pursuit of money. In fact, bookmakers use these two capacities to drain even more capital from the ignorant masses.

The first misconception is that cashing out your bet is a good offer. Most bookies will offer gamblers the chance to buy-out their bets before the event has been finalised. At the beginning of the chapter, we saw Leicester fan John Pryke take a £20 punt on his side to win the 2015/16 Premier League, with his winnings set to be £100k. The Foxes ended up winning the title, but Pryke had decided to cash out his bet a few weeks before the end of the season for just £29k.

Bookmakers advertise cashing out as a helpful service. In television adverts, they often show a punter buying out his bet, only for the team that he originally backed to flop. The bettor would celebrate his triumph, thus indicating how great it is that these particular bookmakers offer the chance to cash out. There is no dispute that the ability to take some money and run *can* be of use. Had the Leicester not ended up winning the Premier League after Pryke cashed out, he would have bagged himself £29k. However, the issue comes in the nonlinearity between the amount that you *should* be able to cash out, and the amount that the bookmakers *actually* offer you. Recall how the bookies overvalue the chance of each result occurring, thus ensuring that your winnings (assuming you do win) are slightly less than you deserve. The same methodology applies for cashing out. The £29k that John Pryke pocketed was far less than the bet was actually worth.

We can work out the expected value of Pryke's bet at the exact moment he cashed out, giving us an indication as to whether or not it was a good idea to buy out the wager. The expected value will tell us how much the bet was actually worth. In this scenario, there were only two possible outcomes; either Leicester win the league or they don't. In order to calculate the monetary amount that Pryke could have expected to make when he cashed out his bet, we must first determine the probability that Leicester would go on to win the title. Most of the bookmakers and leading analysts reached a consensus that, at the point that Pryke cashed out at, Leicester had roughly a 35% chance of winning the league. Thus, there was a 35% chance that Pryke would win £100k, and a 65% chance that he would win nothing. In order to determine the expected value of the bet, we must carry out the following equation:

(Chance of Success x Winnings) + (Chance of Failure x Failure Winnings)
(0.35 x £100,000) + (0.65 x £0)
= £35,000

Thus, the amount of money that John could expect to make was £35,000. Note that this amount of money was *not actually possible to win*, but rather was the *value of the bet*. If the bookmakers were to offer a fair amount of money to buy the bet off John, it would have been £35k. Bookmakers, however, have no interest in offering fair deals. They exist in order to make money. The £29k that Pryke cashed out for was a bad deal, as his bet was worth around £6k more than that. Pryke essentially sold a £35k commodity for £29k. You wouldn't sell a car worth £35k for £29k, thus you shouldn't sell a bet worth £35k for £29k.

Obviously, when dealing with such relatively large sums of money, it may not be as straightforward as working out what the best value is. Different amounts of money carry different weights in our mind. We are not necessarily twice as happy if we are given £100k to if we are given £50k. Perhaps Pryke decided that £100k wouldn't give him over three times the amount of joy as £29k would, and that it was not worth the risk. However, there will be very few situations where we find ourselves having placed a one-off bet of life-altering proportions. If you are looking to make money from placing bets with incredibly long odds, as John Pryke did, you are almost certainly destined for disappointment. Professional gamblers will place lots of bets, each one containing enough of an edge to consistently beat the bookies and make money. For these bettors, cashing out is always a bad deal, because the bookmakers will offer you less money than the bet is worth.

The only instance in which it makes sense to cash out your bet is if you calculate that the bookies have made a mistake. For example, if the bookies had given Leicester a 50% chance of winning the Premier League, and as a result offered Pryke £45k to cash out his bet, it would have made sense for Pryke to take the money if he thought that Leicester only had, say, a 35% chance of claiming the title. Under these circumstances, the bookmakers value the bet at £50k (although they only offer him £45k), and Pryke values the bet at £35k. He should cash out, as he is being offered more money than he thinks it's worth. It is rare, however, that a bookmaker will overvalue the chance of something happening. As a general rule, *professional gamblers will never cash out on bets*, as they would lose money over the long run if they did so.

The second cunning device which bookmakers offer is accumulator betting. In much the same way as cashing out is a bad idea, so too is the placing of accumulator bets. Placing an accumulator, or "acca", is essentially betting that a series of results will all occur. Suppose, one Saturday afternoon, you think that West Ham, Crystal Palace and Millwall all have a strong chance of winning their respective matches. You check the with the bookmakers, and are delighted to discover that they are offering 9/1 for these three teams to win. These seem like great odds (a £5 bet returns a full £45 in winnings), so you place money on the accumulator. Let's assess why betting in this manner is foolish, and how the bookmakers exploit this ignorance for money.

As we have seen, it is crucial to calculate the probabilities surrounding any bet we place. Say that our punter thinks that West Ham, Crystal Palace and Millwall each have a 40% chance of winning their games. This would make them all favourites. How then do we work out the probability that all three of these teams will win? It's easy, we simply multiply the probabilities in decimal terms:

0.4 x 0.4 x 0.4 = 0.064

Thus, the probability that all three sides will win, and the bet succeeds, is 6.4%. When you translate the bookmakers' odds of 9/1 into percentage terms, you are left with 10%. In other words, the bookies are giving all three teams winning a 10% chance of happening, whilst the bettor is giving it a 6.4% chance. The odds that the bookmakers have set are overvalued, meaning there is a negative expected value to the bet. The punter is destined to lose money over the long run.

What has gone wrong? What has made such a seemingly lucrative bet so unappealing all of a sudden? Of course, most bettors don't ask these questions. They will continuously place accumulators, virtually handing the bookmakers their money. If the punter was to stop and question the mechanics in process, he would realise that the problem stems from our incapacity to multiply percentages effectively. We do not realise that when you multiply together the chances of three pretty likely things occurring, the accumulation of odds makes the desired outcome incredibly unlikely. In fact, if our punter was to add another team with a 40% chance of winning to the accumulator (say, Charlton, carrying on our London club theme), the odds of all four teams winning would be 2.6%. This bet would succeed once in every forty or so attempts. Nevertheless, the bookies would only pay out odds of roughly 20/1, assigning roughly a 5% chance to the possibility of all four teams winning. The key to gambling is finding

the outcomes that you think are more likely than the bookmakers are predicting, something that you will hardly ever accomplish with accumulated
bets.

A non-footballing example of our inability to accurately multiply
probabilities can be found in the shuffling of a deck of cards. Ask yourself: have two decks ever been shuffled in the exact same order before?
You might be inclined to say yes. After all, think of how many billions of
times the human race has shuffled decks of cards. Essentially, the question we need to answer is *'how many different ways can a pile of cards
be arranged?'*. To answer this, we must work out 'fifty-two factorial'. As
there are fifty-two cards in a deck, the equation we must calculate is *52 x
51 x 50 x 49, etc.* (there are fifty-two ways to order the first card, fifty-one
ways to order the second card, fifty ways to order the third card, etc.). The
answer to this equation is:

*80,000,000,000,000,000,000,000,000,000,000,000,000,00
0,000,000,000,000,000,000,000,000*

This is the total number of possible ways a deck of cards can be ordered.
There are sixty-seven zeros in this figure. Our inability to multiply probabilities means that we naturally underestimate this sum. This number is
considerably larger than the number of times the human race has shuffled
decks of cards. It is mind-boggling to think that, any time you pick up a
well-shuffled deck, you are almost certainly holding an arrangement of
cards that has never before existed and might never exist again.

Returning to accumulator betting, our emotional fallibility provides
another stumbling block. Everyone loves it when a long-shot bet comes
off, in the same way that everyone loves an underdog success story. The
joy that we feel when we win a bet that originally only had a 2.6% chance
of succeeding is massive. Bettors often pursue this magical feeling, and
in doing so lose a lot of money to the bookies' skewed odds. In accumulators, the luck which is inundated in the eventual outcome all adds
up, making them more like lotteries than informed bets. You are simply

buying a ticket, waiting for numbers to be drawn at random, and hoping that yours come up.

As a general rule, bettors should avoid cashing out or placing accumulators. These are just more ways in which bookies can incur their overround, making it an unfair contest. Bookmakers overvalue the likelihood of outcomes in every single market that they offer. Whether it be first goal scorer, final scoreline, minute of first goal, number of corners, or whatever other market, the bookmakers will have drastically overrated the chances of the event occurring. Match outcomes and Asian Handicaps (which we will study imminently) are the two markets which are easiest to predict. Other markets are filled with too much noise to draw accurate assessments from the data. Bookies laugh at those who bet on the number of corners, just as they laugh at those who bet on the result of a coin toss. The random nature of such markets mean that bettors will get swallowed up by the bookies' overround.

The methods of the bookmakers are analogous to those of a fairground attraction in which customers are invited to shoot round basketballs into an oval-shaped hoop. From the perspective of the shooter, the game is fair and there is the potential to make money (or win a big purple toy giraffe). However, the skewed nature of the hoop means that the shot is almost impossible to make. The customer is fooled into overrating his chance of making the shot, just as the bookies offer gamblers a negative expected value on their bets, accumulators or cash outs. Both the customer and the gambler are partaking in activities which are bad value for money.

THE BATTLE OF THE BETTORS

In order to find the value in the market, and realise when the bookies are undervaluing the probability of an outcome occurring, one requires a reliable model. Of course, the human brain is one of the most complex pieces of equipment that we have at our disposal. It is because of this advanced modelling machine that the average bettor can still make money if he collects and processes enough information mentally. However, professional gamblers will usually supplement their natural judgement with some form of statistical analysis. They aim to collect as much information as possible, thus giving themselves the best chance of making correct predictions.

Matthew Benham has utilised his experience as a city trader to break ground in the gambling community. He recognises the need to find value in the market, but understanding this is only half of the battle won. Those who want to consistently make *a lot*[19] of money will need to develop a system, formula or philosophy that can dependably help you predict the outcome of football matches. Crucially, this system will probably have to be something that no one else has yet discovered. When so many Britons are attempting to make money through gambling, with sports betting being such a saturated market, it is nigh on impossible to think of an original approach. Benham has been able to develop such an approach. The problem then becomes keeping your brilliant system a secret.

Brentford fans can often be heard chanting that *'there's only one Matthew Benham'*, in adoration of their benevolent owner whose pioneering approach has taken the club to incredible new heights. Whilst there is indeed only one Matthew Benham, there are a couple of others like him. The vocation of professional gambling has become more common in recent years. As the betting industry has boomed, so too has the number of people who make a living through beating the bookmakers.

Benham's primary source of income stems from the company which he founded. Smartodds supplies statistical analysis to wealthy clients, who pay for data to inform their gambling. Their offices are based in Kentish Town, and in many ways resemble a Wall Street trading floor. Dozens of computers line the main floor of the office. Televisions cover the walls, each showing different football matches, news channels or other programmes which may be of interest to the men inhabiting the

---

19 The phrase "a lot" is clearly subjective. In this instance, we are talking about the amount of money that Benham has made – enough to buy and run two football clubs. Certainly, the amount that Benham has amassed is far in excess of £100m.

area. Each desk is occupied by an analyst, client or trader. On a Saturday afternoon the atmosphere amongst the group can approach hysteria, as millions of pounds are placed on that weekend's round of football matches. The main difference between a Wall Street investment banker and a Smartodds bettor is that, where the former wears a suit worth a four figure sum, the latter wears khaki shorts and a hoody.

The unique data that Smartodds collects allows them to maintain an edge over the market. Using Benham's system, they are able to consistently succeed in identifying the *true* ability of football teams. This allows the results of matches to be accurately forecast. The clients are essentially buying Benham's data in order to inform their gambling, just like media outlets buy data from Opta to inform their viewers.

Benham is arguably the most successful professional sports bettor in England. Nonetheless, he is not without his rivals. The greatest of Benham's competitors, Peter Bloom, is a man with whom he draws an uncanny number of parallels. Like Benham, Bloom is a former city trader. Like Benham, Bloom owns a football club that he has supported his entire life. Like Benham, Bloom owns a gambling consultancy based in North London. Like Benham, Bloom has used his knowledge of investment and understanding of luck to consistently beat the market.

Before taking over Brighton and Hove Albion FC in 2009, Bloom operated as a professional poker player. He claims that he fell in love with gambling at the same time as he fell in love with football, at the age of about eight. His first major win came in in 2004 when, at the age of thirty-four, Bloom won the Australasian Poker Championship in Melbourne, collecting the first prize of around £180,000. By 2008, his live tournament winnings exceeded £1,200,000. His unwavering poker face led him to be nicknamed The Lizard.

He drew inspiration from this nickname when founding his betting consultancy, Starlizard, in 2006. Besides running this company and forging a successful poker career, Bloom has also been the chairman of Brighton since securing 75% shareholding in 2009. He has invested over £250m of his own personal fortune in the club, steering the Seagulls from League

One to the Premier League in a matter of seasons. His success at Brighton could be likened to Benham's at Brentford, although the former has had a budget over twice the size of the latter. Bloom's net worth is estimated by some to run into the billions. Whilst Brighton have been able to spend their way to Premier League football, Brentford are having to forge the same path through innovation.

Benham and Bloom first crossed paths at Premier Bet, an online bookmaker that Bloom founded. Benham worked under Bloom, but the pair had an acrimonious falling out. After leaving Premier Bet, Benham founded Smartodds in 2004. Two years later Bloom founded his own gambling consultancy, Starlizard. Based in Camden, Starlizard offers a similar service to Smartodds. Both companies found their success on the fact that they can supply better statistical models than the leading bookmakers. Over the years, Bloom has developed and cultivated statistical models that, when fed with the correct information, will calculate a reliable probability of the outcome of a football match. These models are the pride and joy of the company, with only a handful of people knowing the exact formula that Starlizard use.

In order to ensure they maintain their competitive edge, the employees of both Smartodds and Starlizard are made to sign strict non-disclosure agreements. This has allowed the companies to remain a secret outside the world of professional gambling, in spite of the wild success and mammoth amounts of money which both have attained. There are few firms in any line of work that have reaped such great rewards, but that have gone as virtually undetected by the media or general public.

As well as selling his data to clients, in the same way that Benham's Smartodds does, Bloom also uses Starlizard as a mechanism through which he can run what is the UK's largest gambling syndicate. The consortium is made up of high-rolling clients who place hundreds of millions of pounds' worth of bets each year. Employees at Starlizard are invited to share in a stake of Bloom's winnings by entering the syndicate. They simply top up the pot out of their own pocket, and then reap rewards if the matches go as predicted. Thanks to Bloom's models, the syndicate often makes a handsome return. Members of the group can each be due pay-outs of up to £500k every six months.

Both Benham and Bloom's betting consultancies treat football betting like a hedge fund treats stocks. Indeed, it appears that North London has become the Wall Street of professional gambling.

ASIAN HANDICAP EXPLAINED IN THREE PAGES

To make their millions, both Benham and Bloom have used a style of betting that you might not be familiar with. The pair often don't bet on which team is going to win, who is going to score first, or how many corners there will be in a match (which, incidentally, is a completely ridiculous thing to place money on). Professional gamblers tend to use a system called the Asian handicap. The Asian handicap is useful for bettors who can accurately work out not only the chances of a team winning, but the probability of a team winning by a certain number of goals. This betting market is available with most of the notable bookmakers.

As the name suggests, the Asian handicap originated in Asia – or Indonesia to be more precise. The system works by evening the playing field before the match by giving the underdogs a hypothetical goal advantage. This also eliminates the possibility of a draw occurring – either the team wins by the required number of goals or it doesn't. The handicap is designed so that the chance each team will score under the handicap is roughly equal to the chance that they will score over it. This creates a fifty-fifty probability of either outcome occurring, thus completely levelling the playing field.

Let's once again use our Bayern Munich versus Borussia Dortmund match as an example. Bayern are comfortable favourites, so the bookmakers may assign them a 2+ handicap. This means that they must win by at least two goals for a bet on them to return money. A bettor would lose his stake if he put money on them and they only defeated Dortmund by one goal, or if they failed to win at all. Odds are given in decimal format, rather than the more familiar fraction format which bookmakers usually offer. For example, a two goal handicap in favour of Dortmund could be set at 2.0.

Where it gets complicated is when the handicaps become more precise. Often, the handicap for a team would be set more specifically than simply 2+ goals. Bayern could be dealt a handicap of 1.7+, which would more accurately reflect things like their form and injury problems. Obviously you can't win a game of football by 1.7 goals. As a result, pay-outs on these handicaps become more complex. You would win a different amount of money if you won a bet with a 1.3 handicap than if you won one with a 1.9 handicap. The essential thing to grasp is that the Asian handicap system bases itself on how many goals are scored by each team. This works in favour of gamblers like Benham and Bloom, whose algorithms enable them to work out the probabilities of teams winning by different margins.

SMARTODDS VERSUS STARLIZARD

Matthew Benham and Peter Bloom's companies operate in a very similar manner. As we have seen, both companies use mathematical modelling to work out the likely outcomes of any given football match. Smartodds and Starlizard analyse games far beyond the realms of the English leagues. Both companies collect data on virtually every professional football team in Europe, and many from other continents. When I worked at Benham's company, Smartodds, I would often collect data on matches in the Azerbaijan Premier division.

More value can be found in these indistinct leagues than in the distinguished ones. The bookmakers will be more concerned with working out the chances of a Manchester United victory over Arsenal than they will be with estimating the chances of, say, Havelse beating Meppen in the fourth tier of German football. A bettor who focuses his attention on the obscure leagues can find a greater edge, granted he can collect enough information on these teams.

However, Starlizard and Smartodds don't tend to place more than a couple of thousand pounds on bets in these obscure leagues. This may seem like a large sum of money, but to the gambling consultancies that Bloom and Benham run this is merely a drop in the ocean. Placing any more than this on such anonymous divisions would spook the market. The placement of such a large bet may move the odds drastically, thus eliminating any edge that could have been gained. When a large bet comes in on a small team, bookmakers tend to assume that one of the leading betting consultancies has placed the wager. The bookies will realise they have probably missed something, and will move the odds to eliminate the edge that the bettor has found.

Industry experts estimate that roughly twelve large gambling syndicates exist worldwide. An exact figure is almost impossible to approximate due to the fact that each one of them can only survive if they remain surreptitious. If it became apparent that one of these syndicates were placing a bet on a specific team, the whole market would move to reflect the group's prediction. The syndicates have better models than even the bookies, allowing them to make potentially huge amounts of money. Of course, some syndicates are even more covert than Bloom's. These are the groups which are involved in the fixing of matches.

On that note, it would be easy to assume that Smartodds and Starlizard must be partaking in some sort of legal wrongdoing. The companies make huge amounts of money, but still seem to go under the radar. What's more, they operate in a highly secretive manner. Despite the fact that it would be easy to assume the worst, both of these companies actually *depend* on a fair game. It is only through just and unbiased matches that the statistics which both companies utilise can come good. Any fixed matches would render their excellent models redundant.

Both Starlizard and Smartodds are renowned for the corporate nature in which they are run. Whilst many bookmakers are considered laddish and unprofessional, these betting consultancies more closely resemble the atmosphere of an investment bank. At Starlizard, Bloom's betting consultancy, there are four main departments which each perform different roles. These four sectors at Starlizard are closely resembled at Smartodds.

The first subdivision collects the necessary data by watching the relevant football fixtures. They are also responsible for conducting general research on every detail that could relate to the outcome of a match. They make it their prerogative to speak to insiders, journalists and league experts. This group of analysts collect as much useful information as possible; be it on morale, form, training or anything which could impact the performance of a team. Principally, though, this department is responsible for collecting specific match data.

They pass this data onto the second team, who feed it into the complex algorithms that Bloom has developed. These mathematical models compute the information and accurately predict match outcomes. Additionally, the algorithms are able to calculate a probability of every possible scoreline occurring, thus also calculating a handicap to assign the match – Bayern Munich at +1.53, for example. This branch of the operation is filled with the computer geniuses that you would more commonly find working for investment banks. Starlizard's quants are based in a separate office in Exeter. They spend their time curating and developing the algorithms which the data is fed into. They must continuously develop the formulae, deciding which variables are more important than others. This constant aspiration to improve the model is incredibly fox-like. The algorithms are the pride and joy of the company, meaning the work that this second department does is kept strictly confidential.

The third subdivision is responsible for calculating the bookmakers' odds, and comparing them to the odds that the models have gauged. They look for outcomes which the bookmakers have undervalued, using the methodology described earlier in this chapter. This department selects which bets to place, and decide how much money to place on each wager. They do this on behalf of Bloom and his clients. If a bookmaker makes a mistake, you can rest assured that someone in this team will find it and exploit it. This subdivision is essentially searching for the value in the market.

The fourth department are responsible for actually *placing* the bets that the third team tell them to. This bet placement team uses Asian bookmakers to place their wagers, due to the fact that the markets there are far more liquid than they are in Europe. Any large bet that is placed with one of the European bookmakers would almost certainly be detected, allowing the bookies to adjust their odds. In Asia, million pound bets can be placed and go unnoticed by the bookies. Starlizard's odds are tailored to the markets in places such as Thailand, Indonesia and China. Using the Asian markets hides the bettors' predictions from the bookmakers, but it can be difficult to access these markets unless you have the right connections. Starlizard's clients are not just paying for the mathematical modelling provided by the company; they are also paying for the black book of contacts which Starlizard has built up in the Asian markets.

This process, almost identically deployed at Smartodds as well as Starlizard, teaches us a lot about how to approach sports betting. Just like the first department, we must first collect some form of information. Just like the second department, we must analyse this information in order to form a judgement. Just like the third department, we must assess the bookmakers' odds in search of any value that might exist in the market. Just like the fourth department, we must actually place the bet. As we have already seen, the third step of this process is the one that ordinary punters will tend to overlook. We should only place a bet if we believe that the bookies have undervalued the probability of an event occurring.

The exact profits for both Smartodds and Starlizard are unknown. Their incredibly accurate statistical modelling allows them an edge of about 3%. This means that if they were to place £100,000 on various bets, they would make back around £103,000 – a profit of just £3k. Sometimes they will make back more, sometimes less. This may seem like a small margin. In many ways it is, especially when compared to the 5-10% margin that the bookmakers make on most bets. However, Smartodds and

Starlizard place hundreds of millions of pounds' worth of bets each year. This allows them to make a handsome return.

More is known about the finances of Starlizard than Smartodds. Former employees have hinted at the amount of money that Bloom's company makes. The Starlizard syndicate are rumoured to turnover between £20m and £100m each year. Bloom's net worth certainly runs into the hundreds of millions, with some suggesting it runs into the billions. There is no doubt that both Benham and Bloom are two of the most successful bettors in the history of sport.

There is a subtle difference in the philosophies of the two men, one which will become clear after we study Benham's unique system of operation. Whilst Bloom gains an edge through the complex algorithms which he has curated, Benham's approach cuts right to the core of the beautiful game. The Brentford owner's system is based around the *type of statistics* he collects. The methods that Smartodds utilise can by adopted by any football fan. Whilst Bloom has developed an intricate system of analysing data, Benham has developed a simple, yet innovative, form of data collection. Bloom's approach is a science, whereas Benham's is an art. The Brentford owner has established a whole different approach, a new and unique footballing philosophy.

For years, football has been searching for its answer to baseball's Billy Beane, the man who utilised data to revolutionise the American sport. It has searched for the equivalent of the Oakland Athletics, the team who were able to upset all the odds by identifying undervalued players. It has searched for the equivalent to baseball's all important on-base percentage, the piece of data which was drastically undervalued by the sport. It has searched for the eureka moment that transforms the entire way the sport is thought about. For years, football has searched for its own version of baseball's *Moneyball*. Finally, football has found its answers.

THE SECRET FORMULA

In September 2015, those inside the Etihad Stadium witnessed title hopefuls Manchester City lose by two goals to one against West Ham. The hosts from Manchester had seventy-two per cent of the possession, twenty-seven efforts at goal and eight shots on target. West Ham, in comparison, had just twenty-eight per cent possession, six shots at goal and just three on target, two of which hit the back of the net. These stats were the main talking point after the match.

How much does this data really tell us about the game which took place? It gives us the impression that, despite losing, Manchester City dominated the match. They had almost all of the ball, controlled the flow of the game and had four times as many shots as their opposition. Despite this, the hosts conspired to score fewer goals than West Ham. Simple logic would tell you that City should have won.

The stats from this game show that goals are a fundamentally poor indicator of how good a team is. This match, though slightly on the extreme side, is certainly no exception to the rule. In football, the better team often loses. Luck plays a massive role, which makes upsets a regular occurrence. Goals are a rare commodity that are not always fairly distributed to the teams that deserve them.

There is a huge amount of noise involved in the game, not only in a singular match but also over the course of an entire season. As we saw in the first chapter, a last minute penalty kick can decide whether a team is promoted or not. Each goal is of vital importance, whilst simultaneously encapsulating an incredible amount of randomness. One controversial referee decision can cost a team the game. One goalkeeping error can be disastrous for his team's chances of victory. One key player ruled out through injury could end a club's hope of success. Whichever way you look at it, luck plays a colossal part in the proceedings of football matches. Just ask any Manchester City player who played against West Ham.

THE DATA ERROR

As we have already discovered, there are two main parts to prediction-making. First, one must collect data relevant to the event which they are attempting to forecast. Second, the data must be analysed and scrutinised so that a judgement can be reached. These two basic steps are undertaken every time we are asked to make a forecast. If you were asked to predict which route would be the quickest to work tomorrow morning, you would first draw to the front of your mind all of the data which you have collected on your previous trips. You would then assess the information internally before drawing a conclusion. If you were unable to perform either of these steps, your prediction would undoubtedly be flawed.

Those hunting for the best way of predicting the outcome of football matches are looking for new and ingenious ways of analysing data. They are creating complex algorithms which they feed with all types of data; be it possession, shots, shots on target, passing percentages and the like. This seems like the most natural way to improve one's predictions. After all, frequently refining and improving your model until it is as accurate as possible can only be a good thing.

This is where most people have missed the trick. Perhaps, instead of coming up with new ways of analysing data, the best way to become predictive masters is to *improve the quality of information that we are collecting in the first place*. Data such as possession, passing accuracy, territory and the like gives us little, if any, indication of who the best teams are. Football teams often win matches with less possession, a lower passing accuracy, and very little territory[20]. Matthew Benham's system depends as much on the quality of the data that is collected as the methods that go into analysing it.

In order to begin to understand Benham's methods for stripping luck from football, let us start with the basics. The aim of the sport is to score as many goals as possible, whilst at the same time attempting to concede as few as possible. This is the fundamental objective of any football team. You can only score a goal if you create a scoring opportunity. Equally, you can only concede a goal if the opposition create a chance to score. Therefore, football is a sport which revolves around chance creation. This is fairly obvious. After all, television highlights focus on scoring opportunities, whilst match reports describe the various openings which each team produced. During a game, each player tries to create scoring opportunities for their team, at the same time remaining cautious of how many chances they are conceding to the opposition. Thus, we can use data on how many chances a team creates to identify which teams are the best. The data from the Manchester City match against West Ham, for instance, shows that the hosts had twenty-seven shots on target. This tells us that Manchester City had a large quantity of scoring opportunities.

These stats are inadequate, however, at telling us the *quality* of these scoring opportunities. Were all twenty-seven of these attempts long range efforts which didn't trouble the West Ham goalkeeper? If so, it would be safe to conclude that City aren't actually as good as the data suggests. On the other hand, if ten of these shots were from inside the six-yard box, whilst another ten were missed penalties, one could conclude that City were the far better side and were extremely unlucky not to win the game. Clearly, the conventional stats of 'Shots on Target' and 'Shots off Target' are a poor measure of each team's ability. What we must do is dive deeper into the game and collect much more specific data.

This is where the innovation begins.

---

20 Leicester won the 2015/16 Premier League title with some of the worst possession and territory stats the division had ever seen. Out of the twenty teams in the top tier that season, the Foxes ranked 19th for pass accuracy and 18th for possession.

TSR – AN IMPERFECT JUDGE OF PERFORMANCE

Football analysts[21], in their search to find the best way of predicting the outcome football matches, have long since realised the correlation between the number of chances that a team creates and the success of that team. This will seem like an obvious connection to any ordinary football fan. The more you shoot, the more you score, right? Well, not necessarily.

A key metric that generally follows this principle is the Total Shots Rate (TSR) of a team. TSR follows a simple formula, but allows analysts a good indicator of a team's future performance. The formula for TSR is as follows:

Total Shots Rate = Shots For / (Shots For + Shots Against)

The TSR of a team is the number of shots which they take in a match, divided by the total number of shots that took place in the game. Thus, a team who takes any number of shots without reply from the opposition can be assigned a TSR of 1.0. A team who has six shots, but concedes only four attempts, will carry a TSR of 0.6 (six divided by ten). If the number of shots of both teams are equal, then they will both hold a TSR of 0.5. Here is the TSR of both sides if we plug the data from the example match we used at the beginning of this chapter into the appropriate formula:

If Manchester City has 27 shots and West Ham had 6 shots,
Man City TSR = 27 / (27 + 6) = 27/33 = 0.82
West Ham TSR = 6 / (27 + 6) = 6 / 33 = 0.18

Manchester City's TSR is a massive 0.82, whilst West Ham's is just 0.18. The TSR of both sides is always 1.0 when added together, and the average of the two TSRs is always 0.5. This is because, every time a shot is taken by one team, the other team concedes an attempt. There is perfect parity between the two figures.

---

21 An analyst, in this sense, doesn't exclusively refer to those professional analysts who are paid to crunch numbers. Anyone who takes an interest in football statistics could be considered an analyst.

TSR has been proven as a strong indicator for the success of a team. James Grayson, the analyst who first came up with the formula for TSR, has emphasised the correlation between the metric and a team's position in the league. He took a sample of Premier League teams from 2000-2012 and compared their TSR to the amount of points they collected over the course of a season. The correlation that he found was incredibly strong. In fact, no side that has been relegated from the Premier League has ever scored above 0.52. This means that a team who are taking more shots than the opposition on average per match can be almost completely confident that they won't get relegated. Conversely, only one team in the sample achieved a top four spot without scoring above 0.5 in TSR. This team was Everton in 2004/05, who managed to obtain fourth spot with an average TSR of just under 0.45. Generally speaking, the higher a team's TSR, the more points they scored in a season.

Total Shots Rate is a good indicator of success, but it does have large drawbacks. The problem with the formula is that it treats all shots equally. In football, some chances are going to be a lot easier to score than others. An effort from two yards out has a higher probability of hitting the back of the net than a shot from forty yards out. TSR doesn't take into account the quality of shots, only the quantity.

The metric would work perfectly if all teams created an equal amount of good chances as poor chances. However, it is unrealistic to assume that the distribution of low quality shots to high quality shots is equal for all teams. Arsenal, for example, have gained a reputation over recent years for passing the ball to death. The Gunners are often accused of "overplaying", and are encouraged by their fans to take more shots. Whilst their lack of attempts at goal may not see them rank too favourably on the TSR scale, the shots that they *do* take tend to be of very high quality. They work themselves into good positions in order to make it easier to score when they do shoot. Other teams take the opposite approach and choose to shoot on sight. They take lots of long range shots in the hope that a barrage on the opposition goalkeeper will end in a goal or two.

Whilst these teams will rank highly in TSR, they will not necessarily be scoring more goals. Each one of their shots will only have a small probability of scoring.

The Expected Goals Metric

In the coming years, the traditional stats that are used to assess football, the stats regularly promoted by the media, will come to be replaced by a new metric. This form of data is known as "Expected Goals". The main aim of this book was to bring this metric into the mainstream, as it has the potential to be astronomically influential. It offers by far the most profound insight into the ability of football teams that the beautiful game has ever seen. The football analytics community has become obsessed with the idea of Expected Goals. This form of stats, otherwise known as "goal probability", is commonly referred to as "xG". The metric has achieved unparalleled predictive success. You heard it here first: Expected Goals is the future of football.

Essentially, xG indicates *how many goals a team could have expected to score based on the quantity and quality of chances that they create.* Fans often come away from football matches thinking, "We created much better chances then the opposition, we definitely should have won". The Expected Goals Metric is a way of quantifying these scoring opportunities, allowing a better insight into the ability of teams than the *actual* scoreline does.

Teams are often judged by the *quantity* of shots that they have in match, or indeed in a season. For instance, Manchester City's match stats at the beginning of the chapter tell us they had twenty-seven efforts at goal. The central premise of xG is that the quality of those shots is of equal importance to the quantity. Analysts can work out the number of goals that a team would expect to score from a certain amount of shots of a certain quality, thus creating a clearer image of which teams are performing at the highest level. The teams that create scoring opportunities of a greater quantity *and* quality than other teams, whilst at the same time conceding fewer shots and at a lower quality, are clearly the best. The Expected Goals Method is essentially a more powerful version of TSR.

Collecting xG data is very simple. Each shot is assigned a probability that it will end up in a goal. This probability is based on a series of factors. First and foremost, an analyst would tend to look at the frequency that shots taken from that exact position result in a goal. Clearly a shot from inside the six-yard box has a high probability of scoring, say about 85% – an expected value of 0.85 goals. Remember, expected value is the predicted value of a variable, calculated as the sum of all possible values each multiplied by the probability of its occurrence. We studied this formula earlier on with regards to lottery winnings. Two outcomes are possible when a shot is taken in football: either it scores or misses. Thus, the formula for a shot with an 85% chance of scoring and a 15% chance of missing is as follows:

xG = (Chance of goal x Value of Goal) + (Chance of miss x Value of miss)
xG = (0.85 x 1) + (0.15 x 0)
xG = 0.85

Thus, a shot with an 85% chance of scoring is worth 0.85 goals. In football, it is incredibly easy to work out the expected value of a shot. Because the value of a goal is one and the value of a miss is nothing, the xG of an individual shot is simply the decimal probability that the effort results in a goal. A shot with a 10% probability of scoring is worth 0.1(xG), a shot with a 50% chance is worth 0.5(xG), a shot with a 75% chance is worth 0.75(xG), and so on.

How do you determine the probability of a shot's success? The location of a shot has a large bearing on how likely it is to result in a goal. A shot which is taken from a wide position, thirty yards out from goal, will only have a small chance of going in. On the other hand, a close-range shot from a central position will have a high probability of scoring. An analyst could look at a large sample of shots taken from an exact position and find how many beat the goalkeeper. Say an analyst looked at 1,000 shots taken from the right-hand corner of the penalty area. Suppose only 50 of these shots ended up in a goal. He could conclude that future shots from this location have a 5% chance of beating the goalkeeper. Thus, the xG shot probability from this position is 0.05.

It is important to note that most analysts judge a shot by its potential, not by its outcome. A shot from a long way outside the box which finds its way through a crowd of players is assigned a low Expected Goals probability, regardless of whether it misses the target comfortably or actually ends up in a goal. An analyst is essentially pressing the pause button just before the shot is taken, before assessing its probability of success. The outcome of the shot shouldn't affect the chance of it hitting the back of the net. A long range effort with 0.05(xG) will score one in every twenty attempts, but most analysts believe this doesn't mean its shot probability should be upgraded when the anomalous effort does beat the goalkeeper. Most analysts agree that the result should not dictate the narrative[22].

The position of the shot is regarded as the crucial determinant of its chances of scoring. Analysts tend to look at a large sample of previous shots taken from the same point on the pitch, and use this data to determine the chance of the shot going in. Whilst the location of a shot forms the main basis of its danger level, other factors also play their part. Shots which come from crosses are considerably harder to convert than shots which take place when the ball is standing still. Whether the shot is headed or volleyed also affects its chance of success, as does whether the effort is taken on a player's weaker foot. Analysts account for a whole range of such factors in their Expected Goals models.

How can we use these shot probabilities to work out which team deserves to win? This is also simple. The sum of all of the xG shot probabilities from a match will leave you with the xG scoreline for the game. When all the shot probabilities of each team are added up, you are left with the

---

22 Although, a world class player who has a shot from 30 yards out clearly has more of a chance of scoring than a semi-professional footballer. This is where analysts run into difficulty assessing shot probability. *Some players are better at shooting than others.* We will see how Matthew Benham deals with this problem later on.

total number of goals that you could have expected them to score. For example, suppose a match occurred between Arsenal and Tottenham where the following shot probabilities took place:

* *Arsenal Shot Probabilities:* 0.1, 0.4, 0.3, 0.7, 0.1, 0.2, 0.1, 0.3
* *Tottenham Shot Probabilities:* 0.7, 0.5, 0.6, 0.6, 0.8, 0.4, 0.7

Arsenal have taken a total of eight shots, whilst Tottenham have had seven attempts at goal. If you are easily confused by numbers, try imagining it as if the match was actually taking place. For example, Arsenal's first shot (which we have given a 10% chance of hitting the back of the net) might have been a shot from a long way out which comfortably missed. We can assign this shot a probability of 0.1(xG) because it would have only ended up in a goal on one in ten occasions. On the other hand, Tottenham's first shot has been awarded 0.7(xG), meaning it would have found the back of the net 70% of the time. This shot would have probably been a very close-range effort or a one-on-one.

The shot probability data of each team can tell us a lot about the match which took place. Arsenal's chances tended to be non-threatening. The Gunners only had one shot with more than a fifty percent chance of hitting the back of the net. On the other hand, Tottenham got into some good areas. Although they clocked less attempts at goal, the chances that they did create tended to be of high quality.

Working out the Expected Goals scoreline for a match is incredibly easy. In order to calculate the number of goals you could have expected a team to score, you simply have to find the sum of all of their shot probabilities. Thus, the xG scoreline of our theoretical match is **Arsenal 2.2-4.3 Tottenham**. Arsenal's xG shots add up to 2.2, whilst Tottenham recorded an xG score of 4.3.

Obviously goals can't be displayed as fractions in *actual* games of football. This raises an interesting point about the Expected Goals methods; *Expected Goals doesn't tell us how many goals to expect.* By this, I mean that the figure which you end up with in terms of xG (e.g. 2.2 for

Arsenal) isn't the actual number of goals which you expect the team to score. In football, goals are displayed as whole numbers and cannot be broken up into fractions. Arsenal cannot possibly score 2.2 goals.

Expected Goals is calculated by using expected value, a mathematical device that we have come across at several points already in this book. Remember, the expected value of a variable is the long-run average value of repetitions of the experiment it represents. We have seen that the expected value of a roll of a normal six-sided dice is 3.5, because this is the average of all the numbers which come up after a large sample of rolls. Of course, it is impossible for us to roll a 3.5, but this is still the average value that we would expect to come up if we rolled our dice, say, one million times. Likewise, it is often said that the average family has 2.4 children. Obviously, no family in the world possesses 2.4 kids, as it is impossible to break human beings down into fractions. Just like we cannot roll a 3.5 on a dice, or we cannot have 2.4 kids, Arsenal cannot actually score 2.2 goals. This figure is simply a reflection of how many goals we would expect them to score per game over the long-run (i.e. if the match was played one million times).

As a result of this, the shot probabilities will rarely reflect the *actual* scoreline of the match. Let's say that the real scoreline for this match was **Arsenal 1-5 Tottenham**. After the match we would work out the xG scored by each team (2.2 for Arsenal, and 4.3 for Tottenham), and conclude that the outcome was probably fair. Tottenham created much better scoring opportunities, even if they created less of them than their opposition. You would expect Tottenham to win the match based on your xG computations.

However, just because the xG scoreline suggests that Tottenham were the better side doesn't necessarily mean that they will win. As we have already seen, football is a sport in which the worse team often emerges triumphant. The scarcity of goals means that luck plays a large role in determining who is successful. Sometimes the better team will create good chances, but will end up missing all of them. Sometimes the worse team will score with a shot worthy of a very small xG probability. Football can be an unfair and inconsistent sport. Expected Goals strips the luck from the game by showing how many goals each team *deserved* to score.

Variance: The Unfair Determinant

It is clear that the Expected Goals method gives a much more profound representation of teams' ability than TSR does. The Total Shots Ratio only takes into account the quantity of shots that a team amassed. In our example, for instance, Arsenal had eight shots whilst Tottenham only managed a total of seven. Thus, Arsenal were the better side according to TSR, as they scored a TSR of 0.53 (8/15) compared to Tottenham's TSR of 0.47 (7/15).

When the data from the same match is plugged into an xG model, it is clear that TSR has misrepresented the ability of the two sides. We have already calculated that the Expected Goals scoreline of the match is **Arsenal 2.2-4.3 Tottenham**, with Tottenham clocking up an xG total nearly twice as large as their opponents. TSR flopped because it failed to take into account the *quality* of the shots that each team took. What makes xG such a useful tool for analysts is that it takes into account both quantity *and* quality.

The Expected Goals Method gets slightly more complex when you consider the potential variation in each scoreline. This isn't an essential task to carry out. The main usefulness of Expected Goals is studying the xG scorelines of matches, but studying how to account for variance can give us a deeper insight into the ground-breaking metric.

Variance tells us to what extent the score might have differed. A team who takes more shots than their opponents could potentially score more goals, even if their shots are of a poorer quality and they clock up a lesser xG total. In our example, for instance, Arsenal took more shots than Tottenham. This meant that, even though the Gunners could have expected to score less goals than Spurs, the maximum number of goals they could have scored was higher than Tottenham's possible maximum goals total. Variance gives an analyst a more in-depth breakdown of how the match *could* have played out had one team had a little more luck. Crucially, it tells us the extent to which the scoreline could have varied.

Here's an example of the important role that variance plays in football matches. Suppose that we decide to pit two teams against each other; Team Coin and Team Die. Each time we flip a coin it counts as a 'shot' for Team Coin, whilst each roll of a six-sided die counts as a 'shot' for Team Die. Team Coin's shot scores if it lands on tails but misses when it lands on heads. Team Die's shot scores if a six is rolled but misses if any other number comes up.

In our fabricated match, Team Coin amasses four shots to Team Die's twelve shots. Seeing that there is a fifty percent chance of a coin landing on tails, and thus scoring a goal, we can assign each of Team Coin's shots 0.5(xG). Team Die has a one in six chance of rolling a six, meaning that each 'shot' has a 16.7% chance of resulting in a goal. Therefore, each of Team Die's attempts can be assigned 0.167(xG).

Team Coin's four shots of 0.5(xG) leaves them with an xG total of 2, whilst Team Die's twelve 0.167(xG) shots means that they have also amassed a total of 2(xG). The match has played out as following:

Team Coin Shots (xG): 0.5 + 0.5 + 0.5 + 0.5 = 2(xG)
Team Die Shots (xG): 0.167 + 0.167 + 0.167 + 0.167 + (0.167 x 8) =
2(xG)

Essentially what we're saying is that the expected number of occasions that the coin lands on tails when flipped four times is the equivalent to the number of occasions that you could expect to land a six if you roll a die twelve times. You would expect both events to occur twice. The Expected Goals scoreline for this match would be 2-2.

However, this does not tell the whole story. Although the xG total for each team is equal, the range of goals scored by each team differs significantly. Team Coin can only score a maximum total of four goals, seeing that it has only amassed a total of four shots. In other words, if the coin lands on tails every single time, then Team Coin will have scored four goals. Team Die, on the other hand, has the potential to score twelve goals if a six is rolled on every single occasion. If every single shot worth their 0.167(xG) goes in, then Team Die will have tripled Team Coin's maximum number of goals.

Clearly, the chance that Team Coin flips four tails in a row (6.25%) is far greater than the probability of Team Die rolling twelve sixes in succession (0.02%). However, no matter how small the probability of each occurrence, they both still *could* theoretically happen. The scoreline could range from **Team Coin 0-0 Team Die** to **Team Coin 4-12 Team Die**. The Expected Goals score of **Team Coin 2-2 Team Die** does not represent the room for possible manoeuvre within the scoreline. Realising such variance exists is helpful when calculating Expected Goals scorelines.

A More Profound xG Scoreline

We can use three tools to make our Expected Goals scorelines more profound. We can add standard deviation to the scoreline, we can show the win percentage for the two teams, and we can give the expected amount of points that the teams would win per game.

Firstly, let's study how adding standard deviation to the scoreline gives a more comprehensive outlining of the match. It may be helpful at this point to give a general description of what exactly we are trying to calculate: standard deviation describes how points of data may deviate from the average. A low standard deviation means that the numbers within a pool of data are very close to the average, whilst a high standard deviation would mean they are widely spread out.

Standard deviation is another word for consistency, and is used in a range of fields from accountancy to climatology. In order to explain the formula behind working out standard deviation, let's use the example of a race car driver. Each lap the driver does around a circuit is timed. A driver with a low standard deviation of lap times is more consistent than a driver who has a high standard deviation. The more your lap times deviate, the harder it becomes to predict what your next lap time will be. This sounds obvious, right? If a driver clocks the lap time of fifty-six seconds eight times in succession, you can predict with a high degree of confidence that his next lap will be around that same figure. Conversely, a driver whose times vary greatly with every lap presents a real problem for those trying to forecast his next time. The former driver has a much lower standard deviation than the latter.

The formula for working out the standard deviation for a data group is actually fairly simple. Suppose that a driver does eight laps around the track, and the time for each individual lap in seconds is as follows: 49, 51, 58, 53, 52, 48, 51, 56. These results are all fairly spread out, and you wish to determine the standard deviation of this data set.

First, you have to find the average lap time, commonly referred to as the *mean* lap time. You learn to do this at the age of about fourteen. Add all of the numbers in the data set together and then divide by the number of numbers:

$$(49 + 51 + 58 + 53 + 52 + 48 + 51 + 56) / 8 = 52.25$$

The average lap time for our racing driver is 52.25 seconds, as displayed above. Working out the mean alone is a good indication of what future times the driver is likely to record. However, in order to find the standard deviation, we must work out the difference between each of the points of data and the average. For example, the difference between the first of the driver's lap times (49 seconds) and the average lap time (52.25 seconds) is -3.25 seconds. You then square the difference of each of the individual data points. For instance, -3.25 becomes 10.6. Here is each of these calculations in full:

$$(49 - 52.25)^2 = -3.25^2 = 10.6$$
$$(51 - 52.25)^2 = -1.25^2 = 1.6$$
$$(58 - 52.25)^2 = 5.75^2 = 33.1$$
$$(53 - 52.25)^2 = 0.75^2 = 0.56$$
$$(52 - 52.25)^2 = -0.25^2 = 0.06$$

$(48 - 52.25)^2 = -4.25^2 = 18.1$
$(51 - 52.25)^2 = 1.25^2 = 1.6$
$(56 - 52.25)^2 = 3.75^2 = 14.1$

The final step in the process is to find the average of all of these 'difference' numbers, before taking the square root of that figure:

$(10.6 + 1.6 + 33.1 + 0.56 + 0.06 + 18.1 + 1.6 + 14.1) / 8 = 9.97$
$\sqrt{9.97} = 3.16$

Thus, the standard deviation for the driver's lap times is 3.16 seconds. We can now account for the variance in his performance, giving us a more detailed outlining of how the driver's lap times differ. We can compare his standard deviation to that of other drivers, which allows us to work out who are the more consistent. A driver whose standard deviation is higher will be more sporadic in his lap times, whilst a driver whose standard deviation is close to zero will be more consistent in his performance.

When calculating the Expected Goals scoreline of a football match, it can be extremely useful to use standard deviation. Some xG totals will be more subject to variance than others. Accounting for this added variance in the presented scoreline will add an extra dimension to the analysis. Team Die, for instance, are an example of a team with a high level of variance, whilst Team Coin are subject to less variation in their scoreline. The inclusion of standard deviation in the xG scoreline of our match between these two sides reads like this:

Team Coin 2 (±1) v 2 (±1.29) Team Die

Team Coin's Expected Goals total is subject to a standard deviation of just 1, whilst the standard deviation for Team Die's total is 1.29. This reflects that Team Die's xG total is more subject to variance, due to the increased number of shots that they accumulated.

When two teams clock up the same (or a similar) xG total in a match, variance becomes a crucial factor. Our intuition tells us that two teams who score the same number of Expected Goals will win the same number of games in the long run. Surely the chance of victory of two teams with the same xG totals must be equal? In reality, it doesn't play out this way. Two teams who accumulate the same xG total against one another don't always win the same number of games over the long run.

Let me revert back to our match involving Team Coin and Team Die in order to explain. Having accounted for the standard deviation in the xG scoreline of both Team Coin and Team Die (±1 and ±1.29 respectively), we can now create a number of simulations of how the match will play out. The analysts who first attempted this were met with a surprising revelation. They conducted ten thousand simulations of the match between Team Coin and Team Die, a large enough sample of matches to filter out any noise that might corrupt the findings. They discovered that Team Coin won 40% of the games, Team Die won 36%, and a draw occurred 24% of the time.

How, when two teams both carried the xG total of exactly 2, could one team win more often than the other? Both teams are expected to score two goals given the quality and quantity of shots that they have during the game. Surely over 10,000 simulations the number of games that each team won should be equal? Surely Team Die should win just as much as Team Coin?

The results raised an important question: *is it more effective to have a few very good shots than a multitude of poor quality attempts?*

The answer to this question could change the way teams approach football. The old cliché goes that if you don't shoot, you won't score. This phrase is used to encourage players to take long range shots. The theory goes that if you barrage the opposition goal with a host of long shots, one will eventually find its way into the net. Fans and managers alike often encourage their team to have more efforts at goal, whilst the media often imply that a team who had fewer shots than their opposition was weaker.

The notion that one golden chance should outweigh several speculative efforts at goal could be revolutionary to the way the game is played.

This is what Mark Taylor strove to find out when he analysed a game between Fulham and Manchester United back in 2014. Fulham were out-played, managing six efforts at goal to Manchester United's thirty-one. However, just as in the Manchester City-West Ham game at the beginning of the chapter, the better team were unable to win. Fulham scored with their only two real chances of note, and the game finished a draw. Taylor noted that, despite United's success in accumulating a large quantity of low quality chances, the hosts weren't able to score more goals than the Londoners.

Taylor decided to find out whether, when two sides manage to tally up the same xG scoreline, the team with the fewer chances will have the greater probability of winning. In order to test the power of high quality scoring opportunities, Taylor simulated a match between two teams who each amassed an xG scoreline of 1.2. One team, who we will call "Team Golden Chances", managed only two shots in the match, each one being assigned an xG probability of 0.6. By contrast, the second team, who we shall address as "Team Plentiful Chances", managed twelve efforts at goal, with each one only having a 10% chance of hitting the back of the net. Thus, Team GC (0.6 x 2) and Team PC (0.1 x 12) are both expected to score 1.2 goals.

Recognise this kind of test from somewhere? You should do, because it is essentially the same simulation that we carried out with Team Coin and Team Die. Both sides are expected to score the same amount of goals, but one has a larger range of scoreline possibilities than the other. Team GC can only score a maximum of two goals, whilst Team PC can score a full twelve if each of their shots goes in. The standard deviation of Team Golden Chances is much lower than that of Team Plentiful Chances.

After carrying out twenty-thousand simulations on the match between Team GC and Team PC, Taylor had reached some interesting conclusions. Despite our intuition telling us that the two teams should win the same number of matches, it was in fact Team GC who triumphed more than Team PC. The team who took two high quality shots won 37.5% of the time, whilst the team who took twelve low quality shots won just 32.1% of the matches that took place. A draw occurred in 30.4% of the games.

This was not a one off result. Taylor ran several tests with several different xG scorelines and several different shot probabilities for either team. Each and every time, the results showed that teams who create a few high quality chances will win more matches over the long run than teams who create a high quantity of low quality scoring opportunities, despite the Expected Goals total of each team being equal.

He concluded that, when two teams hold the same xG scoreline, it is the team who amassed fewer shots at goal who is more likely to win. Taylor found that as a team produces more and more shots, the range of their likely winning scorelines increase whilst their chance of winning diminishes. If you want to increase your goal difference, then you are better off taking lots of long range shots. However, the priority of teams should be to win as many points as possible. They can do this by prioritising the creation of high *quality* chances over the creation of a high *quantity* of chances.

This revelation is thought-provoking. Instead of players being encouraged to try their luck from long range, it would be more sensible for teams to attempt to work the ball into the box and create close-range opportunities. Arsenal are a team who are often criticised for 'over-playing', for passing the ball to death and for not taking enough shots at goal. I once read a stat which asserted that Arsenal had taken the fewest number of shots from outside the box in the Premier League that season. This was meant as a negative statement on Arsène Wenger's style of play. In fact, Taylor's studies suggest that Wenger has had it right all along. Teams in the modern era have aspired to a "Barcelona-style" of play, where slick passing and flowing attacking moves create a potent threat to the opposition defence. Whilst there is no refuting that Barcelona take a large amount of shots each match, perhaps the factor that gives them the edge is the *quality* of chances that they create. Working the ball into dangerous areas means you will have less shots, but the shots which you do have will be of a higher quality.

A long-range effort that curls into the top corner is a majestic sight. The availability heuristic, studied in an earlier chapter, means that such a goal will certainly stick in the memory of the fans. However, the data strongly suggests that players should pass up speculative shots at goal in order to try and create more clear-cut chances. A single one-on-one with the goalkeeper can carry the same amount of weight as thirty or so long-range efforts.

xG, xP, xAnything

Expected value has proven itself as an important prediction-making tool. Whether it be working out the value of a lottery ticket, how much a bet is worth, or how many goals you can expect a team to score in a football match, it is clear that using expected value gives us a much deeper insight into the *actual* worth of a product, or the ability of a team.

As well as calculating number of goals that each team score and concede in a match, analysts can also work out the number of points the team could expect to collect (xP). Expected Points totals are easy to work out. All that you have to do is work out the xG scoreline by adding all of the shot probabilities together for each team, before accounting for variance in your scoreline as outlined in the previous section. Running a couple of thousand simulations then leaves you with the relatively easy task of working out the average number of points per game that each team would have taken. This is your xP. There are simulators available online which can tell you the Expected Points total of each team when given the shot probabilities from the match.

Following this methodology with the match between Team Coin and Team Die, in which both teams have an xG total of 2 and the standard deviation of ±1 and ±1.29 respectively, leaves Team Coin with a higher xP total. We have already seen that the team with fewer, but higher quality, chances wins more often. Over the long run Team Coin could expect to amass 1.42 points per game, whilst Team Die would only accrue 1.34(xP).

Of course, it would be impossible for Team Coin to *actually* win 1.42 points from the match, or for Team Die to *actually* win 1.34 points. In reality, they could only win either three points, one point, or no points at all. However, as previously stated, the expected value of a product is not necessarily a value that you would expect to be produced. In a previous section, I used an example of the average family expecting to have 2.4 children, or someone who rolls a dice expecting to be met with the value of 3.5. Neither of these things are actually possible, but they do offer a precise reflection of your expectation. Over the long run (say, if the match was played out a couple of thousand times), Team Coin and Team Die would win an average of 1.42 points and 1.34 points respectively. These are their xP totals from the game.

This example gives us a perfect insight into why it is important to consider variance. Team Coin amassed a lesser quantity of shots, but those which they did take had a greater quality. Thus, despite amounting the same xG total as Team Die, Team Coin could expect to pick up an additional 0.08 points per game. This may sound like a small difference, but over the course of a thirty-eight game season Team Coin can expect to amass 3.04 more points than their opponents[23]. If these teams played in the Premier League, those three points could be the difference between winning the division and finishing second, between claiming a Champions League place and finishing fifth, or between survival and relegation.

How can we use these methods to make better footballing predictions? In brief, working out the Expected Points total for each game that each team has played in will give you a *more accurate representation of the ability of the teams in the division than the actual league table will*.

Here's why. The league table only takes into account goals that are scored. The only way to accumulate points is to score goals, meaning that

---

23 The Premier League season lasts for just thirty-eight games. If Team Coin and Team Die were to play in any of the other top three divisions of English football, they would play forty-six matches and the former would clock up an expected 3.68 more points than their opponents.

an incredibly unlucky team who creates lots of good chances but fails to score many of them will not be as high up the table as they should be. An xP table, based on the Expected Goals scorelines of matches, takes into account the quantity *and* quality of shots that each team takes. Thus, it gives a much fuller reflection of each team's ability.

Additionally, in a normal league table teams can only come away with three possible points totals; three if they win, one if they draw, or zero if they lose. Under the Expected Points table, a team will win a far more precise number of points. Assigning a team 1.9(xP) shows that they performed less well than a team who earnt 2.4(xP) in a different game. Both of these teams clearly dominated their matches, and deserved to win. However, the increased specificity with which xP measures performance allows us a more profound insight into the ability of the teams. We can see *by how much* the second team outperformed the first in their respective matches. The closer a team gets to 3(xP), the more dominant they were in the game.

A team who creates several good chances but fails to take them will be rewarded with a high number of Expected Points. Thus, the fact that they were unlucky in front of goal is accounted for. Conversely, a team who is lucky and manages to win a series of games despite performing badly will rank lowly in the xP table. This means that we are assessing the performance of the teams, not the results. The quality of performance that a team puts in tells us more about their ability than the results they achieve, which are heavily influenced by luck.

If football were purely scientific, the success of teams would be based on their xG score. Instead of scorelines of **0-0** and **2-1**, results would be displayed as **0.4-1.3** or **2.8-1.6**. Teams would rarely draw, as a result of the increased precision that would be added to the scoreline. Instead of a team being able to realistically only score a handful of "goals" in any given match, they would be able to score hundreds (they could score 0.1 goals, 0.2 goals, 0.25 goals, etc.). There is no limit to the number of decimal points that you can use to display the Expected Goals total of a team. An incredibly thorough analyst could give a shot probability of 0.284638(xG) if they wanted to[24]. A team could win by 1.54(xG) to 1.53(xG) if this was the precision with which the analyst wished to measure the two sides.

Most importantly, the better team would always win if the result was based on the xG scoreline. This derives from the seemingly obvious point that, if the whole point of football is to create scoring opportunities, then the teams who create the most *and the best* chances to score are the highest performing teams.

Despite the fact that using Expected Goals clearly provides the most accurate gauge of team performance, football will obviously never use xG to decide the *actual* league table. Nor should it. Many would argue that the beauty of football, the most popular sport in the world, lies in the fact that any team has a chance of victory on any given day. Football is a sport that lies exquisitely in the balance between predictability and unpredictability. If our hypothetical daydream of competitions such as the Premier League and the FA Cup using xG scorelines to determine who wins and who loses each match, then almost all of the luck would be removed from the game. The best teams would always win, whilst the worse teams would always lose. The magic of the cup would cease to exist, whilst league tables would become a lot more rigid.

Whilst xG may take away the thrilling element of chance from football, this kind of system is exactly what professional gamblers, fans, pundits and the like have been searching for! The Expected Goals method strips randomness from the game, telling us which clubs are *actually* good and which have just been lucky. This allows us to cut through the noise and work out the true ability of teams. Expected Goals is the tool which most efficiently allows us to sift through the haystack in search of that allusive needle.

---

24 In reality, this would be an over-specification. The assigning of xG probabilities to shots isn't an exact science, and one or two decimal places usually suffice when displaying xG scorelines.

How to Be a Football Analyst

Benham's system is facilitated through Smartodds, the betting consultancy which he owns. We have already seen how Starlizard, Tony Bloom's statistical analysis company, process and utilise the data that they collect. Smartodds have a near-identical structure, with four departments all working alongside one another. There is the subdivision who collect the data, the subdivision who feed it into the algorithms, the subdivision who decide which bets to place, and the subdivision who are actually responsible for placing the bets with the bookmakers in Asia. There is nothing especially pioneering about this process.

The innovation comes in the *type* of data that Benham collects; data which is based on the Expected Goals method.

The first department in the chain of operation at Smartodds, the subdivision who are responsible for the collection of data, are known as "Watchers". These employees are responsible for watching football matches and logging the relevant statistics. This was the role that I performed when I worked at Smartodds. Watchers will typically watch around two to four football matches a day. They are payed £20 for each match that they watch, and are given an extra £20 if that match goes to extra time. I recall one day watching three matches of football, before being given Brentford's League Cup match from the night before to analyse. The Brentford game went to extra time, meaning I earnt £40 from that particular match. I headed home that evening having earnt £100 in one day by watching four football matches, including one involving the team I supported.

Smartodds' Watchers collect data on all of the major leagues, and many of the minor leagues, that exist worldwide. Benham realised the need for more profound statistics to be utilised in football. He recognised the restrictive nature of stats like 'Shots on Target' and 'Shots off Target'. It seemed inexplicable that a glaring miss from three yards and a hopeful effort from thirty-five yards could be lumped in the same 'Shot off Target' category.

In his search for a richer supply of footballing data, Benham came across the Expected Goals method. The principles of expected value were familiar to Benham from his days on the trading floors. Remember, expected value is the predicted value of a variable, calculated as the sum of all possible values each multiplied by the probability of its occurrence[25]. Benham was familiar with utilising this methodology to predict the future value of stocks and the like. The notion of calculating how many goals a team could have expected to score based on the quantity and quality of their shots appealed to him.

One would expect that to become a Watcher at Smartodds, one of the most successful and profitable betting consultancies ever to have existed, you would have to be either a football whiz or a mathematical genius. After all, even the concept of Expected Goals is fairly difficult to understand at first. The idea that a football scoreline could be broken up into decimal points challenges conventional wisdom. However, anyone with a basic level of interest in football can be taught to become a Watcher with some relatively simple training.

The Smartodds offices have a large floor space, filled with over one hundred desks. The high-rolling clients sit in the middle of the space, the analysts sit around the outside, with the Watchers located at the far end of the room. There are forty or so work stations in the Watchers area. When there are very few matches to be watched, there may only be one or two employees sitting in this area. Sometimes I would have to come in early in the morning, probably to watch a match from the Asian leagues, and would be the only Watcher in the entire office. On a Saturday afternoon, on the other hand, the floor would be packed with Watchers. If you wanted to get a spot at favourite computer, you would have to come in long before midday.

---

25 As we have seen, the equation we use to work out the number of goals we could expect a team to score is simple. The value of each goal is obviously 1, so all that we need to do is multiply each shot probability (i.e. 0.2, 0.45, 0.9) by 1. To work out an Expected Goals scoreline, all we need to do is find the sum of all of the shot probabilities added together. Working out the expected value of other commodities (i.e. lottery tickets) can be a lot more challenging.

The clients, those paying for the innovative data that the Watchers collect, are situated in the central area of the main floor. This, incidentally, is where Benham's desk is located. Around the outside of these men, forming almost a circle around the clients, are the desks of Smartodds employees. This is where traders sit, placing bets on behalf of the company and their clients. It is also where the Watcher Operations team sit. These men are in charge of assigning Watchers matches to analyse. Whenever I watched a match, it would be assigned to me by a member of this Watcher Operations team. They sit behind screens showing several of the matches being analysed by various Watchers, and scold any Watcher who makes a mistake. The Watchers area is situated at the far end of the floor, slightly apart from the clients' and analysts' area.

The routine which I performed was almost identical for every match I watched at Smartodds. I would come in about half an hour before the game to carry out some basic research. What were the weather conditions like at the venue? Was the pitch slick or dry? What was the atmosphere inside the ground like? Such details may seem trivial, but to the professional gamblers who sat across the floor tracking every word that I wrote, such information could prove crucial. The clients would be following several matches at once on Smartodds' live platform, watching the Expected Goals data that the Watchers were collecting as it filtered in. This data would allow them to see which teams were looking more dangerous, helping them decide where to place their in-play bets.

When watching a match, Smartodds Watchers must write updates every ten minutes describing the flow of the game. The Expected Goals stats that they log reflect the quality of scoring opportunities that each team is creating, but the overall tempo and flow of the game is not reflected in this data. They must provide this information in their written notes. The Watchers must convey which team is seeing more of the ball, who are showing more attacking intent, which players are having the greatest impact on proceedings, and the like. A match where a team creates a lot of opportunities through counter-attacking football (like Leicester did in 2015/16) has a very different feel to a game where one team is creating lots of chances through sustained pressure and great ball retention (like Barcelona do every season). The notes provided by the Watchers allow the clients an insight into the flow of the game. Watchers are also expected to highlight injuries and substitutions, so that Smartodds' clients who are following and betting on the match in-play can adjust their models accordingly. An injury to a key player could completely change the chances of a certain team winning.

Of course, whilst it may take a keen interest in football to accurately describe the flow of a match, most of the duties outlined above are hardly challenging. Whilst pitch conditions and starting line-ups are certainly important to the Smartodds clientele, the thing which they are *really* interested in is the quality of chances which each team is creating. The innovative Expected Goals data which the Watchers collect is the crème de la crème of the company, as it is these stats which reveal the true performance levels of each team. The training that is required of Smartodds Watchers ensures that they are able to consistently and accurately assess what constitutes "danger" in football. Watchers are taught how to assign each shot a probability of resulting in a goal, a skill which I will now attempt to teach you.

DANGER ZONES

Arguably the most important factor of determining a shot probability (that is, the chance that a shot results in a goal) is the position of the shot. An effort at goal becomes increasingly more likely to succeed the closer it gets to goal. Additionally, a shot becomes increasingly likely to hit the back of the net as it gets more and more central. Shots from wide positions and shots from far out both tend to carry little danger.

Smartodds start training their Watchers by breaking each half of a football pitch down into three areas. The company train their analysts to always visualise these three areas whenever they are logging Expected Goals data. Firstly, there is the Safety Zone, located roughly thirty-five yards out from goal. When a team has the ball in this area of the pitch, they pose very little threat to the opposition goal. The team are too far out to shoot, and the assumption is that the defending team have got men behind the ball. When the ball is over thirty-five yards out from goal, it is hard to even label the state of play as an "attack".

The second zone is known as the Outer Danger Area. This is any area inside the final thirty-five-yards leading up to goal, excluding the Inner Danger Area. Shots from this region are fairly rare, and when they tend to occur they tend to be harmless. It would take an excellent strike to score from this kind of distance. Nonetheless, the defending team should be alert when the ball is in this region.

The final zone is known as the Inner Danger Area. The border for this area is essentially a semi-circle about thirteen yards out from goal, but some consider it to be anywhere within the penalty area. The overwhelming majority of goals are scored from within this Inner Danger Area. In fact, Benham calculated that around 77% of Premier League goals are scored from the zone that stretches from the six-yard box to the edge of the penalty area. Only about one in five goals are scored from either outside the box or inside the six-yard box[26].

These three areas (the safety zone, outer danger area and inner danger area) are used as a guideline with which Watchers can measure the danger of each shot. It is of vital importance that the location of the shot is taken into account when one assesses its chance of success. Ultimately, though, it is down to each individual Watcher to assign each effort an Expected Goals shot probability. If a striker shoots at an open goal from thirty-five yards, clearly the chance will carry a high xG shot probability despite the fact that it has occurred from the Outer Danger Area.

Each time there is an effort at goal, Watchers will assess its danger level and punch the data into the system. After each game, another analyst will go through the footage, watching each of the major chances

---

26 Obviously this isn't to say that shots within the six-yard box aren't dangerous. In fact, shots taken from within the six-yard box have a near 100% record of scoring. The difficulty lies in actually getting the ball this close to goal without a defender intervening. A team who looked to score all of their goals within the six-yard box would struggle.

which took place, and offer a second opinion as to whether the probability which the Watcher awarded each shot accurately reflected its danger. In this sense, Smartodds deploy the wisdom of the collective so that individual mistakes are corrected.

Many football analysts simply use shot locations to determine the danger of each effort at goal. Smartodds have an edge in the sense that they have an actual human being assessing the likelihood of each shot being successful. The human brain can account for much more information than a computer can. Was the shooter under pressure from the opposition defence when he took the shot? Did he use his weaker foot? Was the goalkeeper well positioned? Did the ball bobble awkwardly as it was struck? Did the player have to shoot through a crowd of bodies? There are a large number of variables which contribute to how dangerous each shot is. A Watcher who has been trained by Smartodds can more accurately assess the probability of a shot resulting in a goal than a model which simply looks at the historical probability of a shot from a specific location succeeding.

The whole Watcher process that Smartodds use is fairly straightforward. A Watcher will be assigned a match to watch. He will watch the match, and use his intuition to adjudge the probability that each shot which occurs has of hitting the back of the net. This data will be reviewed by another analyst after the match. The game will then be assigned an Expected Goals scoreline (for instance, Arsenal **2.2-4.3** Tottenham). This Expected Goals scoreline, which details the number of goals that each team could have expected to score and concede based on the quantity and quality of their shots, will more accurately reflect the ability of the two sides than the actual scoreline. This innovative data will offer an analyst a more profound insight into which teams are the best, allowing them to make better predictions and, ultimately, win money through betting. Who said maths was boring?

TURNING STATS
INTO WINS

―――――

IN THE PREVIOUS CHAPTER, WE studied the system used by Matthew Benham to limit the damaging effects that chance has on our footballing predictions. We saw how, by fostering a form of data collection that gives much more insightful information on the ability of football teams, he has been able to filter out much of the noise which exists within the sport. The Expected Goals method outmuscles the more conventional stats of "Shots", "Shots on Target", "Possession" and the like, which give very little information on how a game actually played out. Looking at the quantity and quality of the scoring opportunities that a team creates gives us the most accurate understanding of their ability.

Nevertheless, as we have seen throughout this book, collecting the data is just half of the challenge. Whether or not you use it in the correct way will determine your success.

Smartodds' Watchers collect Expected Goals data on virtually every professional football team in, and many outside of, Europe. This is a vast amount of information, and can be used to reveal which teams are playing the most efficient football. Benham has used this information in two capacities; to found the success of his gambling and to assist in the running of Brentford and Midtjylland. Both of these uses are facilitated by Smartodds, the company he founded in 2004.

It is obvious how the data helps Smartodds make money. In the first instance, Benham and his employees place bets on behalf of the company. Using the chance creation statistics that the Watchers collect to work out which teams are undervalued by the bookmakers has achieved great success. Given that bookies will often base their odds on the form of sides, the data collected using the Expected Goals method can give a much more accurate image of how well a team has been playing.

For example, one might look at the match between Arsenal and Tottenham which is outlined in the previous chapter. Arsenal could have expected to score 2.2(xG) based on the shots that they took throughout the game, whilst Tottenham managed to accumulate 4.3(xG). Spurs could have expected to score nearly twice as many goals at the Gunners. However, let's say that the game *actually* finished two-one to Arsenal. The bookmakers might look at the final score and undervalue Spurs' ability. Thus, Tottenham's chances of victory in their next match would probably also be undervalued by the bookies. A Smartodds analyst could look at the data and see that Tottenham actually deserved to win the match. Thus, if the analyst deems that the bookmakers have undervalued the probability of Tottenham winning their next game, there is the potential to make money. Smartodds look at the odds for their next match and, using the data that they have collected on both Tottenham and their upcoming opponents, make an assessment on which team is undervalued in the eyes of the bookmakers.

Smartodds also acquire money from clients, who pay for their Expected Goals data. The company sells these stats to professional gamblers, who use it to inform their own models. In this sense, Smartodds is similar to data companies like Opta, the key difference being that the latter primarily sell their statistics to media outlets. Most of the stats deployed on television broadcasts, or used by commentators, have been purchased from Opta. Smartodds, on the other hand, only sell their data to professional gamblers who are bound by strict confidentiality agreements. Any leakage of data, or even the means by which Smartodds *collect* the data, could come at a huge cost to the company.

In the gambling world, information is key. Those who have the most informed, accurate and insightful data will inevitably come out on top. The Expected Goals method allows Smartodds to consistently gain an edge over the bookmakers. Benham's philosophy, partnered alongside his innovative data collection, has seen him rob the bookmakers of millions.

THE FOOTBALL STOCK MARKET

The Expected Goals data which Smartodds collect is also used by Benham to assist in the running of Brentford and FC Midtjylland. Special analysts are assigned to watch each of these clubs exclusively. The xG stats are used to assess both the attacking and defensive strength of Benham's two sides. What areas of the teams can be improved on? How many chances are they creating and conceding? Should the managers focus on developing attacking or defensive skills?

Brentford and Midtjylland also utilise Smartodds' data to profile opponents. How strong are their upcoming opposition offensively and defensively? When do they tend to create their chances? Do they start games quickly or slowly? Do they tend to create high quality or low quality chances? These questions can all be answered by looking at Expected Goals data that Smartodds have collected on the other teams.

Primarily, though, Benham uses the information collected by his Watchers to recruit players for Brentford and Midtjylland. Before explaining how the Expected Goals data helps Benham find the best footballers, it may be useful to explain how Benham approaches the transfer market. His approach to buying and selling players is similar to his approach to the stock market. Each football player represents a value; a sum of money that he is worth to the club. In football, the wealthiest clubs are generally the most successful. The correlation between the depths of the owner's pockets and the loftiness of his club in the league table is overwhelmingly strong. Thus, Benham's simple aim is to build a squad which is as valuable as possible, whilst at the same time spending as little money as possible.

Both Brentford and Midtjylland are comparatively poor clubs. The former has been languishing in the third and fourth tiers of English football for most of its existence, whilst the latter has been a mediocre member of the top tier of Danish football. However, since Benham has taken over, both clubs have been enjoying their most successful period for decades. The key to Benham's success has been his ruthless approach to buying and selling players. Smartodds' Expected Goals data allows him to identify undervalued prospects. The key to being wily in the transfer market is to find the unappreciated players, the hidden gems which can add more to your team than their price tag suggests. Benham has developed a system which highlights such players, allowing him to build a squad far more valuable than the money it cost him to buy.

However, importing players is only half the story. It is obvious that you want to buy the best commodities for the cheapest prices. In our everyday lives we live by this principle. When all other things are equal, we will always plump for the inexpensive options. What makes Benham's approach so shrewd is his approach to *selling* players.

Most football supporters are desperate to see their club retain their best players. The fan favourites who grace the turf every week are loved and cherished by those in the stands. Benham's philosophy is to be just as eager to sell your best players as to buy new ones. This may seem counterintuitive, but Benham is always aware which of his players might be overvalued by other clubs. Benham would be happy to sell a player who other sides are willing to pay in excess of his *actual* value for, regardless of the footballer's reputation amongst the fans. That money can then be reinvested into finding more undervalued prospects. If one of his players then becomes overvalued, Benham will look to sell him.

There are plenty of inefficiencies within the transfer market. We have already seen how human biases can lead to some players becoming criminally overrated. Regression to the mean is another phenomenon which can cause a misevaluation of players. In short, most humans are radically insufficient at successfully determining the value of footballers. Benham is always looking for clubs who might be willing to pay more for a player than he is worth, as well as looking for undervalued talent which he could bring to his clubs. By buying cheap and selling for an inflated price, Benham has been able to keep constantly upgrading the value, and therefore the ability, of his playing staff.

The most illustrious example of Benham's philosophy's success comes in the form of Andre Gray. Benham's statistical models highlighted the striker when he was playing in the Conference for Luton Town. Gray was in fine scoring form, but few clubs in the higher divisions were willing to take a chance on a player who was playing in the fifth tier of English football. Nevertheless, Benham's models projected that Gray was performing at the level of a decent Championship forward. Benham saw the undervalued potential of Gray, and Brentford snapped him up for a measly £500k.

Gray's transfer was met with a fair amount of scepticism from fans of the West London club. The striker had never played professional football before in his career, having only ever performed in non-league. Despite the doubts over Gray's ability, he took to the Championship with ease. The striker scored eighteen goals in his first season at Brentford. He helped the team reach fifth place in the league table, and scored in the Play-Off semi-final against Middlesbrough. Andre Gray quickly became a fan favourite.

Benham's system had succeeded in identifying an extremely talented player who was undervalued by the rest of the footballing world. However, the story doesn't end there. Gray's whirlwind first season had seen him draw attention from several other clubs. Benham realised that Gray had become greatly overvalued in the eyes of potential suitors. As we have already seen, players who have an exceptional season often regress to the mean. Benham anticipated that Gray would not do as well the following season if he remained at Brentford. The striker's stock was nearing its peak, Benham concluded. Just as in all markets, the right time to sell is when the price of an item is as inflated as it will get.

Benham decided to enter talks with other clubs over the signing of Andre Gray. A few weeks later Gray was transferred to Burnley for a whopping £9m, comfortably the largest sum that Brentford had ever received for a single player. The West London club had bought a player for £500k and sold him for £9m just one season later. Benham had traded Gray for eighteen times as much as he had acquired him for. Gray's transfer to and from Brentford represents one of the most rewarding deals in the history of football.

Benham's philosophy is all about using his innovative recruitment techniques to find undervalued players. Whether that be bringing in a free agent whose signing carries little risk, or spending a little more cash on a prospect who could become a top level footballer, the key is to spot the players who add more value to the squad than they will cost you to bring them in. Conversely, by selling players who other clubs are willing to pay over the odds for, Benham makes sure that his clubs steadily become richer and richer. In a sport where the wealthiest teams have a far greater chance of succeeding, Benham has mastered the art of steadily increasing the affluence both Brentford and Midtjylland.

Billy Beane highlighted the need to be constantly "upgrading" the quality of his playing staff. This is exactly what Matthew Benham is doing. He is investing money on players, seeking a large return on those investments, then looking to reinvest the money he has made on even better players. Benham spent £500k on Andre Gray, an investment which made him with £9m. That £9m could then be reinvested into buying more undervalued prospects. Benham, should he so wish, could have bought eighteen more undervalued prospects for £500k. Should those players all boom in the way that Gray did, Benham would make a total of £216m back on those investments[27]. That £216m could then be invested on 432 Gray-like players, and so on. Obviously, Gray's transfer worked out exceedingly well for Benham and Brentford. Even by Benham's incredibly high standards, Gray was an outstanding purchase. In fact, there almost

---

27 Feel free to check the maths. Eighteen multiplied by twelve is indeed two-hundred and sixteen. This figure reveals the true impressiveness of the return that Benham made on Andre Gray.

certainly aren't eighteen other players in the vast pool of English footballing talent out there who are undervalued to the same extent.

The English football pyramid, though only holding four professional football leagues, possesses countless non-league divisions. The recent examples of Charlie Austin, Jamie Vardy and, indeed, Andre Gray suggest that there are plenty of players who play non-league football who would be comfortable competing in the top divisions. The task for clubs is filtering the diamonds from the rough. Teams in the loftier tiers of English football are reluctant to gamble on players who wallow in non-league. Benham's mission is to find the undervalued players like Gray who are ignored by the rest of the footballing world. The more undervalued the player, the greater return you could expect to receive on your investment.

Despite Benham's philosophy of buying and selling players working wonders at Brentford, fans often misunderstand the logic behind it. When Andre Gray was sold to Burnley, for example, Brentford supporters didn't see it as a shrewd piece of business. The supporters simply saw a Gray-shaped whole in their starting line-up. They didn't understand why Benham had sold one of their best players to a rival in the same division. The selling of a fan-favourite does seem to defy intuition, even if it makes economic sense. Football fans must try to accept that their club will sell its best players. In fact, fans should *encourage* and *want* their club to do so. Similarly, owners and managers should learn to spot signs of decay in their squads. Alex Ferguson always looked for players who were past their peak, and shipped them off for more money than they were worth.

One of the greatest mistakes that a club can make is overpaying for an aging player. Managers sometimes spend too much money on a player because he is a big name, or has played for a series of big clubs. These are external factors which will not help the performance of your team. In the second chapter we saw how players can be undervalued for a number of reasons – for instance, a slightly awkward gait. Players can be overvalued in a similar fashion. Teams should be paying for the impact a player will have on their side in the future, not the performances they have made in the past.

Strikers are particularly prone to becoming overvalued in the transfer market. A one-off season in which a forward scores a mass of goals will often lead him to become vastly overrated. *This is when the club should be looking to sell him.* Take the example of Michu at Swansea. The Welsh side should have realised the Spaniard would regress to his mean level of performance after his spectacular season, and should've sold him to Arsenal for £25m when they had the chance. Try to picture football in the way that Benham does; by viewing each player not as a player, but as an amount of money. Each player represents an intrinsic value of worth, like stocks in the stock market. A team is essentially a portfolio of financial assets. When signing a player, Benham always considers their re-sale value. Younger players are clearly much more profitable than older ones. They can be developed and sold for a much greater sum than they were bought for. It is little coincidence that Brentford had the second youngest Championship squad in the 2016/17 season.

When a club is willing to pay more money for your player than he is actually worth, you should sell him. When you spot a player who you could buy for less than he is worth, you should buy him.

These are simple principles of investment, yet they are criminally neglected in the world of football. Why is football so ignorant in this regard? For one, owners, managers and fans alike are blinded my emotion. Football is an incredibly sentimental game, and it is hard to keep an unbiased view of what is going on around you. Fans become emotionally attached to players, and when they leave it can be hard to let them go. Managers must separate themselves from such sentiments and act in a rational manner to ensure the best possible future for their football club. Benham has demonstrated in recent years his willingness to let his best players leave should his terms be met, and it has seen Brentford upgrade their squad time and time again.

LOYAL OR SPOILS?

You must be ruthless to succeed in the world of football. The notion of loyalty ceases to exist in the sport anymore – that is, if it ever did in the first place. Players, managers and agents all search for the most high-profile jobs, the jobs which pay the most amount of money. This is a given in any other field of work. When a normal employee is offered a promotion, or a more highly paid position at a different company, they don't tend to turn it down because of a sense of loyalty to their current department. Yet in football, when a player wishes to join a bigger club which pays a more lucrative salary, he is labelled a mercenary.

There is a clearly defined food chain which exists within football. At the top are the clubs owned by men with seemingly bottomless pockets. These sides will almost always finish at the top end of the league table. Anything less than the best is a disappointment. There is no need for these clubs to innovate in the way that Brentford and Midtjylland have. Goliath doesn't need to update his methods when fighting against David. The clubs at the very top end can use their financial brawn to dominate the world of football.

The majority of teams are not in quite a luxurious position. I would suggest that ninety-five per cent of professional football clubs could be tagged as both predators and prey. These sides are in a constant battle to try and increase their affluence. They all have teams who are richer than them, who will often swoop for their best players. Similarly, they all have teams who are less well off than themselves, whom they can lure players away from. Footballers are drawn to money like moths to a flame. The best players will naturally gravitate towards the richest clubs. This is common sense.

One of the most merciless techniques that a club can deploy to lure a player to their side is to submit a derisive bid to their current team. Submitting an offer which is substantially smaller than the value of the player, in the knowledge that the bid will be rejected by the host club, unsettles the player. It puts the host club in a difficult situation, and often leads to the player submitting a transfer request. Smaller clubs find it very hard to prevent larger clubs signing their players. When a wealthy, successful team offers a smaller team's player higher wages, it is unlikely that they will remain at the smaller club for much longer.

The only way for a club to work their way up the food chain is to become more wealthy. Only then can you offer larger wage deals and attract a higher calibre of player. Benham realised this, and set about implementing his philosophy at Brentford and Midtjylland. He had found the trick to succeeding in investment banking was finding the undervalued stocks. He had found the trick to succeeding in professional gambling was finding the undervalued bets. Now he had found the trick to increasing the stature of his football clubs was to find the undervalued players.

BENHAM'S BRENTFORD TRANSFERS

Money is the main ingredient to success in football, besides luck. Matthew Benham, however, has managed to turn the tables. Both of his clubs are performing at a much higher level than their wealth should allow them to. He has used brain to combat the financial brawn of other teams. Through exploiting the inefficiencies of the transfer market, Benham has managed to steadily increase the prominence of both Brentford and FC Midtjylland.

Finding great players that are unrecognised by the rest of the footballing world is incredibly hard. It requires a unique recruitment system, something that Benham has cultivated using the Expected Goals data outlined in the previous chapter. We will soon look at how these statistics are utilised in the actual recruitment of players. First, though, let us study the phenomenal results that Benham's philosophy has produced.

Benham became the majority shareholder of Brentford FC in 2011, at which point he started implementing his innovative philosophy at the club. The stats which Smartodds collected started having more and more influence on the decision-making process behind transfers. Benham bought FC Midtjylland in 2014 with the aim of testing his philosophy to its logical extreme before he attempted to fully revolutionise the structure of Brentford. The purchase of the Danish club was a low-risk move. Midtjylland were in huge financial trouble and needed someone to bail them out, meaning that Benham could purchase them on the cheap. Once again, the master investor spotted an undervalued prospect. Benham restructured the Danish club to incorporate his mathematical approach to football. Midtjylland became Danish champions in Benham's first year in charge.

The success that was reaped at Midtjylland using Benham's approach gave him the confidence to install a similar system at Brentford. The West London club had been using Smartodds' stats to assist in recruitment since he took over in 2012. However, in 2015, after seeing Midtjylland's success, Benham decided to completely revolutionise Brentford's structure so as to fully incorporate his analytical methods. He was going all in.

There was just one problem, which came in the shape of Mark Warburton. The incredibly popular Brentford manager resisted the changes that Benham wished to make. Warburton was a traditionalist, believing that conventional scouting methods should take precedence over statistical modelling. Ultimately, though, Warburton couldn't accept Benham's wish to remove the manager's power of veto over transfers. The owner wanted to include his manager in transfer discussion, but in the end it would come down to a transfer committee to decide whether or not to sign a player. Benham's committee would include the manager, assistant manager, the directors of football, a handful of analysts and, of course, himself. Warburton, on the other hand, saw it as the manager's prerogative to have final say over the departure and arrival of players.

In February, Warburton and Benham mutually agreed not to renew the former's contract at the end of the season. This was much to the bemusement and displeasure of Brentford fans, who were in the dark about what was happening behind the scenes. The media made Benham out as the villain, criticising the owner for "sacking" the manager that had taken Brentford to fifth place in the Championship.

What the fans and media didn't understand was that Matthew Benham and his philosophy were infinitely more important to Brentford FC than Mark Warburton was. Managers come and go, and it wouldn't have been long until a bigger club noticed Warburton's meteoric rise and poached him from Brentford anyway. Benham and his unique recruitment system were indispensable to the club. It wasn't just the money that the owner had pumped into the West London side that made him such an important asset, but his vision and innovation. Warburton's managerial ability may have contributed in some part to Brentford's rise from mid-table in League One to the top end of the Championship, but the focal point of Brentford's incredible overachievement was Benham and his philosophy.

Most important, perhaps, was Benham's exploitation of the transfer market. The owner has used his data to consistently bring undervalued players to Brentford and Midtjylland. Benham's statistical analysis started to impact the Bees' signings at the beginning of the 2012/13 season, and with every season that followed his philosophy had more of an impact. *Figure 6-1* shows just some of Brentford's successful transfer endeavours that have been facilitated by Benham's system.

Figure 6-1: Benham's Successful Transfer Activity at Brentford FC

Player	Year Purchased	Fee	Year Sold	Fee	Profit
Stuart Dallas	2012	Free	2015	£1.3m	**£1.3m**
Will Grigg	2013	£250k	2015	£1m	**£750k**
James Tarkowski	2013	£350k	2015	£6m	**£5.65m**
Moses Odubajo	2014	£1m	2015	£3.5m	**£2.5m**
Andre Gray	2014	£500k	2015	£9m	**£8.5m**
Scott Hogan	2014	£750k	2017	£12m	**£11.25m**
Total	--	**£2.85m**	--	**£32.8m**	**£29.95m**

A profit of £29.95m on six players may seem unremarkable to the fans of Premier League clubs, who possess wealth to rival even nations. However, this is a huge amount of money for a club the size of Brentford, who had considerable financial problems before Benham took over. The owner bought Dallas, Grigg, Tarkowski, Odubajo, Gray and Hogan for just £2.85m, an investment which returned £32.8m. That money has since been invested in the next generation of Brentford players, whose value Benham hopes will inflate to a similar extent.

It is possible to put an exact monetary value on the players who Benham has sold to other teams, some of which are listed in the table above, but many of the players that Benham has signed in the last couple of years are still playing for Brentford. Almost the entirety of the Brentford playing staff are now worth in excess of what Benham paid for them. Several have been subject to bids from Premier League clubs, whilst others have performed exceptionally well in the Championship. A fifth place finish in the second tier in 2014/15 is a testament to the ability of the squad at Brentford. This exceptional achievement was followed by a ninth place finish in 2015/16, and a tenth place finish in 2016/17. In a division where previous English heavy-weights such as Aston Villa, Fulham, Nottingham Forest, Leeds, QPR, Derby and many more have struggled, Brentford's consistency has been outstanding. Their three successive top ten finishes have been achieved with one of the lowest wage bills in the division. If the league table was determined by finances, the West London side would be fighting relegation. Brentford, alongside Midtjylland, have consistently punched well above their financial weight under Benham's guidance.

NECESSITY: THE MOTHER OF INVENTION?

The advancement of technology has revolutionised the way that clubs recruit players. Old fashioned methods of scouting have become supplemented with statistical analysis, allowing clubs a deeper insight into the ability of transfer targets. Companies such as Opta and Prozone collect vast amounts of information on teams and players. They sell this data to football clubs, who are willing to pay big money for accurate stats.

The rise of statistical analysis within football has created friction between the number crunchers and the traditionalists. We have already seen how Mark Warburton struggled to accept Matthew Benham's mathematical approach to the beautiful game. One of the key themes of *Moneyball*, the book which tracks the revolutionary introduction of statistical analysis to baseball, is the conflict between the advancers of Bill James' radical new sabermetrics and the orthodox scouts who based their decisions on "gut feeling". The analysts would explore the data whilst the scouts would scorn, sneering that you cannot measure the size of a player's heart.

Back in the footballing world, Arsène Wenger has been at the forefront of the data revolution. The long-serving Arsenal manager is unusual in that he never played the sport at the top level. The Frenchman went to the University of Strasbourg, where he studied politics and economics. This is where Wenger's strong economical foundation was laid. His appointment at Arsenal was met with a fair bit of scepticism; Arsène Wenger was an unknown name in English football. The spectacle-wearing, nerdy-looking economist was certainly not a trendy appointment.

When he started out at the Gunners, Wenger did not have a single statistical analyst at his disposal. By 2016, he had over twenty mathematicians crunching the numbers for him. Wenger's use of stats was ahead of his time. He was one of the first managers to turn to data to identify undervalued prospects, a practice which is now common amongst the smarter football clubs. In 2012, Arsenal made one of their most important signings of all time for just £2m. This signing did not make many headlines, and certainly didn't create a buzz amongst fans of the North London club. In fact, the acquisition went almost entirely under the radar. The 'secret' signing which took place was Arsenal's purchase of StatDNA, a US-based football analytics company.

StatDNA was one of the fastest growing data collection organisations, and offered expert analysis on sporting performance. The measly sum of £2m that Arsenal payed is just a drop in the ocean for a club of their size, especially considering the revolutionary impact that the company had on the club's recruitment system. Statistical analysis within football is a growing field, and will only become larger and larger as technology progresses. The purchase of StatDNA was a wily investment by Wenger. Just as the manager has proved over the years that he has a knack for spotting undervalued players, he showed in this instance the ability to identify an unrecognised field (that of data analysis) which was on the verge of booming. StatDNA was in itself an undervalued prospect, one which Wenger could purchase on the cheap and use to great effect.

Arsenal and Brentford are clubs which greatly differ in fame, wealth and size. However, both are at the forefront of the statistical revolution within football. These are the only clubs in English football that possess their own personal data companies. Whilst every other team has to purchase data from companies such as Opta, Arsenal and Brentford's ownership of their own statistical analysis companies, StatDNA and Smartodds, enables them to generate their own unique information. The inimitable nature of the stats that they can collect allows them an edge over other clubs. Moreover, they don't have to pay money to purchase the data which they use.

We have already studied the innovative chance creation data which Smartodds collect, based on the Expected Goals method. The statistics which Arsenal collect are more orthodox. What Arsenal's data lacks in innovation, it makes up for in meticulousness. StatDNA are much closer to Opta than Smartodds in the way that they collect information. Whilst the Watchers at Smartodds are instructed to rate the danger levels of shot, the analysts at the other companies are trained to 'code' the matches they scrutinise. There is much more of an interest in individual match actions, such as passes, tackles and dribbles. For instance, they may look at a mere pass and focus on its specific features. How heavy was the pass? Did it reach its intended target on his stronger foot? Was it played aerially or along the ground? Every match action is assessed and coded by StatDNA, whereas Smartodds focus solely on logging Expected Goals data.

The data collected at Arsenal is incredibly specific. This can be advantageous when attempting to scouting individual players. However, when it comes to identifying which teams are inherently the best, the data which Smartodds collects is far more useful. Looking at the quantity and quality of chances that a team creates is far more *relevant* than looking at passing percentages, aerial duels and the like. The Expected Goals method is tailored to reveal which teams are the most effective, both in attack and in defence, without the need to highlight the ability of specific individual players.

Furthermore, the data that is utilised at Smartodds is far easier to collect. Watching a match and logging the probability of each shot resulting in a goal only requires one analyst, and takes ninety minutes – or however long the match lasts. Coding a match in the style of StatDNA, Opta and other data collection companies can take much longer, and often requires in excess of two analysts. Opta have three analysts logging the statistics for most games: one for each team and another one overseeing the whole procedure. These analysts collectively log between 1,600 and 2,000 actions in a typical football match. Smartodds employees will tend to log between 10 and 40, the number of scoring chances that tend to take place. This enables Benham's company to collect stats on far more teams across the globe, and pay to employ less analysts. Benham's data collection methods are far more efficient.

Another major difference between Arsenal and Brentford's use of data companies is that the latter are *required* to innovate in order to succeed. Arsenal have enough wealth that they can outspend most of the competition, ensuring that they will remain one of the heavyweights of English football for a long time to come. Brentford, on the other hand, are in unrelenting competition with richer clubs. They do not have the finances to outspend the opposition, and therefore must *outthink* their opponents if they are to succeed. Just as Arsenal's edge comes from their superior monetary backing, Brentford's edge comes in their unique form of operating. Benham's pioneering footballing philosophy has allowed the West London club to continuously punch above its financial weight.

In a sense, this is what makes Wenger's approach so admirable. Other clubs, such as Chelsea, Manchester City and Manchester United, are prone to making mistakes in the transfer market due to the fact that they have the wealth to do so. Arsenal, should they so wish, could easily join the likes of these other super-wealthy clubs in splashing cash left, right and centre. These clubs can afford the luxury of over-spending time and time again on big names who eventually flop. Manchester United spent in the region of £250m between 2014 and 2016, a figure that only managed to buy them fourth-place in 2014/15, a fifth-place in 2015/16 and a sixth-place finish in 2016/17. This kind of brainless spending is permitted because United are wealthy enough to lose such large sums with little consequence, other than some jibing from fans of less well-off clubs.

Brentford don't have the budget to be so inefficient with their spending. One mistake in the transfer market could leave the West London club in serious financial trouble. Arsenal, on the other hand, could adopt the kind of spend-for-spending's-sake approach that is deployed at clubs like Manchester United. The fact that Wenger is tight with his money often opens him up to criticism from Arsenal fans. The truth of it, however, is that Wenger is a member of a rare breed of *smart* managers. He understands the principles of investment, and he realises that spending ludicrous amounts of money on overvalued players will not dependably guarantee you success. Wenger's efficiency in the transfer market is reflected in the consistency of Arsenal's league position during his tenure. Arsenal didn't drop out of the top four places in the twenty Premier League seasons from 1995/96 to 2015/16, a remarkable achievement.

The underpinning of Billy Beane's philosophy was that, in order for the poor teams to succeed, they had to invent different ways of operating to the rich teams. When David and Goliath fight with the same weapons, there will only ever be one winner. David must outsmart his foe if he is to achieve any success. This is what Beane did in Oakland, trading out conventional scouting methods and replacing them with an emphasis on statistical recruitment. This innovative way of operating allowed Beane's team to compete with much larger sides.

The smartest clubs are those who *need* to be smart in order to compete. Whist the richest teams can win by simply outspending the opposition, the poor teams need to find a different sort of edge.

If you were to start running a football club tomorrow, and you wanted to know the best ways of operating, the trick would be to look at the clubs who are overachieving relative to their wage budget. The poorest clubs in each division are at a natural disadvantage, and thus must have some other reason for being able to compete. Brentford are one example of such a club; Benham's team have overachieved their financial expectation drastically in the last few years.

Another notable example that springs to mind is Stoke City. When the Potters were promoted to the Premier League for the first time in their history in 2008, they were one of the poorest clubs ever to grace the top division. Many tipped the Potters for immediate relegation. Nonetheless, Stoke managed an incredible 12th placed finish. Over the next few seasons they finished comfortably safe of relegation, despite having one of the lowest budgets in the top flight. They consistently outperformed the expectations that could be made based on their finances.

The reason for this overachievement wasn't pretty. Whilst Matthew Benham's unique philosophy has given Brentford an edge over the competition, and Billy Beane's statistical analysis had allowed the Oakland A's to punch above their weight, what set Stoke apart was the brand of football that they played. The Potters have become famous for playing the game in an "ugly" manner. They were incredibly physical off the ball, and displayed little finesse when on it. The philosophy which Tony Pulis had installed demanded that the players get the ball forward as quickly as possible, aiming for a target man up top, whilst sitting deep in defence. Although not exactly beautiful, Stoke's style of play proved very effective in the Premier League. When foreign players are assessed by fans, it is often contemplated whether they could perform well 'on a cold Tuesday night at Stoke'. Their aggressive approach shocked the Premier League. Other clubs didn't know how to counter it, and it gave the Potters an edge that allowed them to overachieve. Pulis fixed his team with a tactic that allowed them to survive in a league filled with much wealthier sides.

Brentford, Stoke and Oakland all had something which set them apart, an edge which gave them an advantage over the competition. However, they have all been rebuked for their methods in one capacity or another. Sport is incredibly entrenched in its ways and any deviation from the norm is met with scepticism. Beane was scorned for trying to introduce statistics into baseball, a sport which traditionally emphasised characteristics like personality and "heart", the type of features that can't be mathematically analysed. Pulis was disdained for the ugly brand of football that he implemented at Stoke, despite the fact that the Potters would have probably been relegated had they tried to play the same style of football as the rest of the Premier League.

When one assesses the manner in which each of these three men were criticised, it is probably Matthew Benham who has had the worst of it. This book exalts the Brentford and Midtjylland owner for his bold and innovative approach. The reader may not have grasped that Benham has been subjected to a large amount of disparagement, from fans of other clubs, from the media and, indeed, from some supporters of his own teams. There have been many keen for Benham's "*Moneyball*" experiment to fail. Benham's journey has not always been smooth. His methods have been met with resistance from the more traditionalist corners of the footballing world. Indeed, "sacking" popular manager Mark Warburton left Benham exposed to a barrage of abuse from all corners. Furthermore, the transition period at Brentford after the owner revolutionised its structure was a time of great uncertainty for the club.

"The first one through the wall always gets bloody", notes John Henry, the Boston Red Sox owner who tries to tempt Beane away from Oakland in the film adaptation of *Moneyball*. The cases of Pulis, Benham and Beane seem to verify this claim. Running against a rushing crowd can be difficult, but if you do it well enough then everyone else will turn around and run with you. Those who do not do it well enough will get stampeded on. There is a fine line between changing the direction of the horde and being trampled. Often, you will need to take a bit of a battering before you make any progress.

The question still begs as to why you would want to go up against the masses in the first place? Surely the safer option is to just follow the crowd? One answer is that lucrative rewards beckon for those who successfully find a novel approach. More importantly, those at the back of the stampeding herd must find some way of barging their way to the front. Pulis, Benham and Beane would all agree that necessity is the mother of invention. Had these men not steered their teams in a new direction, they would have remained last in the race. By creating a new path for their teams, they were able to lead our metaphorical herd on a new course.

Let us turn away from our running analogy and return to the world of football. Small clubs who emulate the approach of the top clubs will be doomed for failure. Tony Pulis' Stoke would have probably been relegated from the Premier League had they not tried a different approach. Billy Beane's Oakland Athletics would never have found considerable success had he not used mathematical modelling in their recruitment of players. Matthew Benham's Brentford would have remained languishing in the bottom tiers of English football had he not introduced his groundbreaking philosophy to the club. The smartest clubs are the ones who *need* to be smart.

"Necessity is the mother of invention". Who knew that the works of Plato could be so relevant to the sport of football?

Conventional Statistical Recruitment

Whilst Brentford and Midtjylland have embraced statistical analysis to its rational extreme, they are by no means the only two clubs who utilise data to inform their recruitment of players. All Premier league clubs, and many lower down the football league pyramid, have a team of analysts crunching numbers and using stats to highlight potential transfer targets. We have already seen how Arsenal purchased their own statistical analysis company. Other clubs are restricted in the sense that they have to buy data from companies such as Opta and Prozone. The latter company provide in-depth data on more than 350 professional football teams worldwide, cover over 12,000 games each year, and have statistics on more than 80,000 players. Clubs can purchase this data and use it to narrow down that list of 80,000 potential transfer targets to a shortlist of just several prospects.

The process will tend to start with the manager, who will give a detailed outlining of the kind of player he wants to recruit. The statisticians will then filter through the tens of thousands of players that are on the Prozone system. Finding a player who is the right fit is like finding a needle in a hay stack. The analysts are tasked with weeding out as much of the hay as possible, with the ultimate aim of finding a needle who will fit perfectly into their team. In the manager's detailed report of the sort of player that he wishes to sign, he will often include a list of key characteristics. Does the player need to have a high pass accuracy? How many of his aerial duels does he win? Does he cover long distances per ninety minutes?

That last question was of particular importance to Arsène Wenger when he was looking to replace star midfielder Patrick Vieira back in 2004. The most important attribute that Wenger wanted in Vieira's replacement was the ability to run long distances. Statistical analysis back in 2004 was limited, but the distances that a player covered in a match could still be accurately measured. Wenger consulted stats from various European leagues, before stumbling across a young midfielder by the name of Mathieu Flamini. The Frenchman, who was playing for Marseille at the time, was clocking an incredible eight miles (14km) per match. Wenger travelled to Marseille to see whether Flamini had the technical ability to match his dogged stamina. The Gunners boss was impressed by what he saw. He signed Flamini on a free transfer, and the player went on to become a great success at Arsenal. Four years after he signed, Flamini was sold to AC Milan in a deal nearing £10m.

When coaches are looking for a new player to sign, they will almost always highlight key attributes that the player must have. Once the analysts feed these specifications into the system (i.e. players who run over 14km each match, or players who have a pass accuracy of above 85%), they are left with a much shorter list of potential targets. The metrics that are fed into the system can be persistently refined and made more specific, thus leaving fewer and fewer players who still match all the criteria. For example, you could search for a midfielder who runs over 14km *and* has a pass accuracy of over 85% *and* a shot accuracy of over 60%, and so on and so forth. Eventually, the analysts will be left with just a handful of players who still meet every condition. The overwhelming number of potential targets has been weeded down to just a handful.

Once the data highlights the needles hiding in the giant haystack of players, analysts are employed to find out everything they can about the remaining shortlisted targets. Information on the player's injury history, wages, personal life and even their temperament will be assessed before any decision over signing the player is made. In player recruitment, just as in sports gambling, an analyst leaves no rock unturned.

Analysts will often have access to hundreds of hours of footage showing each transfer target playing for their club. This allows the scouts to provide an in-depth analysis on the playing style of each target. This evaluation is supplemented with the stats that are purchased from companies like Prozone. The level of the team and league that the player currently plays in is also assessed. You wouldn't want to assume that a player who is performing well at a vastly inferior level would make a natural step up.

If the scouts are impressed by what they see, then they hand their reports to their superiors. The most forward-thinking clubs now have a transfer committee which will read the reports and make a decision on whether or not to sign each player. Do they match the initial brief of the type of player that the manager wants to sign? If a player gets the all-clear from the transfer committee, then the club enter negotiations over a potential deal.

In reality, the data crunching part of the process is generally a lot more complex than I have outlined above. Each club differs in the models and algorithms that they use, and each analyst values certain metrics more highly than others. Teams keep their models as closely guarded secrets. A leakage of how they recruit players could eliminate any competitive advantage over other clubs in the market.

More and more football clubs have supplemented their orthodox methods of scouting with statistical analysis carried out by quants who would more commonly be found on trading floors in London and New York. Even managers of an older generation, who might be expected to lie on the traditionalist side of the argument, are converting. Claudio

Ranieri, the Italian who led Leicester City to the most remarkable title win in English football history, embraced the role of statistics within football. West Ham are another side who have adapted to the modern game by placing a strong emphasis on data analysis in their player recruitment. Rory Campbell, technical recruitment scout for the East London club, points out that whilst clubs like Manchester United are throwing hundreds of millions of pounds away on players who consistently underperform[28], players like Dimitri Payet at West Ham and N'Golo Kante and Riyad Mahrez at Leicester are being signed for a combined cost of just £16m. Using data to unearth hidden gems is helping clubs like Leicester and West Ham punch above their financial weight.

A Global League Table

Whilst most football clubs are slowly adopting the use of analytics, Brentford are leaps and bounds ahead of the rest. Matthew Benham has used the Expected Goals data which Smartodds collect to guide his player recruitment for a handful of years now. His two clubs, Brentford and Midtjylland, go several steps beyond the use of traditional statistical analysis.

For those who need a refresher; xG is a metric that analysts use to work out which teams are performing at the highest level, based on both the quantity and quality of shots that the teams take. The teams who create the largest amount of high quality chances are clearly the best teams, regardless of how many goals they *actually* score. Expected Goals are calculated by assigning each shot a probability of succeeding. For example, a missed penalty would be worth around 0.7(xG) to a team's total xG scoreline, as around 70% of penalties result in a goal. This 0.7(xG) reflects the probability of that shot scoring. In order to work out the total number

---

28 Memphis Depay (£25m), Matteo Darmian (£12.7m), Morgan Schneiderlin (£24m), Ander Herrera (£29m), Luke Shaw (£27m), Maroc Rojo (£16m), Angel Di Maria (£59.7m) and Daley Blind (£13.8m) are examples of players that Manchester United have arguably over-payed for in recent years.

of goals that a team could have expected to score in a match, one must simply add up all of the shot probabilities that were amassed.

Conventional Expected Goals analysts have measured the likelihood of individual shots hitting the back of the net based on simply the location of those efforts. This undoubtedly offers a better insight into the skill of football teams than looking at conventional stats such as shots, shots on target, possession, and so on. However, there is still the potential for a vast amount of noise to inundate this conventional xG data. For example, a shot where the ball is bouncing awkwardly has less chance of hitting the back of the net than a shot from the same position in which the ball is motionless. One of Benham's greatest innovations was to train his employees to incorporate such factors into their assessments when logging Expected Goals data. The position of a shot gives a decent indication of its danger level, but a more holistic approach is needed when assigning shot probabilities. The Watchers at Smartodds learn to more accurately assess shot probabilities than other analysts, who only use the location of the shot to inform their judgements.

Benham realises that goals are completely random events. They are therefore a poor reflection of a team's ability. Good teams can be unlucky and score few goals whilst creating lots of chances, whilst bad teams can be fortuitous and score lots of goals whilst creating few chances. Each goal is inherently random, making it hard to correctly predict the outcome of football matches. Whether a team wins or loses is often governed by blind luck.

It follows that the league table offers an inaccurate depiction of the teams' ability. The world of football tends to view the league table as the all-important deciding factor in which teams are the best. Fans quarrel incessantly about which teams will finish higher than others, which team will win the league and which teams will get relegated. The team who wins the title is considered the best team. It would be illogical to suggest anything otherwise. League tables are taken as gospel.

However, thirty-eight games (or forty-six for those Football League fans among us) is still a small sample size. The fact that so many teams are separated by just a handful of points at the end of a campaign is a testament to this. Very rarely is there nothing to play for on the last day of the season, whether it be in deciding the title, the Champions League places or the relegation zone. We have already seen how entire campaigns can be decided with the final kicks of the ball. When each individual game is governed by so much luck, and each season often comes down to an individual game, it follows that the fortune of many clubs comes down to complete and utter randomness.

This may be hard for some to hear. We would like to believe that factors such as skill and work-rate determine success. It can be difficult to accept that a whole season can come down to what is effectively chance. It seems unfair that luck can play such a large role in football, and this is probably why we tend to undervalue the impact that it has on the game. We would prefer to believe that football is deterministic; that managers and players have control of whether they win or lose. In reality, randomness heavily influences who are the winners and who are the losers.

This is good news for those who are able to quantify the uncertainty of the beautiful game. Benham has stated that he will never judge his managers on where they stand in the league table, he will judge them based on their *performances*. The difference between the two is that, whilst the league standing of a team will fluctuate due to luck, the performance of a side is completely within the managers control. This vital definition is what Benham bases his whole philosophy on. All a manager can do is ensure his team puts in decent performances. If they are unlucky, losing when they perform well, an owner should take this into account. Performance is deterministic, league ranking is not.

By monitoring the Expected Goals results of every club in Europe, Benham can work out which teams are *performing* at the highest standard. This data strips luck and randomness from football. As well as seeing how many goals each team is scoring, Benham's analysts can monitor how many goals a team *deserves* to be scoring based on their performances (the quantity and quality of chances that they are creating).

In every match that Benham's employees watch, each team is assigned an xG score based on the quality of shots that they took during the match. This method is described in Chapter 5, and relies on the Watchers at Smartodds accurately assessing the probability of each shot resulting in a goal. Each shot probability is given as a decimal; for instance, a long-shot may be assigned 0.1(xG), whilst a shot from very close range may be awarded a shot probability of around 0.7(xG). When all the decimals are added up you are left with an xG scoreline for the match. At the end of the game you will have a score that reads something like 3.2-1.4. This Expected Goals scoreline may be vastly different to the *actual* scoreline of the match, but it will be immensely more informative of the ability of the two sides. Calculating these Expected Goal scores can tell an analyst which teams have been lucky (those who are creating low quality chances, but scoring lots of goals), and which have been unlucky (those who are creating lots of high quality chances, but scoring few goals).

Benham's chance creation data can tell you more than just the xG scoreline of a match. Once you calculate this scoreline it is possible to work out the Expected Points (xP) that a team could hope to take from the game. This is done by running thousands of simulations of the game, then computing the average number of points that each team could have expected to win. The larger quantity of high quality chances a team creates, the higher number of points that they can expect to take from a game. Obviously, the highest number of points that a team can expect to take from any given fixture is three. A team who creates a plethora of scoring opportunities, and who simultaneously manage to concede very few dangerous attacks, can expect to take just below three points from the game (say, 2.8(xP)). Two very evenly matched teams will each earn about 1.3(xP)[29].

---

29 It could be easy to assume that two evenly matched teams would share around 1.5 Expected Points, seeing that there are 3 points on offer for the winning team and 1.5 is exactly half of 3. However, in the occurrence of a draw only two points are awarded, one for each team. Thus, the xP total for two evenly matched teams tends to place itself just under 1.5(xP), around the 1.3(xP) mark.

Remember that, just as with Expected Goals, the stated allocation of Expected Points is not the number of points you would *actually* expect the team to gain. It is obviously impossible for a team to actually win 1.3 points from a match. This figure simply reflects the number of points that a team could expect to win over the long run. If the game was played out thousands of times, this is the average number of points they would win. Similarly, analysts do not expect a team to achieve the impossible feat of scoring 4.3 goals. They are simply quantifying the fact that a team could expect to score just over four goals based on the quantity and quality of shots that they took.

In every game that Benham and his employees watch, each team is given both an Expected Goals total and an Expected Points total. In much the same way that points and goals translate into the league tables in real life, the analysts feed the xG and xP into a league table format. This table reflects where each team should be positioned based on their Expected Goals data, thus giving a more accurate gauge of the ability of the teams.

Let's use an example. Suppose that, in their first match of the season, Juventus are dominant and create several very good scoring opportunities. When the Shot Probabilities from the match are tallied up, the Expected Goals scoreline reads 3.2-1.1 to Juventus. This data is then keyed into a simulator, and it is calculated that the Italian side could expect to win 2.63 points from this match. However, suppose that Juventus failed to take any of their multiple chances, whilst the opposition managed to score from one of their few. The actual league table will award Juventus zero points, as they lost the match, but the xG league table will recognise that their performance was worthy of 2.63 xP.

In their second match Juventus find it much harder going. They struggle to create chances, and only manage to accumulate 0.6 Expected Points. They manage to get a draw from this match, however, and now have accumulated a total of 1 point in the *actual* league standings (zero points from the first game added to the one that they earnt in the second). The analysts at Smartodds follow the same procedure, adding the 2.7(xP) from the first game to the 0.6(xP) in the second game. Thus,

Juventus could have expected to collect 3.3 points from their opening two games of the season based on their performances. The analysts can conclude that Juventus are unlucky to have only accrued one point from their opening two games. The xG league table will suggest they should be higher up the *actual* table than they are.

This is the methodology that Matthew Benham has used to classify teams, creating a ranking system that acknowledges the *true ability* of each side. The Expected Goals data that he collects eliminates most of the luck from football. Additionally, using xP allows one to assign each side a more specific number of points (say 1.4 instead of 1). The league table can become much more precise as a result of this, as well as giving a much more profound indication as to which teams are performing the best and which have simply been lucky.

The implications on each individual league table are obvious. Whichever leagues Smartodds cover across the globe can be translated into an Expected Goals table. These xG league tables will incorporate Expected Points instead of actual points, and Expected Goals instead of actual goals. One can even calculate the Expected Goal difference of a team; simply take the total xG that a team has scored, and subtract the number of xG they have conceded.

Whether it be Premier League, La Liga, League Two or the Azerbaijan Premier League, if Smartodds have collected the chance creation data on the division's matches, they have the ability to create an Expected Goals league table. This table will show an analyst where each team deserves to be based on their level of performance. It will offer a more accurate reflection of each team's ability than the *actual* table. Rasmus Ankersen, co-director of football at Brentford, stated that "telling people the league table lies is like telling people that the Earth is flat. All their preconceptions are being challenged, and the media won't accept it".

The innovation goes even further. From looking at past matches between sides from different divisions, Smartodds' analysts have the ability to create a *global league table*. This is one giant league table which incorporates every professional football team that Smartodds collects data on.

Each season, hundreds of matches take place between teams from different divisions. Within England, the majority of these matches take place in competitions such as the FA Cup, the League Cup and the EFL Trophy. Almost every team in England is eligible to take part in the FA Cup, a tournament which often pits lower league sides against the giants of the Premier League. The League Cup is similar, but only includes teams from the top four divisions of English football. The EFL Trophy is contested between teams who reside in League One and League Two, the third and fourth tiers of the English pyramid. Most of the games in these competitions feature teams from different divisions playing against one another. By collecting the Expected Goals data of matches between teams of different divisions, Smartodds analysts are able to accurately gauge the difference in ability between leagues.

For example, let's say that Smartodds collect data on hundreds of matches in which one team is from the Premier League and one is from the Championship. The analysts can create algorithms and formulae to determine the extent to which the Premier League sides tend to dominate the game. Do they create far more scoring opportunities than the teams from the division below, or do the Championship clubs tend to hold their own? From analysing the data, they can formulate a concise image of the gap in standard between the two divisions. The same process can easily be repeated with matches between teams from the Championship and League One, and from League One and League Two.

Every league in Europe is, in fact, comparable to one another, as long as there are fairly frequent matches between sides from the different divisions. The European competitions, principally the Champions League and Europa League, facilitate matches between clubs of different countries throughout the continent. Additionally, multiple friendlies are played between teams from different European leagues. Thus, any league in Europe can be compared to any other league in which teams from the two countries compete. Smartodds analysts can take data from matches between, for example, Premier League and La Liga sides and see who tends to perform better. They can utilise their advanced models to see which league generally operates at a higher level.

However, one cannot simply state that one league is better than the other, for a team who is at the bottom of one division will almost certainly be worse than a team who is at the top of the other. Although one could argue that the Premier League is of a higher quality than Ligue 1, very few would contest that Bournemouth are a better side than Paris Saint-Germain. European football is like an enormous spider web, with each match that takes place between two clubs of different divisions being the equivalent of a single thread. By plugging the information from each individual thread into their models, the analysts at Smartodds can create an accurate assessment of each team's ability based on their ranking in their own "domestic" Expected Goals league table, coupled with the ranking of their division amongst Europe's other divisions.

At the end of this data analysis, the Smartodds analysts are left with a league table that incorporates every team that they collect data on. Every single team in Europe is lumped into one giant league table, each competing against one another as if in one huge division. Whenever your club plays a match, you naturally consider the implications on your league standing. "If we win, and that other team lose, we could move up to seventh place", the anonymous fan might state. However, within Matthew Benham's framework, each club is not just competing with teams in its actual division (be it Premier League, Championship, Moldova Second Division, whatever), it is also competing with *every other professional football team in Europe*. A fan with access to Benham's global league table could support Oldham Athletic and excitedly exclaim, "If we win today, and Ordabasy of the Kazakhstan Premier League lose, we could move up to 675th in the table![30]"

Actually this is not what the fan would be saying at all. Wins, draws and losses do not count for anything in Benham's system. What counts

---

30 Note that I have no idea where either Oldham Athletic or Ordabasy reside in Benham's global league table. Nor do I know how many teams are accounted for in his rankings, although I do know that Smartodds collect data for almost every professional football club in Europe, and many on other continents.

is the quantity and quality of attacking opportunities that you both create and concede. The fan would be more correct in exclaiming that, "If we create a large number of high quality chances, whilst simultaneously conceding very few, we will amass a dominant Expected Goals scoreline and thus win a large number of Expected Points. This means that we will move higher up in both our domestic xG league table and the global xG league table!"

Benham's system gives analysts an idea of which teams are performing at the highest level when luck is stripped from the equation. For coaches, scouts and gamblers, performance is all that should matter. The rest is all down to randomness. You may not be able to win titles by scoring lots of xG, by accumulating a large number of xP and by finishing first in the Expected Goals league table, but you certainly give yourself the best chance of doing so.

BRENTFORD'S REVOLUTIONARY RECRUITMENT SYSTEM

The data that Smartodds collects has two primary functions; to inform the professional gamblers who buy the stats from the company, and to assist Brentford and Midtjylland in their recruitment of players.

Benham's Expected Goals league tables can aid the professional gamblers who purchase such data. The fundamental objective of xG is to eliminate chance from football. This is the aim of anyone who forecasts the sport for a living. Those who make the most accurate predictions will be the most successful. Bettors who use Benham's formula and buy into the general Smartodds philosophy will almost always make a large profit. Anyone with a solid grasp of the principals covered in the first few chapters of this book, supplemented with the Expected Goals data that Smartodds collects, has the potential to make a lot of money.

The professional gamblers who work with Smartodds simply have to cross-reference Smartodds' Expected Goals league tables with the *actual* league tables. Remember that gambling is about finding the value in the market. If the bettor spots that the bookmakers have undervalued the chance of a team winning, he should place a bet on it. Whilst a conventional gambler may look to the league table to provide an assessment on the ability of a team, Smartodds' clients are able to look at the much more informative Expected Goals league table. This tells them how well each team is performing once luck is removed from the equation, thus giving them an edge over other bettors and the bookmakers.

Gamblers also tend to focus on the form of the two sides to inform their betting on a match of football. How well has each team performed in their last five or six matches? A conventional gambler might see that a team hasn't lost any of their previous six games, and decide to place a bet on this in-form side. However, a Smartodds gambler can look at the xG scoreline of each of the team's last six matches. Perhaps the team has simply been lucky, and should have lost three or four of those matches. In this instance, they have been performing at a lower standard than their results suggest, and placing a bet on them to win is clearly a bad idea.

Conversely, the bettors who work with Smartodds will look out for teams who have had a bad run of results, but who have actually been *performing* well. These teams have been unlucky but, as we found out earlier in the book, their form will generally regress to the mean. A team who have been creating a lot of good scoring opportunities, but who have not been scoring many, are likely to be undervalued by the bookmakers. Goals scored and points gained are the key performance indicators when it comes to football. This gives Benham and Smartodds, who are able to utilise their more profound data based on the Expected Goals method, an edge over those who set the odds.

Here is a summary of Benham's innovative system. First, Smartodds' Watchers watch matches and gather the shot probabilities for each team. Second, they add up all of the shot probabilities to leave an xG scoreline for each match. Third, these matches are simulated thousands of times (a task which takes less than a second with modern technology), and work out the Expected Points that each team takes from each match. Fourth, they generate an Expected Goals league table based on the number of xP and xG that each team has scored. Fifth, analysts trawl through the bookmakers' odds looking for outcomes that they might have undervalued. Sixth, a bet is placed if the data suggests the bookmakers are undervaluing the chance of an event occurring. This simple methodology has allowed Benham and Smartodds to consistently beat the bookmakers.

The second function that Smartodds serves is to assist in player recruitment for Brentford and FC Midtjylland. We have already studied the conventional methods of statistical recruitment that other clubs practice. Benham's two football clubs both operate with a similar process, but take things one step further. The signing of players is where Benham's global league table really excels. Remember how Benham views player recruitment; each signing is an investment that he will look to sell on for more money than he bought them for. Hence, the trick is to spot the undervalued talent.

Brentford have signed a lot of players from abroad in recent years. There are a number of reasons for this. Firstly, the English football leagues are easily accessible to most managers and scouts. Even League Two, the lowest of the four tiers in professional English football, is very popular compared to other leagues in Europe. The average attendance in the English fourth tier surpasses that of the top divisions in many other European countries. Thus, there are very few "hidden gems" within English football. A great player languishing in the lower regions of the English Football League will quickly be spotted and recruited by one of the top clubs (who will often overpay for his services, something that Benham is incredibly wary of doing). Just as bets on obscure European Leagues are of better value because the bookies pay less attention to such leagues, so too are the players of these leagues of better value because British scouts pay them less attention.

The second reason that Brentford have tended to sign foreign players is that they are a lot cheaper. The transfer fee for an English player will be reasonably more than the fee for a player of equal ability from a less accessible country. Similarly, the wages that Brentford would have to pay the player would be a lot higher if he was from another English club. This seems counterintuitive. Why should one player be more expensive than the other when both are of equal ability? The answer lies in the generally accepted notion that the English Football League takes a certain amount of time to acclimatise to. It is regularly suggested that English football is a lot more physical and high tempo than other leagues around the world. Thus, when you pay for a player from another English club, you are paying for his ability *as well as* the fact that he is proven in the English game. Signing foreign players is seemed as risky as they may flop in a new country. They might not be accustomed to the physicality of their new league. They might become unsettled and get homesick. Such risks can be averted by signing a player from another English club, but it comes at a price.

Benham is sceptical of the belief that the English divisions are vastly different to other European leagues. Indeed, many of the foreign players that the Brentford owner has brought in have been huge successes in English football. There is no palpable evidence to suggest that players from abroad tend to struggle when they come over to England. Thus, transfer targets at other English clubs tend to be unnecessarily overvalued, prompting Benham to look abroad to find the best deals.

Smartodds collect data on almost every professional football team throughout Europe. The stats that companies like Opta and Prozone supply, the stats which most clubs buy and use for their recruitment, is only at its most accurate for the top European divisions. Remember that the data which Opta collect is complex and takes time to log. Measuring every single action that takes place in a football match, as Opta do, takes hours and requires three analysts. Thus, there is little incentive for the company to collect stats on smaller European leagues, as there is much less demand for this data.

On the other hand, Smartodds are able to easily collect information on even the most indistinct of leagues, due to the fact that Benham's data collection method is so simple. Anyone who is able to accurately determine the probability of a shot resulting in a goal has the ability to calculate a match's xG scoreline. The simplicity involved in collecting chance creation data, rather than logging every pass, shot, tackle and the like, means that very few other football clubs will have such a large sample of information to analyse than Brentford and Midtjylland.

Not only does the Expected Goals data that Smartodds collect allow them to analyse a greater number of teams, it also provides much more profound insights. The xG global league table is a tremendously useful tool. Analysts are able to rank all European clubs in order, as if they all play in one enormous league. Benham scours the table for clubs who are performing at a much higher level than their *actual* league position would suggest. Are there any small sides who are playing a standard of football that is much higher than you would expect? In other words, are there any teams who might be *undervalued* by the rest of the footballing world? These teams, the ones performing much better than their results or league position are letting on, are more than likely to have underrated players in their squad.

Finding the undervalued teams leads you to the undervalued players. As with gambling, the recruitment of players is about spotting the value in the market. If Benham finds a team who are performing at an exceptionally high standard, he will ask his analysts to file a report on the reasons why. Benham looks for high quality footballers who play for indistinct-yet-overachieving clubs, footballers who he might be able to sign for rock-bottom prices.

Tim Sparv is not a name that many English football fans will be familiar with, but he is perhaps one of the most important signings in football history. Sparv was the first major success of Benham's system, and is an ideal example of how Benham utilises his global Expected Goals league table in player recruitment. The Midtjylland owner spotted that Greuther Fürth, a German second division side, were sitting unusually high up in his global xG league table. The small club were performing at a level much higher than was being reflected in their results and league standing. In other words, the side were creating a high quantity and quality of chances, and conceding a low quantity and quality of chances, but had been unlucky with their results. In fact, Benham's model suggested that, although they were languishing in the second division of German football, Greuther Fürth were actually playing at an English Premier League standard. Benham realised that the players at Greuther were worth checking out.

He asked his analysts to compile a report on the team, wanting to know if there were any individual players who were responsible for Greuther's exceptional performances. One obvious player stood out; a central defensive midfielder named Tim Sparv. The analysts identified Sparv as one of Greuther Fürth's key players, and decided to buy him. Despite only signing for a reported £255k, Sparv excelled at Midtjylland and has become one of their star players.

Another example, one that we have already covered in an earlier section, is Andre Gray. In 2014, Benham's models showed that Luton Town were playing at an incredibly high standard considering they were a non-league side. Benham and his analysts had a look at their squad, and identified Gray as the primary reasons for Luton's good performances. The Hatters were creating an abundance of high quality chances, and Benham's analysts concluded that this was down to the attacking prowess of Gray. Brentford bought the striker for £500k and sold him a year later for a fee rising to £9m.

Benham and his analysts look at the Expected Goals league table to inform Brentford and Midtjylland's signings, but they also have the ability to be even more specific in the metrics that they use. If one of these clubs needs a new defender, the analysts can look for teams who are not just ranked highly on the global xG league table, but who are also conceding very few scoring opportunities. A team who have very few high quality shots counted against them are more likely to have a strong defensive line, meaning their defenders are worth a closer look at. Conversely, a team who are creating a high number of dangerous attacks are likely to have a strong set of forward players.

Benham's transfer record at both Brentford and Midtjylland has been exceptional. The growth of both clubs has been founded on their ability to continually upgrade their squads. Sign players on the cheap, sell them for a profit, re-invest that money in buying more undervalued players, before selling them when they become overvalued. By repeating this cycle, Benham has been able to raise his clubs to new levels. This is the blueprint that every team should follow; the difficulty lies in actually identifying undervalued players. When everybody is trying to spot the diamond in the rough, the most sparkling of jewels will be quickly spotted by the clubs with the best recruitment networks. The top clubs have the most money to spend on infrastructure, but Brentford have managed to turn the tables through innovation. Benham's pioneering recruitment system based on the Expected Goals method has allowed Brentford and Midtjylland to achieve accomplishments beyond their fans' wildest dreams.

The Undervalued Nature of Set-Pieces

One insight that the Expected Goals data has given Smartodds analysts is that set-pieces are drastically undervalued in football. A large proportion of dangerous shots are a result of dead ball situations; be it corners, free kicks or even throw-ins. These set-piece situations represent positions of maximum opportunity – otherwise known as "POMOs". There are not many areas of football which allow set routines to be developed. The fluid nature of the game means that training is more about developing technique and working on fitness than devising the kind of rehearsed 'moves' that exist in sports such as rugby or American football. Set-pieces provide the only real opportunity for football coaches to develop a series of strategic routines which can be deployed in a match situation. They can be devised and practiced in training, then replicated in-game.

Rasmus Ankersen has suggested that human sentiment creates an inefficiency when it comes to set-pieces. "People in football tend to feel that a set-piece goal is not worth as much as a normal goal, which is obviously romance", the Dane lamented. Benham's right-hand man highlights that teams neglect set-piece practice in training, despite the fact that around one-third of goals come from such routines. "Could you imagine a company that spends 10 percent of its time on an area which produces 35 percent of its revenue? That's what happens in football."

Benham has adopted the same stance, and has made set-pieces a major focus for both of his teams. In 2015, the Brentford owner caused a stir by bringing Bartek Sylwestrzak to the club. Sylwestrakz is a professional free kick coach who focuses primarily on the technique that players use to kick the ball. This job description prompted derision from various corners of the footballing world. Surely professional footballers don't need to be coached on how to kick the ball? Nevertheless, when one considers the implications of Sylwestrakz's coaching, it begins to make sense.

The specialist kicking coach trains players to hit the ball with top-spin, as opposed to the more standard side-spin. When curling it with the inside of their boot, players rely on gravity to bring the ball back towards ground, whilst it simultaneously swerves irrepressibly off to one side. This type of shot is much harder to get on target and is much easier for a goalkeeper to save. The path of the ball remains constant, making it simpler for a keeper to predict where he needs to catch it. On the other hand, shots with top-spin are renowned for swerving and dipping erratically, whilst also carrying a greater momentum towards goal. They are much easier to get on target, as their projection is essentially in a straight line, and can easily trouble the goalkeeper with dip. Over the years free-kick takers such as Ronaldo and Bale have mastered the art of striking the ball with top-spin, otherwise known as hitting a "knuckle-ball".

Sylwestrakz even has his own website which he uploads videos onto. In these clips he gives a few basic tips on how to strike the ball well, often using players such as Juninho, Marcos Assuncao and Ryan Williams as examples of how to do it. In fact, when Sylwestrakz moved to Brentford, he recommended that they sign Ryan Williams. The young midfielder had just been released by League Two Morecambe, but Championship side Brentford decided to sign him on a free transfer. Williams featured heavily in Sylwestrakz's videos as a case study for his training methods. Benham's dedication to set-piece excellence was such that he was willing to listen to his specialist kicking coach and recruit this anonymous midfielder. Ryan

Williams didn't really get a look in at Brentford, but was used to train the other squad members in how to strike the ball. When Benham reflected on the fact that Williams had made few appearances for the Bees, he said his transfer had carried "very little risk, with the potential for large returns should it come off".

Brentford's other main staffing recruitment in the Summer of 2015, the period when Benham was overhauling the structure of the club to facilitate his analytical philosophy, was Gianni Vio. The Italian joined Brentford from AC Milan, having previously worked at Fiorentina and Catania. His unique approach to set-piece training meant that he was regarded as one of the best free kick coaches in Europe. His capture was quite a triumph for the West London club.

Whereas Sylwestrakz focused on the actual striking of the ball, Vio was dedicated to the set-up surrounding set-pieces. At points in the 2015/16 season, Brentford would draw mockery from fans in all four corners of the ground because of their bizarre free kick formations. At one point, the Bees set up a four man wall of their own in front of the opposition wall, and aligned another three players in front of *that* wall, leaving seven of their own players between the ball and the goal. As Alan Judge ran in to take the free kick, Brentford's three players in the first wall splintered off to the side, whilst the four men in the second wall backed into the Birmingham wall. The aim was to unsight the opposition wall and goalkeeper, allowing Judge a greater chance of scoring.

Making marginal gains is a cornerstone of Benham's philosophy. For every dangerous free-kick that a team is awarded, the opposition goalkeeper has a limited amount of time to react to which way the ball is travelling. The further out the free-kick, the more time the goalkeeper has to react. Placing some of your players in the opposition wall unsights the goalkeeper, thus reducing the time he has to work out which way the ball is directed. This essentially makes the target that little bit bigger for the free-kick taker. In a sport decided by such thin margins, and where you can guarantee yourself several set-piece opportunities during a match, devising innovative tactics such as Brentford's is very intelligent.

Rumour has it that Benham even has a Whatsapp group chat involving analysts, coaches and a couple of players in which they post ideas of potential set-piece routines, supplemented with the occasional video of inventive dead ball sequences which have worked for other clubs in the past. Both the logic behind Benham's set-piece emphasis and the execution of the philosophy have proved to be valid.

Let's start with the logic. In Gianni Vio's book *Dead Balls: The 15-Goal Striker*, the Italian outlines the undervalued nature of set-pieces. A striker who scores fifteen goals a season can get ruled out through injury or suspension. Football players are unreliable, and will not always be able to create scoring opportunities each week. However, set-pieces occur in every single game, without fail. A coach who is able to devise specialist set-piece routines, from which around fifteen goals can be scored in a season, is equally as valuable as a striker who scores fifteen goals – if not more valuable, as the set-piece coach cannot get injured. The logic behind utilising set-pieces to create a larger quantity of high quality scoring opportunities makes footballing sense.

The execution of this theory has validated the logic. Brentford scored far more goals from set-pieces in the 2015/16 season, following the appointment of Sylwestrakz and Vio, than they did in the previous campaign. Benham's other club, FC Midtjylland, have had even greater success. The Danish side employed the services of Sylwestrakz a season before Brentford did[31] – the campaign in which they won their first ever Superliga title. Midtjylland's set-piece prowess was a big contributor to their title success. The Danes scored an average of around one goal a game from set-plays. Remarkably, on four separate occasions Midtjylland scored four goals from set-pieces in one match. Atletico Madrid were the only European team to score more set-play goals than FC Midtjylland in 2014/15.

When FC Midtjylland faced Manchester United in the Europa League the following season, one of Sylwestrakz's routines caught the eye of

---

31 Benham saw the success that Sylwestrakz's methods were having at Midtjylland in 2014/15, and decided to move him to Brentford for the 2015/16 season.

United manager Louis Van Gaal. United used one of Midtjylland's set-piece routines in their following match, a cup tie against Shrewsbury Town. The Red Devils erected a wall of their own behind the Shrewsbury wall. As Juan Mata ran up to take the free kick, the United wall splintered, unsighting the Shrewsbury keeper, and the ball ended up in the back of the net.

Just as Benham searched for undervalued stocks in the world of finance, searches for undervalued odds in the world of betting, and searches for undervalued players in the transfer market, he has identified set-pieces as having undervalued potential when it comes to creating scoring opportunities. Every single innovation that his teams adopt can add an extra percentage point or two to their chances of succeeding. The professional gambler truly is one of the smartest footballing thinkers that the beautiful game has ever seen.

CONCLUSION

IN MANY WAYS, FOOTBALL IS a stupid sport. Moreover, centuries of tradition are preventing it from getting any more intelligent. If Isaiah Berlin could extend his theory of the hedgehog and the fox to cover modern-day football, it would be diagnosed as a stone-wall hedgehog. There is an enormous reluctance within the beautiful game to adapt to new ideas. Making bold and outlandish predictions, whilst living life by broad and overarching principles, is what makes hedgehogs awful forecasters. Foxes are much more sensitive to new information, and are keen to adapt their predictions as often as possible. However, it is exactly these qualities which make foxes awful pundits. Foxes will tend to sit on the fence, giving answers in probabilistic terms. They are tedious and mathematical in their approach to prediction-making. On the other hand, despite being over-confident in their forecasting abilities, hedgehogs make for more entertaining viewing.

The hedgehog is stubborn, inflexible and bullish. The world of football is inundated with such characters. Almost every prominent manager in the sport leans more towards the tag of hedgehog than fox. José Mourinho, whose emotional blinding we studied in the second chapter, is a model hedgehog. The Portuguese is unwilling to change his ideas about the way football is played. He is overconfident in his ability as a manager, and overvalues the impact that his presence has on a team. These qualities make him the ideal candidate for a post-match interview, or the focus of a back-page piece in the national newspaper. They also make him a flawed prediction-maker.

Whilst the hedgehog thrives off the attention of the masses, the contrary could be said for the fox. Benham is a prime example of a fox; the Brentford and Midtjylland owner is continuously updating his forecasts, allowing for new information. Most importantly, Benham thinks probabilistically. When asked by Rasmus Ankersen whether he thought Brentford would get promoted in 2013/14, he responded, "there is a 42.3% chance that Brentford will get promoted". A hedgehog would have perhaps given an emotional "yes" or "no" answer, but Benham's awareness of the impact of luck allowed him to give a more accurate answer.

The other foxes in this book, of which there are few, display similar characteristics. Tony Bloom, the owner of Brighton and Hove Albion and Benham's closest rival, tends to be cautious in his approach to prediction-making. The professional gambler is always gathering and analysing as much information as he can. Billy Beane is another who could be appropriately described as a fox. The Oakland Athletics general manager showed immense flexibility to embrace a more statistical approach to baseball. Beane's adopting of new ideas that were being rejected by the rest of the sport was incredibly fox-like.

Hopefully this book will inspire the birth of a new race of foxes. A more open approach to sporting methods can only lead to progress, and embracing analytics is the first step.

THE FUTURE OF xG

The overall aim of this book has been to promote a smarter footballing philosophy. The first few chapters focused on the predictive flaws in our conventional statistical inference, in our emotional bias and in the world of media. For those who struggle with vices like alcoholism, the first step to recovery is to admit to the problem. In the first half of this book, we confessed to ourselves that we are imperfect predictive entities. Humans are very poor at forecasting the future, yet, incredibly, we are almost always overconfident in our prophecies. Having admitted and studied our flaws, we can hopefully start to make more accurate and truthful predictions.

The second half of the book highlighted methods which we can use to analyse the sport of football. The first half asked *why* we are flawed predictors, whilst the second half asked *how* we could improve. It is crucial that we understand the principles laid out in the first half if we are to deploy the pioneering techniques laid out in the second. Hopefully, through learning how to calculate the bookies' odds, and seeing how such establishments make their money, readers can successfully bash the bookmakers.

Of course, a primary intention of this book was to reveal and explore the innovative way that Matthew Benham has used statistics, particularly the Expected Goals method, to achieve success in the world of football. For years, people have been searching for a footballing equivalent of baseball's *Moneyball*. Many concluded that data couldn't permeate the beautiful game in the same way, due to the dynamic and flowing nature of football. These people were simply looking at the wrong stats. The general consensus was that there must be a new way of analysing possession, passing accuracy, distance covered, and other conventional statistics. Benham did not find a new way of analysing old data, but developed a whole new system for creating data altogether.

This system, based on the Expected Goals method, cuts right to the core of footballing knowledge. The best teams are not those who score the most goals, but those who create the highest quantity and quality of scoring opportunities. Whilst everyone else has been trying to create complex algorithms into which they can feed irrelevant statistics, Benham has taken the very essence of football (the ability of teams to create and prevent scoring prospects) and found a way of quantifying it. Goals are what *really* matter. Stats that don't directly relate to scoring opportunities are, to some extent, just background noise.

Studying Expected Goals offers a much more accurate reflection of the ability of football teams than looking at stats such as 'Shots', 'Shots on Target' and 'Possession'. Thus, it is reasonable to assume that fans, clubs and the media are all likely to embrace it as a new method of analysis. In addition to Expected Goals, the xG league table methodology that Benham has deployed at Smartodds would be of similar interest to the footballing world. This new method of assessing football is likely to enter the mainstream in the coming years.

Almost any metric could be made more accurate by calculating its expected value. For example, we could assign midfielders an Expected Assists (xA) total. Luck influences the amount of assists that a player clocks up in a season. Consider a midfielder who has a prolific striker playing ahead of him. This player is likely to clock up a larger number of assists than a player of identical quality who is playing behind a poor forward. How can we tell how good each of these players *actually* are at providing assists? We can take each key pass that they make in the final third and assess the probability that the average forward would score from where the ball is received. A pass which is accurate and precise could achieve an Expected Assist score of 0.7(xA), whilst a poor pass which forces the forward to stretch for the ball could be just 0.15(xA). Over the course of each game, or each season, a player would accumulate a total number of xA. Each player's Expected Assists total could be compared to that of other players, and an xA Table could be formed to rank the ability of the individuals. This would provide a much more accurate reflection of who the best assisters are, due to the fact that luck and randomness are being stripped from the equation.

We have seen how Benham has used the Expected Goals method to assess the ability of teams, but analysts are also using the metric to analyse individual player ability. For example, Harry Kane scored twenty-nine goals in the 2016/17 Premier League season. An analyst could look at every shot that he took in this particular campaign and give each one a probability of finding the net. Adding up all of these shot probabilities would give you the total number of goals that you would have expected the striker to score. Suppose the Englishman took seventy-five shots over the course of the season, thirty of which with a shot probability of 0.1, twenty with a shot probability of 0.3, fifteen with a shot probability of 0.5

and ten with a shot probability of 0.7. The following expected value equation will tell us how many goals Kane should have scored:

(0.1 x 30) + (0.3 x 20) + (0.5 x 15) + (0.7 x 10) = Expected Goals
*3 + 6 + 7.5 + 7 = **23.5***

Based on the prior probability that Kane had on scoring each of his shots, he should have amassed 23.5 goals over the course of the 2016/17 campaign. This leaves us with an interesting question: how do we account for the fact that Kane actually scored twenty-nine goals, 5.5 more than we could have expected him to? Some analysts attribute this to striking efficiency, claiming that players who outperform their expected goal totals are clearly high quality players. Others would assert that Kane was simply lucky to score a higher amount of goals than expected, acknowledging that there will always be variance in such metrics.

Members of the football analytics community often debate over whether teams should look to sell strikers who are outperforming their Expected Goals. In other words, are strikers who are scoring more goals than is expected of them likely to regress to their mean level of performance? If so, it would be wise for clubs to sell them whilst they are overvalued. The debate appears to have reached a consensus that, ultimately, a substantial sample size is needed in order to reach a conclusion. Players who consistently outperform their Expected Goals totals, players such as Lionel Messi, are clearly excellent footballers. Their overachievement can be accredited to skill over luck. Messi creates space for himself to shoot that other players wouldn't, and is an excellent finisher. There are other players who outperform expectations for brief periods, but who have simply been lucky. An example is someone like Charlie Austin, who just happened to go through a spell of scoring lots of hard chances. In reality, we must accept there is probably a blend of both skill and luck at play when a striker who is outperforming (or underperforming) their Expected Goals total.

Whilst Benham's system allows a team's performance level to be accurately assessed, individual player ability is much more difficult to accurately measure. Further problems arise when assessing whether a forward with a higher Expected Goals total is better than one who could have expected to score less goals. Is Kane, who amassed 23.5(xG) in the 2016/17 season, a far better player than Jermain Defoe, who accumulated 12.8(xG) in the same campaign? Some would argue that Kane worked himself into better positions, made better runs and created better shooting opportunities for himself, making him the superior player. Others would point out that Defoe played for a much weaker team. His Sunderland teammates, who were relegated in this campaign, would have provided Defoe with a much less shooting opportunities than Kane's Tottenham comrades.

Clearly there is still a lot to be learnt about the Expected Goals methods, in particular when assessing individual player performance. Nonetheless, expected value has the potential to dominate the statistical sphere within football. Benham only has the manpower to collect data on Expected Goals, the key indicator of a team's performance. However, should his philosophy be embraced by the sport, the increased interest would lead to more thorough analysis of expected value. We have seen how assists can be assigned a probability of resulting in a goal, allowing us to work out xA totals. Indeed, each cross, tackle, pass, save or any other action which takes place in football could be given an expected chance of succeeding.

The beautiful thing about Benham's Expected Goals method is that *it can be used to analyse absolutely any football team*. Whether you are watching two Premier League titans going head-to-head live on your high definition television, or simply sitting on a park bench watching your local Sunday League team, you can use Benham's data collection system to work out the Expected Goals scoreline of the two sides. Even if you are coaching a schoolboy team and wish to work out your true level of performance, you can collect chance creation data by assigning each effort at goal a probability of scoring. Working out the sum of all of each side's shot probabilities will give you the number of goals that you could expect to have been scored, and to have been conceded.

It doesn't matter in what setting, or in which era, a match took place. If you wanted to, you could watch a recording of England's 1966 World Cup final and work out the Expected Goals scoreline of the game. It would be interesting to find out whether England really deserved to win the most important match in the nation's history. A firm grasp on what constitutes a dangerous shot is all that is required to deploy Benham's system.

Whatever the future holds for football analytics, Matthew Benham's utilising of the Expected Goals method to guide his two football clubs has been a huge stride forward. The Brentford and Midtjylland owner has used pioneering statistical methods to massively outperform financial expectations. Over time, it is inevitable that Benham's edge will be eliminated, as other clubs gain wind of his philosophy and adopt it as their own. The playing field will level again, before another individual arrives to innovate the sport once more. Benham's story is unique in that never before has such a large advance taken place in a sport that is so strongly averse to change.

THE NEXT THOUSAND YEARS OF ENGLISH FOOTBALL

Prediction-making is hard, and it gets harder the further into the future you attempt to predict. Analysts could fairly accurately forecast the Premier League table next season. However, they could not even attempt to predict the position of each Premier League team in twenty years' time. As time progresses, the ever-increasing randomness that is induced makes it more and more difficult to make an accurate forecast.

Consider a game of chess. After the very first move, there are only twenty possible ways in which the board could lie. If one was tasked with predicting where every piece lay after the first move of a chess match, they would have about a 5% chance of being correct. After the second move of the game, the black side's first move, there are 400 possible ways in which the board could lie. After four total moves, this figure becomes 8,902. After six turns, it rises to 197,742. After ten moves, there are 4,897,256 ways in which the board could be arranged. Any chess game that has lasted more than a handful of turns is unique. As the game progresses, more and more noise enters the picture, making it harder to predict how the board will lie.

The task of predicting what the English Football League will look like in just a handful of seasons' time is equally as challenging as predicting the lay-out of a chess board. There are so many different possibilities that could take place, and as time goes on we become more and more uncertain. The potential variance gets increasingly larger as time progresses.

Even the most successful predictors of football struggle to separate the signal from the noise a couple of years down the line. *Football Manager* is perhaps the most fox-like entity that has been described in this whole book. The video game uses an incredible amount of information, displaying hundreds of stats on each footballer that exists worldwide. The *Football Manager* database is by far the largest collection of team and player data that exists. The machinery which processes the game has no unfounded biases, as computers can act a lot more rationally than humans. Technology is dispassionate in a way that human beings never can be. The game thinks entirely in probabilistic terms. It assesses the chance of each team winning each match based on form, injuries and the like. *Football Manager* follows all of the rules for predictive success that are laid out in this book.

Fansites and blogs often use the video game to simulate how developments within the real world of football will affect the future. For example, when José Mourinho was appointed manager of Manchester United, a blogger simulated the next three years in the game to see what impact his appointment would have on the club[32]. Of course, we should not take these *Football Manager* replications too seriously. They are simply a bit of predictive fun, but can still offer a good insight into the role that chance plays within football.

The most intense simulation that has been carried out using *Football Manager* forecasted the thousand-year period of the English leagues

---

32 For those interested, the game predicted that United would win the Premier League in Mourinho's third season in charge (2018/19).

starting from the beginning of the 2015/16 season. It took fifty-eight days of continuous real-life simulation for the millennial landmark to be reached. Studying the shifts in footballing power between the present day and 3015 highlights the extreme impact that randomness has on the sport, as well as demonstrating how data becomes increasingly noisy as time progresses.

So, how did *Football Manager* forecast the next thousand years to play out? Here is an extract from the report:

2000s: The first surprise of the simulation was Derby winning the Premier League in 2021, with Southampton coming in third position. Their success faded pretty quickly, but a surprisingly dominant Stoke took over, trading titles with Manchester United and occasionally Newcastle. Coventry also had a dominant spell, winning 6 titles in 7 years. Arsenal and Burnley entered the mix as contenders as well as Nottingham Forest and Blackburn. The century ended with a very dominant Manchester United.

2100s: This century started with a very powerful Stoke, as they won 7 titles in a row as well as 14 titles in 17 years. Later, Burnley became dominant as the Premier League turned into a power struggle between the two teams. Newcomers West Brom and Barnsley also stole some titles, especially Barnsley, who won quite a few in the last couple decades.

2200s: With Stoke on the decline, a newcomer filled their spot: Sheffield United. They traded titles mostly with Man U, though later with Barnsley and Southend United. This century had no real dominance, as teams struggled to string titles together. Though teams such as MK Dons, Hull, and Plymouth came and went, the five big players were Sheffield United, Arsenal, Barnsley, Southend, and Burnley.

2300s: Southend replaced Sheffield's position of dominance, winning many titles early on. Cambridge, Chesterfield, and Hull were also contenders. 7 titles in a row marked an all-time high for

Southend, as they hammered their opposition for the rest of the century, with occasional wins from Brighton, Barnsley, and Man City.

We will not dwell on the brief reports from each of the ten simulated centuries. The four centuries charted above adequately demonstrate the difficulty in predicting footballing outcomes. We should not be surprised if Derby do indeed win the Premier League in 2021, or if Stoke City become the dominant force of English football for the remainder of the century. Chance dictates which clubs will succeed and which will fail, particularly as you move further and further into the future. Consider that most of the clubs who *Football Manager* predicts to succeed in the 2000s are fairly big establishments within English football. Arsenal, Manchester United, Southampton, Stoke and Newcastle are all big players in the English game who are amongst the most successful teams, as well as Championship teams like Derby, Nottingham Forest and Blackburn. A large proportion of the teams who are predicted to succeed in the next century are already well-established sides.

Let us now fast-forward to the 30th Century. In the hundred years between 2900 and 3000, the clubs predicted to be competing for the Premier League title are teams who, in the real life present day, are fairly innocuous in the English game. The 30th Century begins with a rivalry between Bromley and Burnley. Granted, Burnley are a well-renowned club, but most football fans will not be familiar with the small side of Bromley. In the present day they play their home fixtures at Haynes Lane, a stadium with a capacity of just 5,000. It is safe to say that Bromley have very little chance of becoming a Premier League super-power in the next century. However, as more and more time progresses, and more and more chance is inducted into proceedings, the likelihood that Bromley will dominate the English game will become as great as any other club.

The current race of dominant teams can expect to keep succeeding for a while. Their astronomical finances assure them a place in the loftier regions of the league table for the foreseeable future. However, as time progresses, these teams can become less and less certain of their providence. The increased impact that chance will have means the probability of the current race of leading clubs continuing to dominate the English game will diminish. The probability of Arsenal winning the Premier League in the year 3000 is almost certainly equal to the probability of Bromley doing so, such is the large volume of luck that both sides will endure in the intervening time period.

The drastic natural variance that exists within football can also be highlighted by looking at the past. Only nine of the twenty-two teams who played in the first season of the Premier League (1992/93) resided in the top division of English football at the beginning of the 2017/18 campaign. Additionally, only one of the teams who finished in the top five positions in 1992/93 (Manchester United) are still playing in the top tier of English football. The historical league tables show that no club has a divine right to succeed. Some teams will acquire good fortune and shoot up the Football League, whilst others will have luck go against them and almost disappear off the face of the footballing world.

When it comes to football, the only certainty is uncertainty. It may entertain some readers to note that, in the one thousand years that were simulated between 2015 and 3015, Chelsea FC only managed to win one Premier League title, the same number as both Forest Green and Alfreton Town managed.

A FOOTBALL REVOLUTION OR EVOLUTION?

Friction between the traditionalists and revolutionaries will always occur in football. Whilst some will promote new ideas, others will feel more assured sticking with what they know. Sport, generally, is very fixed in its ways. A heavy reliance on data-driven methods makes many coaches and scouts uncomfortable. It is an alien methodology which they struggle to understand. It threatens the way they operate. They fear that it might put them out of a job, and that they will be replaced by nerds sitting at computers, crunching numbers.

Harry Redknapp summed up this outlook perfectly after he experienced a defeat as Southampton manager. Redknapp turned to one of his analysts and snapped, "I'll tell you what, next week, why don't we get your computer to play against their computer and see who wins?" Redknapp was the type of traditionalist who naively believed that his eyes wouldn't lie to him. He once accused a player of not working hard enough in training, only to be told by a medical analyst that the player's heart rate had exceeded the expected level. Redknapp refuted this, stating "I don't care, my eyes tell me that he hasn't run enough and I don't need a heart monitor to tell me that."

However, just because the advancement of technology and statistical analysis is clearly beneficial to the sport of football does not mean that we should disregard the traditionalist completely. There must be a balance between the two schools of thought. Data should be used to supplement our own judgements and opinions, leaving us better informed to make accurate predictions. Analytics is a language through which we can express what we believe to be correct. It is a way of formally quantifying what we know to be true. Mathematics is synonymous with logic, but stats mean nothing without context. There will always be a place in football for thinkers who use their footballing experience to draw accurate conclusions from data. The dynamic nature of the sport means it can never be completely broken down into a series of numbers; we will always need to use our eyes to some extent.

Over time, the general approach to football has become standardised, meaning that everyone has adopted a similar attitude to the sport. Writers have called this the "Firehouse Effect". The essential theory goes that firemen, whilst waiting for fires to break out, will do a lot of talking. They will share and debate their political views. As they discuss and deliberate more and more, the opinions of the firemen become increasingly in sync, until they eventually come to an agreement and hold the same political attitudes. The firehouse could be taken as a metaphor for the world of football. As fans and pundits discuss their theories about the sport more and more, everyone acclimatises to the most popular beliefs. Clichés are often thrown around carelessly without much consideration, whilst myths are generally accepted without supporting evidence[33]. The general approach to football has become standardised, meaning that anyone who takes a different approach has the potential to develop an edge over the competition.

There have been teams who have defied conventional footballing wisdom. For instance, clubs who have used pioneering mathematical modelling to find an edge have been able to perform above their financial expectations. Brentford and Midtjylland are the two most extreme examples. Football is slowly realising that statistical analysis is the way forward. However, although positive strides are being taken in terms of the mind-set of football, the actual application of the new analytical approach is still in its infancy.

We must first realise the need to change the way we think about football, admitting that utilising statistics will tell us far more about the beautiful game. The second step is to actually collect and analyse the data. The current brand of stats which are used by media outlets are of low quality. It is hard to tell which teams are performing at a higher level by using data such as possession, shots on target, passing accuracy and the like. The Expected Goals model which Benham uses is a much better indicator of which teams are better. Any forward-thinking media company would do well to adopt this metric as their primary statistical focus.

The simplicity of Matthew Benham's ground-breaking methodology gives us hope for the future of statistical analysis. By collecting data on the quantity and quality of shots which each team creates, Benham has managed to gain an enormous edge. Whilst an edge of this magnitude is unlikely to be found again for quite some time, we should be excited by the possibility of other means of data collection having a similar impact. As football clubs realise that analytics is the way forward, they will begin hiring more analysts. It follows that, as more analysts are hired, more

---

33 For instance, it is generally accepted that "you are most likely to concede a goal immediately after you have scored one". Football fans use this saying so much that it has become established as a fact. In reality, the data shows the exact opposite: you are actually *least* likely to concede after you have just scored.

progress will be made in defining how to form an even clearer image of the sport. Better predictions will be made, and the game will become much more efficient. Those clubs who do not adopt a smarter brand of thinking will be left behind. Teams must adapt in order to survive.

The dynamic nature of football means that there is an incredibly large amount of information to collect and analyse. As technology progresses, our data collection systems will evolve and become even more accurate. Who knows what metrics we will be using to measure player ability in a couple of decades? One prediction that I can make with a fair degree of confidence is that the demand for football analysts will increase hugely over the course of the next few years. The traditionalist who rejects analytics will soon be required to convert, or else will be forced out of the game.

On-pitch decisions would also benefit from an increased digitisation. Steps have been taken in the right direction. Goal-line technology has been installed in a large number of professional football stadia. The next logical step, one which has been taken in a variety of other sports, would be to allow referees technological assistance when making important in-game decisions. Replicating the referral system in cricket, where each team is gifted two chances to ask for a decision to be reviewed with the assistance of TV replays, will remove a lot of the luck which surrounds football. Less decisions will be incorrect, meaning the sport will become much fairer.

The natural following question is one which threatens to undermine the entire contents of this book: do we actually *want* the element of chance to be removed from football?

The Prediction Test

Shortly after I was introduced to the world of football betting, I recognised the need to study the tactics of the bookmakers. I saw the bookies as my direct opposition, an entity that needed to be out-predicted if I were to have any success in making money. I decided to find out if there was any particular kind of football match, or a particular outcome, which the bookmakers tended to undervalue, thus leaving an opportunity for me to exploit. Perhaps the bookmakers thought draws were less common than they actually were? Or maybe, when they predicted that a team had between a 40% and 45% chance of winning, they actually won far more often?

With hindsight, this was a fairly pointless task to undertake. The bookmakers ensure that there is no area of betting which they undervalue. In fact, because they overestimate the odds of each outcome occurring, almost all the markets they offer are vastly overvalued. We have already seen that their overround, the adding up of the outcome probabilities to over 100%, is how they make money. However, one interesting thing did come out of my futile attempt to exploit potential errors of the bookmakers; I stumbled across the perfect method to test predictive ability. This methodology could be used to test the analytical success of bookmakers, pundits, fans, or anyone who wishes to forecast to the outcome of an event.

Using an Excel Spreadsheet, I devised a table with twenty columns, each one representing a set of probabilities. The first column was labelled 0-4.9%, the second 5-9.9%, the third 10-14.9%, the fourth 15-19.9%, and so on until the column marked 95-99.9%. Each football match which the bookies had offered a prediction on was given a row. In each of these rows, I would write the name of the team in the appropriate column correlating with the percentage chance that the bookmakers were giving that side. For example, say there was a match between Arsenal and Chelsea. The bookmakers were giving Arsenal a 46% chance of victory, Chelsea a 38% chance and a 26% chance of a draw[34]. I would write the word *Arsenal* in the column labelled *45-49.9%*, the word *Chelsea* in the column labelled *35-39.9%*, and the word *Draw* in the column labelled *25-29.9%*. After the event took place, I would fill in the box with the outcome that

---

34 Notice that the probabilities add up to 110%. This reflects the fact that the bookmakers are overvaluing the chance of each event occurring. As we have seen, this is called the overround and is how they make their money. The bookies are, in essence, cheating our predictive game.

did occur green, whereas I would fill in the outcomes which didn't occur red. Say Arsenal and Chelsea end up drawing the match, I would fill the box marked *Draw* in green, whilst filling in the boxes marked *Arsenal* and *Chelsea* red.

In the next row, I would repeat the same steps for a different game. The bookies might give Liverpool a 47% chance of winning their match, meaning I would put them in the same column as Arsenal (*45-49.9%*). Suppose that Liverpool did win. The column marked *45-49.9%* would now have one fulfilled outcome out of two. Seeing as Arsenal didn't win and Liverpool did, the column has a success rate of 50%.

After analysing a large sample of games, I would go through each column and tally up the fraction of outcomes which actually took place. Let's take the *45-49.9%* column, the one that Arsenal and Liverpool oc-cupied, as an example. Suppose that I had a sample of 1,000 matches, in 150 of which an outcome was given a *45-49.9%* chance of occurring. Thus, this *45-49.9%* column has a sample of 150 predictions. I would then go through each of these forecasts, and work out how many of them actu-ally came into fruition. If the bookmakers are predictive masters, then the fraction of events which did occur would be similar to the probability that is assigned to that particular column.

Let's say that 74 of the events that the bookies gave this chance of happening did occur. 74/150 is the equivalent of 49.3%, meaning that the bookies were spot on with their forecasting. 49.3% of the events which they said had between a 45% and 49.9% chance of occurring *actually did take place*. Had only 40 of the 150 events taken place, we could have cause for concern with regards to the bookmakers' predictive abilities, as would we if 100 of the 150 predictions were fulfilled. The proportion of events which came into fruition should be close to the speculated prob-ability of these events occurring.

I would go through each column and implement the same method. It would be expected that about 3% of the events in the first column, labelled *0-4.9%*, would actually occur. Equally, the column labelled *95-99.9%* should have virtually all of their predictions fulfilled. My original aim was to find a column which was drastically undervalued by the bookmakers, but I found that the bookmakers were incredibly accurate in their predictions. In fact, each outcome was slightly overvalued. For example, the column which was labelled 60-64.9% achieved a success rate of around 58%. This is because, as you will recall, the bookies overestimate the chances of events occurring in order to make a profit.

Having taken a large sample size, I concluded that the bookmakers were just too good at predicting the probability of outcomes to even attempt to defeat them without a more powerful model. Professional gamblers are able to make money because they have more advanced predictive systems than even the bookies. Matthew Benham's powerful formulae, into which he feeds his Expected Goals data, allow him to precisely calculate the odds of each team winning, and thus enable him to find value in the betting market.

Whilst I was unable to achieve the futile task of spotting an error in the bookmaking system, the type of spreadsheet that was developed as a result is a fantastic way of assessing the ability of predictors. Say you wanted to analyse the ability of your local weather forecaster. You could devise a similar table, with each probabilistic column increasing by 10% from the last. Each time the forecaster predicts the chance of rain occurring, place this prediction in the suitable column (depending on the probability that the forecaster has assigned), look out for whether it rains or not, and assess their performance once you've collected a large sample of data. If it rained on 15% of the occasions that the weather forecaster predicted a 10-20% likelihood of rain, you can conclude that they are an accurate prognosticator. If a forecaster carries such an accurate record across all of the columns, they can be deemed a great predictor[35].

Creating a table like the one I stumbled across when assessing the precision of the bookmakers' forecasts would also be a much better way

---

35 In reality, weather forecasters tend to overestimate the chance of rain. When they predict it won't rain and it does, the public curse the weather channel. When they predict it will rain and it doesn't, the public forget about the prediction. Thus, in order to please their consumers, weather forecasters tend to overvalue the probability of rain occurring.

to assess the predictive qualities of football pundits. Instead of asking for a predicted scoreline (which is possibly the most useless question one can ask), presenters should ask pundits to predict the probabilities are of each team winning. The TV broadcaster could then log each of these predictions in the same sort of table that I described above, and keep tabs over the predictive success of each pundit. When Ian Holloway says he thinks a team has a 60% chance of victory, how often does this team actually win? Does the regularity of the event occurring match the probability that he has assigned to the column? This type of predictive scrutiny forces us to think probabilistically, whilst also holding us accountable to our poor predictions. It is an excellent way of separating the hedgehog from the fox.

ENTERTAINMENT BETTING

During a Summer holiday in Croatia, my undying thirst for football led me to attend a game between two teams I hadn't previously heard of. As I sat watching the match, a fierce rivalry between Split and Hajduk, it occurred to me how wholly disinteresting I found the fixture. I suddenly felt the urge to put a bet on the match. I understood that I was likely to lose money; I knew nothing about either side and understood that the bookmakers' overround will always allow them to defeat uninformed bettors over the long-run. Why, then, did I still end up placing a bet on Split to either win or draw the game? Naturally, Hajduk ended up scoring a last minute winner and I lost my money.

As I left the match, I reflected on whether it was worth placing the bet. I had lost money, but the occasion had been made far more interesting due to my increased stake in the fixture. Fans dedicate hours of their week travelling up and down the country in order to watch their team play. This induces a large amount of emotional investment, meaning the outcome of each match greatly effects their happiness. Supporters who invest a large amount of time, money and emotion into a football club will be largely impacted by their results. The problem with watching the anonymous Croatian match was that I had no stake in the fixture. The only way that I could replicate the buzz I get from watching the team I support was to invest some money in the match.

Despite losing £7, I had actually gained a lot of entertainment from cheering on Split, a team that I had no previous connection with whatsoever. My evening had been more exciting than if I had simply watched the game as a neutral. This was a new concept to me; betting not in order to make money, but in order to be entertained. Clearly, doing this regularly would drain your bank balance. You need to exercise rationality when confronted with a craving for gambling. However, when one takes betting in this sense, as an act of enjoyment rather than a quest for wealth, we could think of the bookmakers as the providers of a sort of service. They offer a form of entertainment, in turn taking a share of the money.

Earlier in the book, I likened the bookies' practices to a rigged fairground attraction in which you are tasked with shooting balls into a hoop. Unbeknownst to the player, the hoop is shaped in a way that makes it harder to get the ball in. The player will overvalue his chances of winning a prize, resulting in his losing of money. Nevertheless, whilst he will likely end up walking away from the fairground emptyhanded, there is a certain value to the entertainment that he has experienced by taking part in the game. Perhaps, occasionally, we can abandon the need for predictive success in the pursuit of cheap thrills.

OUR LOVE-HATE RELATIONSHIP WITH LUCK

This book has tried to convey a smarter approach to football. We have studied various statistical phenomena which will help us make more accurate predictions. We have learnt to control our emotional biases. We have seen how to be more fox-like, and why hedgehogs are poor forecasters. We have studied how the bookmakers tax those who don't understand the laws of probability. We have uncovered the methods that Matthew

Benham has used to remove luck from football, and how he has used these methods in both his gambling and in the running of his two clubs.

There are clear advantages to identifying and eliminating the role of chance from football. It leaves us with a clearer image of what is true, and what is simply noise. This is particularly important in the betting world, as defining which teams are the best is crucial to making money. This book will hopefully have left you more prepared to go and make accurate footballing predictions, thus allowing a more insightful perception of the beautiful game.

However, detractors of *The Football Code* may rightly ask whether it is necessary to remove the luck from football. Do we actually want football to become more predictable? After all, as I have pointed out at several points in this book, one of the most beautiful things about the sport is its balance between predictability and unpredictability. From the perspective of fans, in particular, is there a risk of football becoming a stale, mathematical entity? If we were able to forecast perfectly who was going to win every game, there would surely be no point going to watch football. In this totally pre-decided world, we could simply award each team the number of points that they are predicted. The sport would become incredibly dull.

Similarly, if every football pundit were to adopt the fox-like qualities that we studied in the third chapter, then television coverage would become tedious and boring. Despite being able to offer more precise and insightful predictions, I would argue that if pundits were to become more rational then an intrinsic entertainment value would be lost. It is enjoyable watching hedgehogs such as Alan Hansen make bold, outlandish and ultimately foolish predictions. We like to disagree with these pundits, debating with our peers whether their assessments are correct or not.

Whilst a pre-match build-up featuring the best mathematical analysts the sport has to offer would certainly give us the most refined probabilities of each team winning, it would not be nearly as interesting as watching hedgehogs remonstrate amongst themselves. As long as we recognise the shortcomings of the pundits we watch, and do not fall victim to the same deficiencies in our own predictions, then there is certainly a place for them within the game.

Nonetheless, whilst they may provide entertainment value, you would not want to employ a hedgehog to run your football club. Owners, managers, scouts and others whose profession it is to make accurate footballing predictions should all aim to be the model fox. Their purpose is to succeed in understanding and forecasting the beautiful game. Those inside the sport have a responsibility to take a much more rational approach than the fans, who are naturally emotional and unreasonable.

Hedgehogs will always pervade the sport of football. There will always be people who fall victim to their emotions. There will always be people who are unable to think probabilistically. There will always be people who live by broad and overbearing rules, and who are too inflexible to adapt to new and more sophisticated ways of thinking. Indeed, for all of my preaching, there have been several points during the writing of this book where I have had to check myself, remaining acutely aware of falling victim to hedgehog-like tendencies.

Some features of football are non-changeable. The sport will always be heavily influenced by luck. Underdogs will beat favourites, and entire seasons will hang on a knife-edge. Teams will search for an edge which sets them apart from the opposition. The rich clubs will dominate the poor, all other things being equal.

All of these things will remain the same, but some things look set to change. Matthew Benham and his innovative system have advanced our understanding of football. Smartodds' Expected Goals method is likely to enter the mainstream in the coming years. They have cracked the seemingly unbreakable code of how to use data to achieve footballing success. As technology continues to progress, analytics will throw up exciting new tools which we can use to measure the beautiful game. Benham has kick-started a more intelligent and fox-like era within the sport. In the past, the words *smart* and *football* have been juxtapositions. Hopefully, using the philosophy laid out in this book, we can craft a world of smarter football.

Commonly Assigned Odds Translated into Percentages

1/1 = 50%	2/1 = 33.3%	3/1 = 25%
4/1 = 20%	5/1 = 16.7%	6/1 = 14.3%
5/2 = 28.6%	7/2 = 22.2%	9/2 = 18.2%
11/2 = 15.4%	13/2 = 13.3%	1/4 = 80%
3/4 = 57.1%	5/4 = 44.4%	6/4 = 40%
7/4 = 36.4%	9/4 = 30.7%	11/4 = 26.7%
15/4 = 21.1%	17/4 = 19%	21/4 = 16%
2/5 = 71.4%	4/5 = 55.6%	6/5 = 45.5%
7/5 = 41.7%	8/5 = 38.5%	9/5 = 35.7%
11/5 = 31.3%	12/5 = 29.4%	13/5 = 27.8%
14/5 = 26.3%	16/5 = 23.8%	17/5 = 22.7%
18/5 = 21.7%	5/6 = 54.5%	4/6 = 60%
4/7 = 63.6%	11/8 = 42.1%	13/8 = 38.1%
15/8 = 34.8%	4/9 = 69.2%	7/10 = 58.8%
11/10 = 47.6%	13/10 = 43.5%	17/10 = 37%
19/10 = 34.5%	21/10 = 32.3%	23/10 = 30.3%
29/10 = 25.6%	4/11 = 73.3%	8/11 = 57.9%
10/11 = 52.4%	8/13 = 61.9%	8/15 = 65.2%
9/20 = 69%	17/20 = 54.1%	19/20 = 51.3%
21/20 = 48.8%	23/20 = 46.5%	29/20 = 40.8%
37/20 = 35.1%	100/30 = 23.1%	

BIBLIOGRAPHY

Barnes, H. (2013, August 17). *Does It Make Statistical Sense to Sack a Football Manager?* Retrieved from BBC News: http://www.bbc.co.uk/news/magazine-23724517

Flanagan, A. (n.d.). *Statistics Don't Always Tell the Whole Story.* Retrieved from The Mirror: http://www.mirror.co.uk/sport/football/news/arsene-wenger-statistics-dont-always-7040459

Hassan, N. (2013, October 26). *The Life of a Football Scout.* Retrieved from BBC Sport: http://www.bbc.co.uk/sport/0/football/24653124

Hytner, D. (n.d.). *Arsenal's Secret Signing.* Retrieved from The Guardian: https://www.theguardian.com/football/2014/oct/17/arsenal-place-trust-arsene-wenger-army-statdna-data-analysts

Innes, R. (2016, April 10). *11 Things That Were More Likely Than Leicester Winning the Premier League.* Retrieved from The Mirror: http://www.mirror.co.uk/sport/row-zed/11-things-were-officially-more-7320326

Innes, R. (2016, February). *Gary Neville Record at Valencia.* Retrieved from The Mirror: http://www.mirror.co.uk/sport/row-zed/valencias-record-under-gary-neville-7327790

James, G. (2006). *Manchester City - The Complete Record* (Derby: Polar Publishing)

Morris, B. (2014, July). *Billion-Dollar Billy Beane*. Retrieved from FiveThirtyEight: http://fivethirtyeight.com/features/billion-dollar-billy-beane/

Page, D. (n.d.). *Expected Goals Just Don't Add Up*. Retrieved from https://medium.com/@dannypage/expected-goals-just-don-t-add-up-they-also-multiply-1dfd9b52c7d0#.ecnn3zbyu

Simendinger, T. (2011, October 27). *Why First Impressions Are Hard to Change*. Retrieved from Ocean Palmer: http://oceanpalmer.com/2011/10/why-first-impressions-are-hard-to-change/

Sorene, P. (2013). *The History of Football Goalposts*. Retrieved 2015, from Who Ate All The Pies: http://www.whoateallthepies.tv/retro/158123/the-history-of-football-goal-posts.html

Stuart, K. (2014, 8 12). *Why clubs are using Football Manager as a real life scouting tool*. Retrieved from The Guardian: http://www.theguardian.com/technology/2014/aug/12/why-clubs-football-manager-scouting-tool

Taylor, D. (2014, July 3). *Massimo Cellino Axes Paddy Kenny from Leeds Over Date of Birth*. Retrieved from The Guardian: http://www.theguardian.com/football/2014/jul/03/massimo-cellino-leeds-united-paddy-kenny

Taylor, M. (2014, February 12). *The Power of Goals*. Retrieved from http://thepowerofgoals.blogspot.co.uk/2014/02/twelve-shots-good-two-shots-better.html

Williams, J. (2009, April 22). *Penalty Kicks By The Numbers*. Retrieved from Science of Soccer: http://www.scienceofsocceronline.com/2009/04/penalty-kicks-by-numbers.html

Williams-Grut, O. (2016, February 10). *Inside Starlizard*. Retrieved from Business Insider: http://uk.businessinsider.com/inside-story-star-lizard-tony-bloom-2016-2

INFLUENTIAL WORKS

Anderson, Chris and David Sally, *The Numbers Game: Why Everything You Know About Football is Wrong* (Viking, London, 2013)

Buchdahl, Joseph, *Squares & Sharps, Suckers & Sharks* (High Stakes Publishing, Herts, 2016)

Ferguson, Alex, *My Autobiography* (Bantam Books, London, 2007)

Haigh, John, *Taking Chances* (Oxford University Press, New York, 2009)

Hornby, Nick, *Fever Pitch* (Indigo, London, 1996)

Kuper, Simon and Stefan Szymanski, *Soccernomics* (HarperSport, London, 2014)

Lewis, Michael, *Moneyball* (W.W. Norton & Company Ltd., New York, 2004)

Peace, David, *The Damned United* (Faber and Faber, London, 2006)

Silver, Nate, *The Signal and the Noise: The Art and Science of Prediction* (Allen Lane, London, 2012)

Taylor, Peter, *With Clough by Taylor* (Sidgwick & Jackson, London, 1980)

Tomkins, Paul, Graeme Riley and Gary Fulcher, *Pay as You Play: The True Price of Success in the Premier League Era* (GPRF Publishing, Wigston, 2010)

ACKNOWLEDGEMENTS

―――――――

DOZENS OF PEOPLE MADE THIS book possible. I would like to thank Adam Manley and Anne Griffiths for instilling me with a passion for sport. Their energy, enthusiasm and support has inspired me, and this book was written in memory of two of the best people I ever had the pleasure of knowing.

My parents, Sarah and David, have been as encouraging as ever. They have refrained from placing unnecessary restrictions on me, and have wholeheartedly supported this project. Their hard-work is what drives my ambition.

Thank you to my siblings, Oliver, Anna and Isabel, for providing a dull background glow to my burning flame. Their shortcomings make my achievements even more noticeable. Despite being younger, and indeed less wise, they have all contributed ideas and additions to the book. I am forever grateful.

Jonah Manley has been incredibly influential. Over the course of the last decade or so, he has led me down many of the paths that ended up with the production of this book.

I received help in editing from Piers Blofeld, Julian Tippett, Anna Tippett and David Tippett. Nik at BookBeaver designed the exceptional cover.

I am grateful to the following for listening to my incessant rambling about football, writing, analytics and the rest: Nick Macnee, Tom Krum, Alex Carrie, Olivia Thorniley-Walker, Issy Brown, Anna Trafford, Kit McCrystal, Max Stevensen, Kitty Froggatt, Lexie Turner, Sue Manley, Sheila Ward and many more.

43369983R00160

Printed in Poland
by Amazon Fulfillment
Poland Sp. z o.o., Wrocław